I0901055

IMAGES
*of America*

# MANCHACA

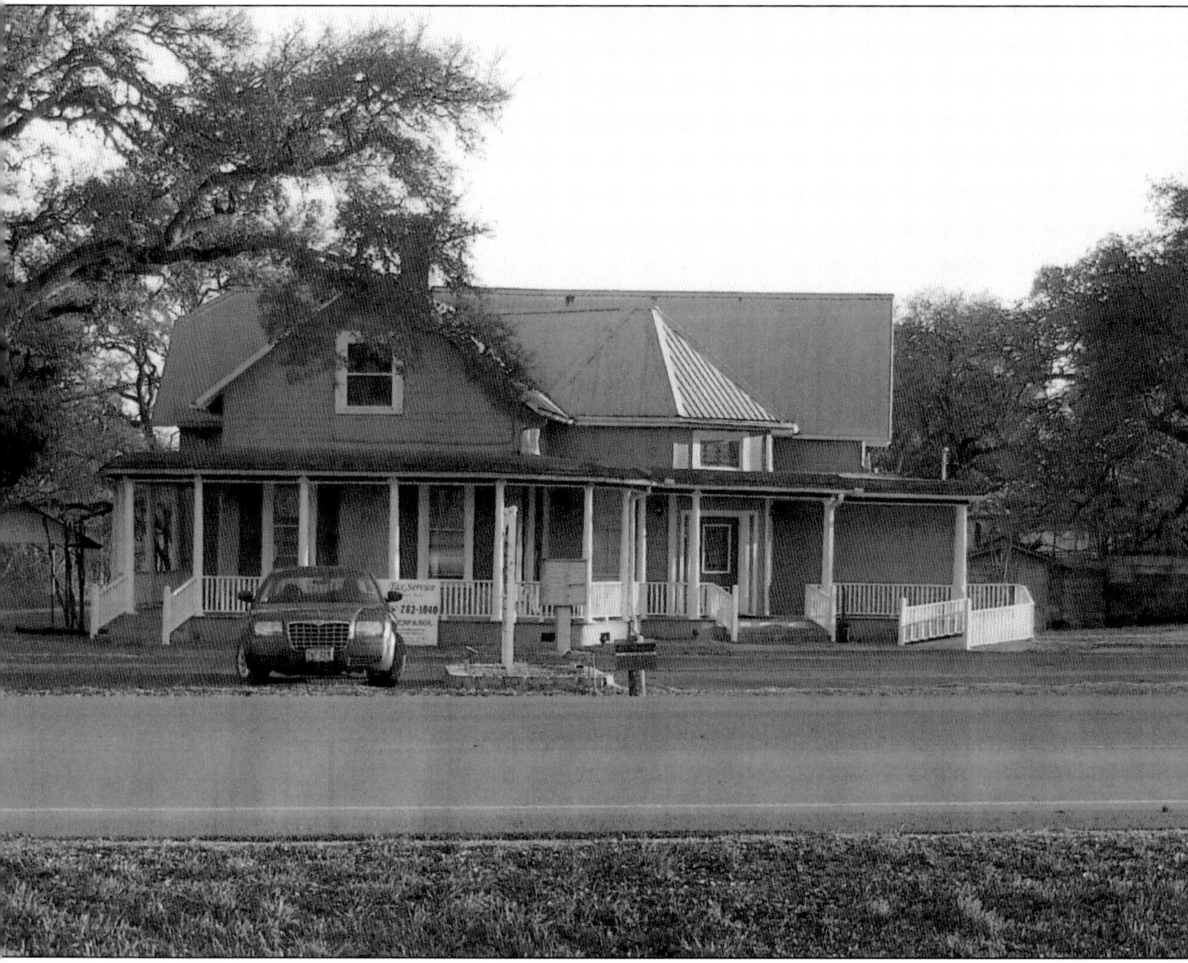


The two-story "Carpenter House" has been a familiar landmark on the main street of Manchaca for over 100 years and is now home to several local businesses. The home takes its name from Edna and Tommie Carpenter, who raised their family there in the early 20th Century. (Courtesy Ann and Barry Trask.)

**On the Cover:** The students of Manchaca School are shown in this 1917 group photograph. The school was located on the present-day northeast corner of Manchaca Road and FM 1626. (Courtesy Lillie M. Moreland.)

IMAGES
*of America*

# MANCHACA

The Manchaca Onion Creek
Historical Association

ARCADIA
PUBLISHING

ISBN 978-1-4671-3051-6

Published by Arcadia Publishing
Charleston, South Carolina

Printed in the United States of America

Library of Congress Control Number: 2013935594

For all general information, please contact Arcadia Publishing:
Telephone 843-853-2070
Fax 843-853-0044
E-mail sales@arcadiapublishing.com
For customer service and orders:
Toll-Free 1-888-313-2665

Visit us on the Internet at www.arcadiapublishing.com

*Dedicated to the residents of Manchaca, past and present, who made this book possible*

# CONTENTS

# Acknowledgments

*The challenge of history is to recover the past and introduce it to the present.*

—David Thelen

For an organization filled with members who love history, old photographs, and historical maps, the compilation of this book has been an escape into the beloved past of an area we treasure. With the discovery of each old photograph or bit of information, our enthusiasm soared.

We wish to express our heartfelt thanks to each and every person who took the time to help us along the way. There have been many kind individuals who took time out to search for family photographs and endured our many questions with grace and a smile; thank you.

Manchaca residents Joanne Deane and Lillie Moreland have been the backbone of our support in the community, freely lending their treasure trove of historical photographs and anecdotes for our use in this book. We hold you in highest esteem.

We must commend the staffs of The Texas General Land Office and the Austin History Center, who were so accommodating to our needs, providing us with fabulous maps and photographs. Their expertise and professionalism are very much appreciated.

We would like to extend a very special thank-you to archaeologist Doug Boyd of Prewitt & Associates, the staff at Texas Department of Transportation, and the University of Texas, who allowed us to use photographs of the historic Ransom and Sarah Williams archaeological dig. We feel so fortunate to have those photographs included here. We wish to thank Terri Meyers of Preservation Central for her extensive research. Finally, we would like to thank Dr. Maria Franklin, who worked with Prewitt & Associates by interviewing local residents, coaxing them to share what life was like in the old days. Her publication of those interviews in "I'm Proud to Know What I Know" will remain as a permanent record of history for those who will come after us.

A special word of thanks must go to the members of the Manchaca Onion Creek Historical Association (MOCHA), who are dedicated to preserving the history of the area and have given so much of their time and effort to make this book possible. Please visit our website at www.mochaonline.org to learn more about the organization.

# INTRODUCTION

Nestled in the richly forested and picturesque rolling hills of south Travis County, Manchaca lies in an area that has been occupied by man for thousands of years. As the frontier was pushed farther and farther west, indigenous people moved with it, and early settlers eyed the land with great interest. The Spanish land grants issued in the 1830s opened up the area for settlement, and growth has come at a steady pace in the decades following. El Camino Real de los Tejas, represented today in sections of the Old San Antonio Road, was instrumental in the development of Manchaca by pointing the way through the Texas wilderness as early as the 17th century. At the Onion Creek Bridge along this old artery, wagon wheels have worn ruts in the limestone creek bottom, put there long before a bridge afforded travelers an easier crossing.

Manchaca takes its name from the Manchaca Springs that lie to the south of the community along the Old San Antonio Road. When New York landscape designer Fredrick Law Olmsted traveled to Texas in 1854, he stayed at an establishment owned by Adolphus Weir, located at Manchaca Springs. He recorded his experiences in his famous book, *A Journey through Texas*, published in 1857. Below is an excerpt from his publication, detailing an unexpected picture of early life in the area:

> We found a plantation that would have done no discredit to Virginia. The house was large and well constructed, standing in a thick grove, separated from the prairie by a strong worm fence. Adjacent, within, was the spring which deserved its prominence of mention upon the maps. It had been tastefully grottoed with heavy limestone rocks, now water-stained and mossy . . . Everything about the house was orderly and neat . . . We were ushered into a snug supper-room and found a table set with wheat-bread, ham, tea and preserved fruits waited on by tidy and ready girls.

Upon leaving, Olmsted added an afterthought regarding one large shortcoming he noticed during his time spent there. He noted that even though they had been offered drink in silver cups, there was "no other water closet than the back of a bush or the broad prairie—an indication of a queerly Texas incompleteness in cultivation of manners." This was the area as seen through the eyes of a cultured, well-educated easterner.

Several stagecoach lines ran along Old San Antonio Road, stopping at Manchaca Springs to rest and refresh both passengers and horses alike. By today's standards, the stagecoach was a rough and tumble way to travel, with bumps and jolts and dust perpetually flying, but it was a definite upgrade from mounting a horse and traveling the route alone. "Scott's Stage Line" ran an advertisement in the Austin City Directory in 1877, claiming just 14 hours travel time for their coaches from Austin via Manchaca Springs to San Antonio. Many stage travelers liked what they saw and returned to settle their families in the area.

In 1880, when the International & Great Northern Railroad laid track in Manchaca, the population increase spurred the building of a new school and various mercantile establishments to service the burgeoning populace. By the turn of the century, Manchaca was a booming community with stores, blacksmith shops, schools and at least one church. Citizens had several doctors at their disposal, and those doctors could attest, through the many babies they delivered, to the population growth taking place among the townspeople.

The cotton gin was operating by 1899, giving the farmers of the area a convenient place to get their cotton ginned. Its location close to the train depot made it easy to get their goods to market as well.

During the years of the Great Depression, families depended heavily on each other, using a barter system that provided each with what they needed. The Depression was felt in Manchaca, but not as painfully as it was in large cities, where the populace was dependent upon paying jobs to cover rent, food, and transportation.

Today, Manchaca and the area surrounding it is bursting with new growth and building. Homes, businesses, and apartment complexes are going up on virgin ground that in previous decades knew only the horse and occasional red-tailed hawk as it slowly circled the sky, scouting for its next meal. Unfortunately, we have permanently lost several historic structures that played pivotal roles in Manchaca's development. Many of the new residents moving into the area are unaware of the rich history of the town. The huge and ancient oaks along the train tracks in the middle of town that once shaded the old depot, cotton gin, and mercantile establishments, stand on parched and barren soil, a testament to a time gone by.

As Manchaca was the stage where many a bygone citizen lived out his or her life, Live Oak Cemetery, down Twin Creeks Road just outside of town, is testament to the cast of characters who called the town home. There, beneath the spreading canopy of the oak and pecan trees, lay the men who cleared the fields behind their horses and mules, and farmed the land. There also lay the mothers, who nursed their infants and sang them to sleep, cherishing every moment with them, only to lose that child to one of the many childhood diseases. And there too lay the children and infants whose lives were too short, but who will forever be remembered. Live Oak is still a very active cemetery, and a stroll through its rows of headstones reveal generations of families buried close to their kin, and often visited by those who remain.

While it is so true that times have changed a great deal, we hope that those times will not be forgotten. It is our fervent hope that this publication will spark a resurrection of awareness of a time gone by, and appreciation for those who have lived here before us. In some ways, their life was much more difficult than ours; yet recalling "the good old days" sparks our imagination, enticing us with the charm of a country life and a time that can never be relived or experienced again, but only kept alive in memory.

# *One*

# The Earliest Records

Evidence found by archaeologists indicates that man settled in the Manchaca area at least 6,000 years ago. The sparkling creeks and lush forests provided a rich environment for the early Indian cultures of central Texas. Settlements of the Tonkawa and their predecessors, the Toyah culture, enjoyed the gifts that nature provided in the rolling hills of this area.

As settlers moved west into central Texas, they also discovered the beauty and resources of the rich land. Native Kentuckian Benjamin Rush Milam would play a very important role in the development of land that would one day be Manchaca. Milam petitioned the Mexican Government for the right to settle colonists on Texas land. On January 12, 1826, Mexico granted an Empresario contract to Milam, consisting of a large piece of land that was later known as Milam's Colony. The grant encompassed 11 leagues of land, and Milam agreed to settle 300 families within the grant's boundaries. The property that makes up Manchaca today was part of that colony. By 1835, leagues from this original grant were being settled by pioneers who carefully chose their property and paid to have it surveyed.

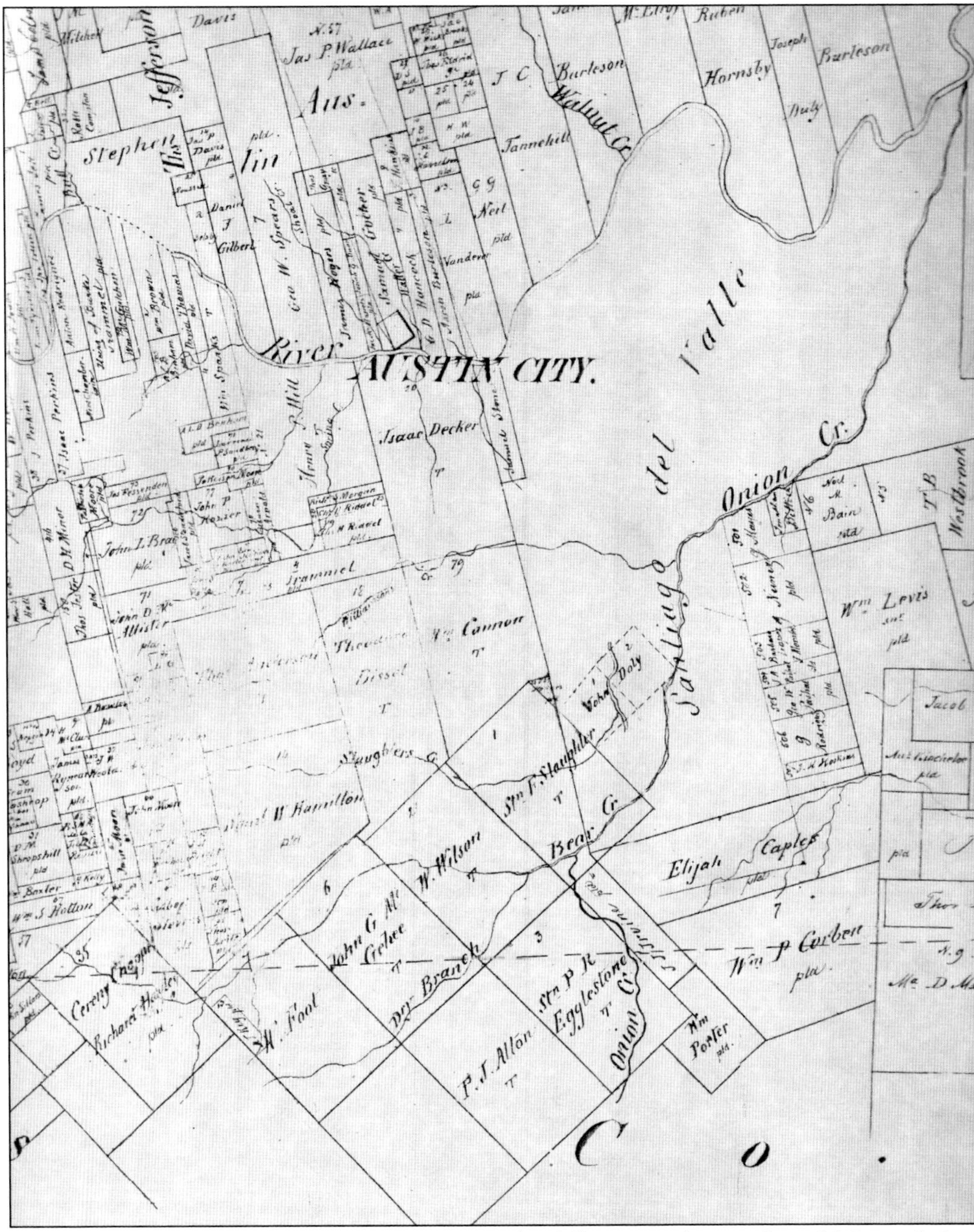


The land that makes up the Manchaca area today falls primarily into five old Spanish land grants. These grants were given to Stephen F. Slaughter, Walker Wilson, John McGehee, Josephus S. Irvine, and Stephen Egglestone. Several of these grants contain a league of land, which is equivalent to 4,428.4 acres. Residents in the area today often discover that one of the original land owners mentioned above appears on the title to their own property. This map is just a small portion of a wonderfully old, but undated, Travis County map. Running left to right across the page is a dashed line that depicts the county line dividing Travis County on the north from Hays County on the south. (Map of Travis County, no date, No. 4090. Courtesy of the Texas General Land Office, Austin.)

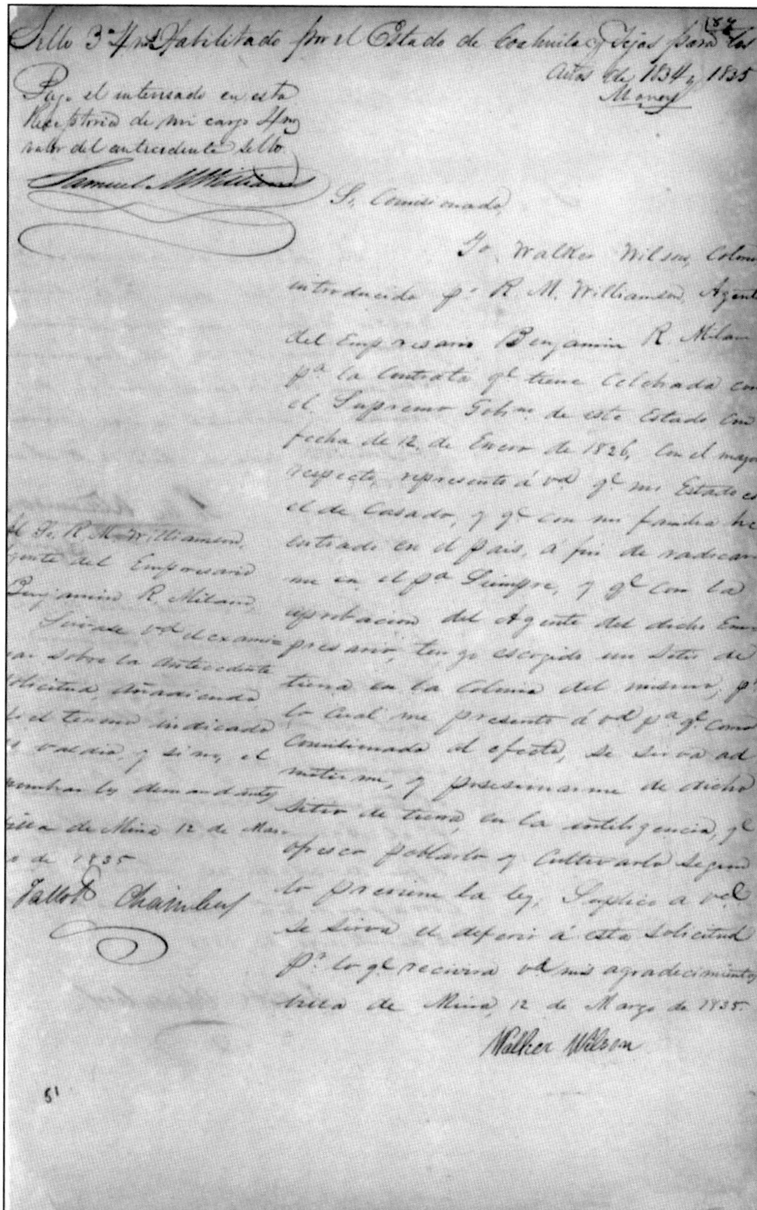

Sr. Comisionado

Yo, Walker Wilson, Colono introducido p.r R. M. Williamson, Agente del Empresario Benjamin R. Milan p.a la Contrata q.e tiene Celebrada con el Supremo Gob.no de este Estado con fecha de 12 de Enero de 1826, con el mayor respecto, represento á vd. q.e mi Estado es el de Casado, y q.e con mi familia he entrado en el pais, á fin de radicarme en el p.a siempre, y q.e con la aprobacion del Agente del dicho Empresario, tengo escogido un Sitio de tierra en la Colonia del mismo, p.r lo cual me presento á vd. p.a q.e como Comisionado al efecto, se sirva admitirme, y posesionarme de dicho Sitio de tierra, en la inteligencia, q.e ofrezco poblarlo y cultivarlo segun lo previene la ley. Suplico á vd. se sirva el deferir á esta solicitud p.r lo q.e recivira vd. mis agradecimientos. Villa de Mina, 12 de Marzo de 1835.

Walker Wilson

The Walker Wilson land grant, shown above, is written in Spanish, and carries the date of March 12, 1835. After carefully selecting the land he wished to settle on, Wilson signed this grant, swearing that he and his family would permanently settle and cultivate the land according to the law. This transaction took place in the town of Mina, which is present-day Bastrop. The Mr. R.M. Williamson mentioned in this grant was also known in Texas history as "Three Legged Willie." He served as the agent of Empresario Benjamin R. Milam. Mr. Williamson acquired this unusual nick name due to a teenage illness that affected his right leg, drawing it back and making it useless for walking. An artificial limb was fashioned for him from the knee down that gave him walking mobility. During his illness, he read extensively, resulting in his admission to the bar at the age of 19. (Spanish title for Walker Wilson, March 12, 1835. SC 000039:12 Spanish Collection, Archives and Records Program, Texas General Land Office, Austin.)

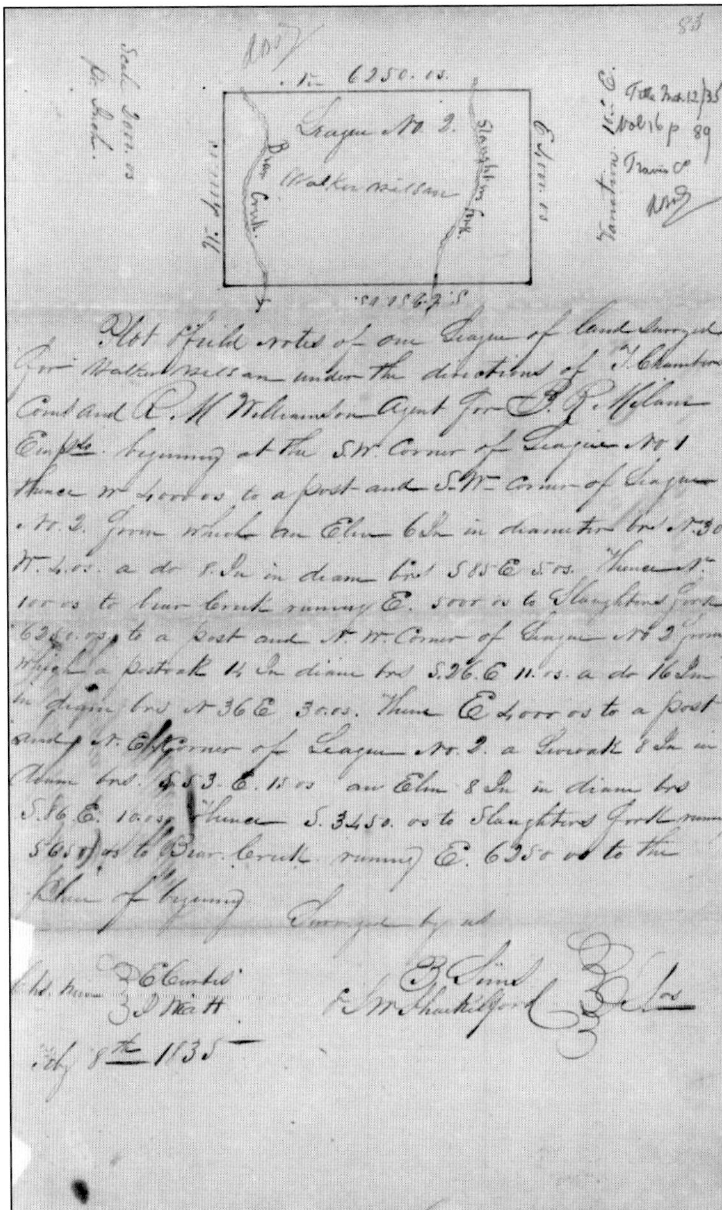

This document is a wonderful window into the history of Manchaca. It contains the field notes of the men who surveyed the land for Walker Wilson, documenting two very important creeks. Wilson received a full league of land consisting of 5,000 varas, or 4,428.40 acres. This was a prime piece of property, with both Bear Creek and Slaughter Creek (noted here as Slaughter's Fork) running through it. Stephen F. Slaughter, who had also been awarded a league of land, was Wilson's neighbor to the east. Papers at the Dolph Briscoe Center for American History reveal that when it came time for Wilson to pay the survey and registration fees for his land, he could not afford them. Slaughter offered to buy half of Wilson's property. Walker Wilson sold that land for the tidy sum of $500 on March 12, 1835. (English Field Notes for Walker Wilson League, February 8, 1835. English Field Notes S-83. Spanish Collection, Archives and Records Program, Texas General Land Office, Austin.)

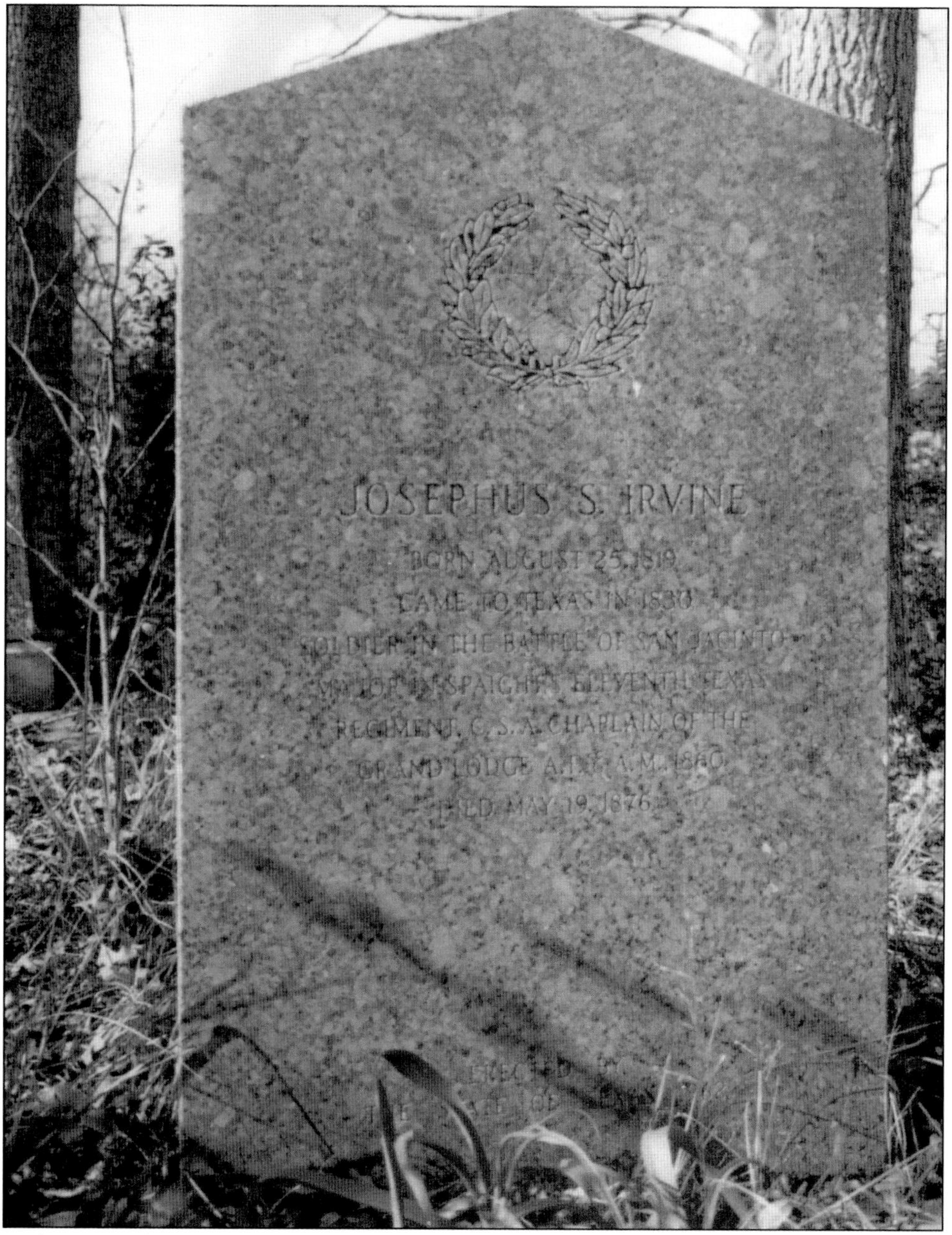


Texas hero Josephus Somerville Irvine is buried in historic Wilson Chapel Cemetery in Newton County, Texas. The land grant he received for his service in the Texas Revolution makes up part of the land that is Manchaca today. The grant lies along the Old San Antonio Road as it winds its way through south Travis County into northern Hays County. Irvine was born in Tennessee in 1819 and came to Texas with his family in 1830. He is acclaimed to have been the youngest participant at the Battle of San Jacinto. Irvine received his certificate for a land grant in 1838 and patented his grant in October 1846. He volunteered for military service to Texas three times during his life, participating for the last time as a major in Spaight's 11th Texas Regiment, CSA. Irvine was also a respected Methodist minister in Newton County, Texas. He died May 17, 1876. (Courtesy E. Barry Gray.)

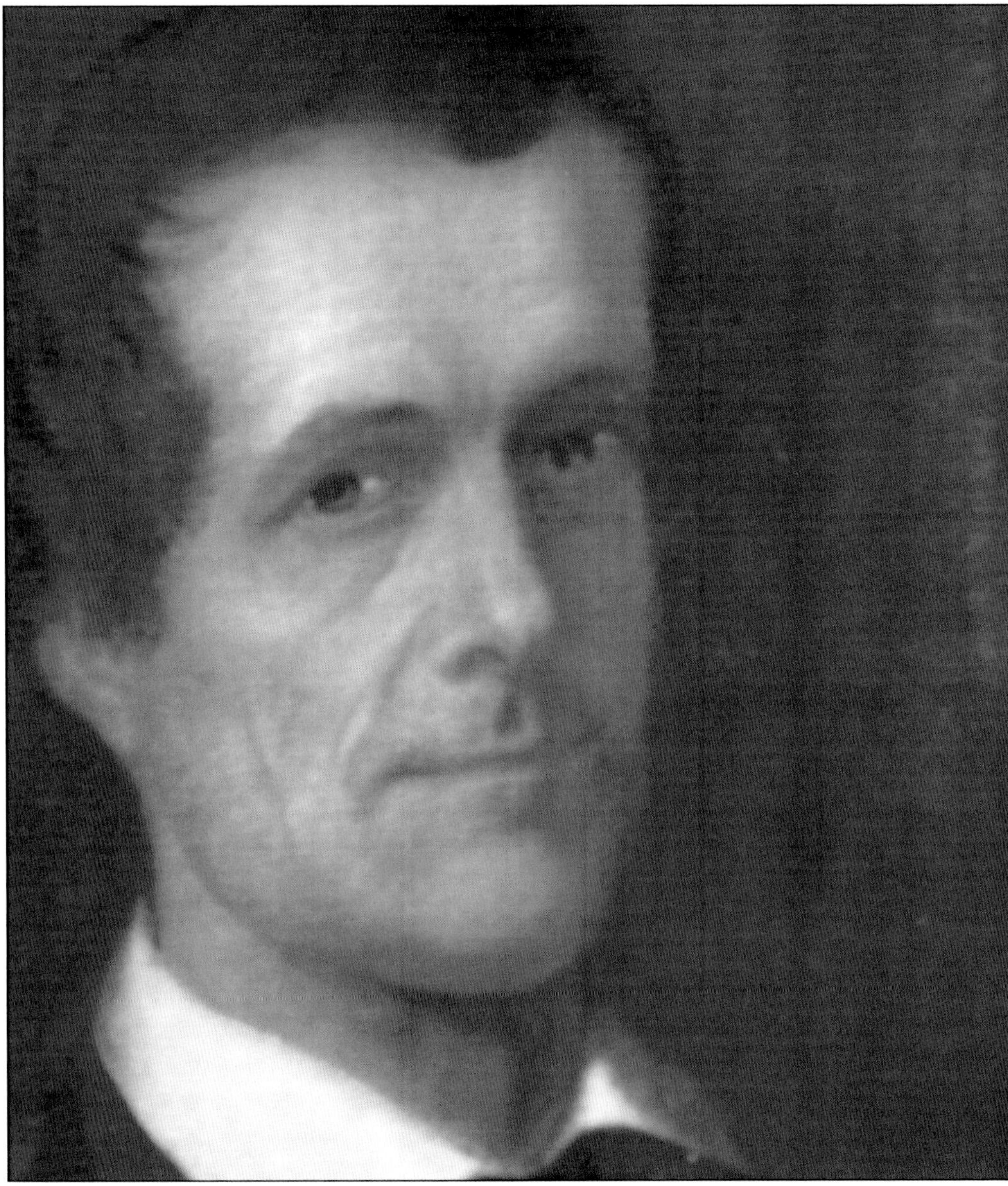

Mississippi resident Adolphus Weir first saw the country around Manchaca when he passed through on the stagecoach. He was duly impressed with the climate and beauty of the land. In 1851, he purchased 553.5 acres that included Manchaca Springs. A "Title Bond" was negotiated with Washington D. Miller, who had been the private secretary to Sam Houston. In the book *A Journey through Texas*, published in 1857 and written by Frederick Law Olmsted, the father of American landscape architecture, we find the following quote regarding his stay at the home of Mr. Weir: "The house was large and well constructed, standing in a thick grove, separated from the prairie by a strong worm fence. Adjacent, within, was the spring which deserved its prominence of mention upon the maps. It had been tastefully grottoed with heavy limestone rocks, now water-stained and mossy . . . Everything about the house was orderly and neat . . . We were ushered into a snug supper-room and found a table set with wheat-bread, ham, tea and preserved fruits waited on by tidy and ready girls." (Courtesy Sharon McClure Reinhard.)

When Adolphus Weir died in 1860, he was buried on his property at Manchaca Springs. His widow, Martha, moved to Austin shortly after that. In 1875, he was reinterred at Oakwood Cemetery in Austin. During his lifetime, Weir was an active public servant and was friends with many state officials. He was elected Travis County Sheriff in 1857. (Courtesy Sharon Reinhard.)

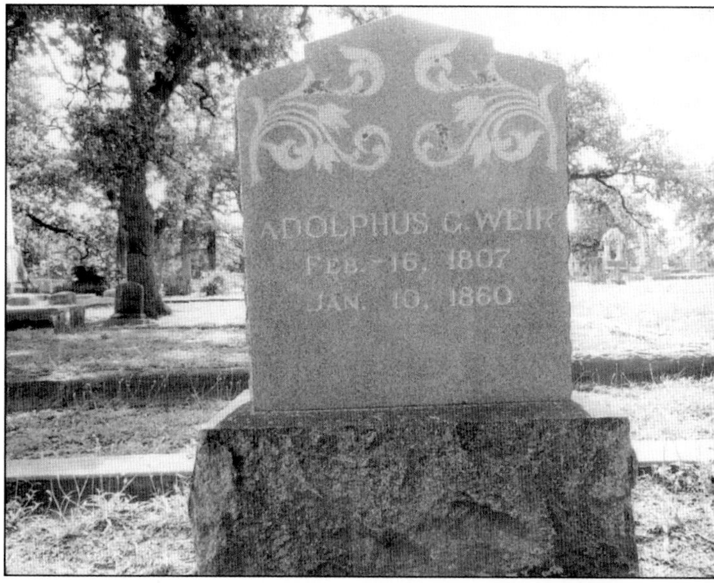


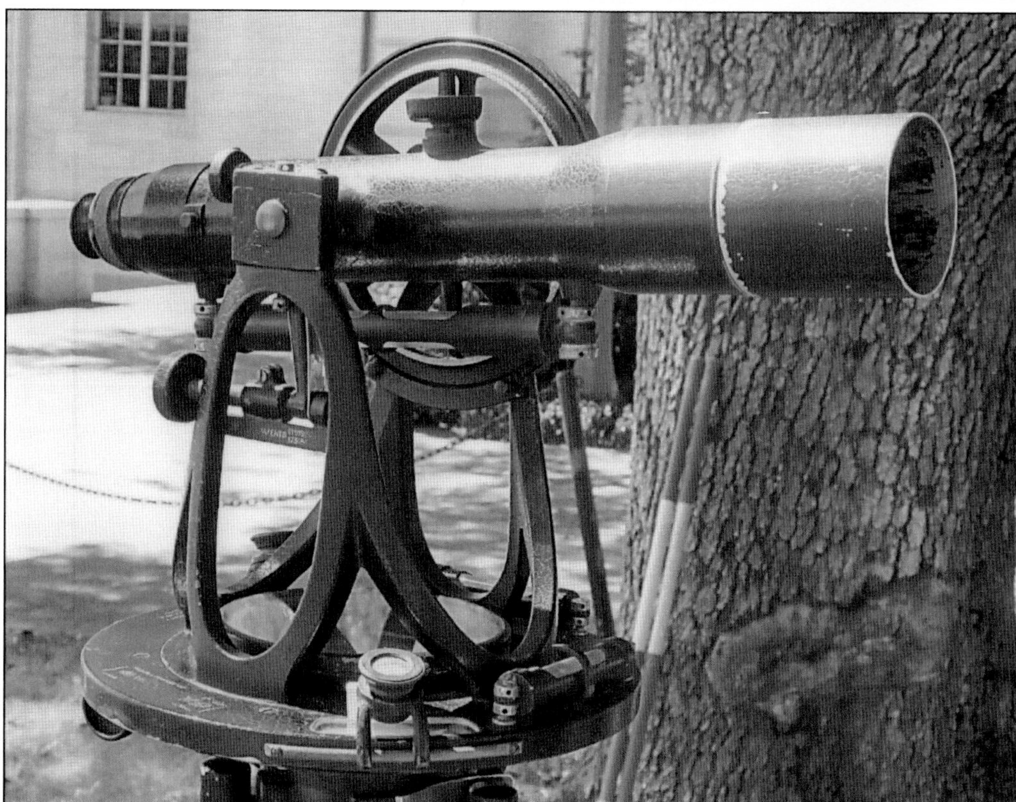

In February 1835, Bartlett Sims and a Mr. Shackelford surveyed the original leagues of land that now make up Manchaca. They may have used this old piece of surveying equipment, called a transit, which is now owned by the Texas General Land Office. Surveying was not for the faint of heart. They often encountered Indians and other perils when they ventured onto the virgin frontier. (Courtesy Ann and Barry Trask.)

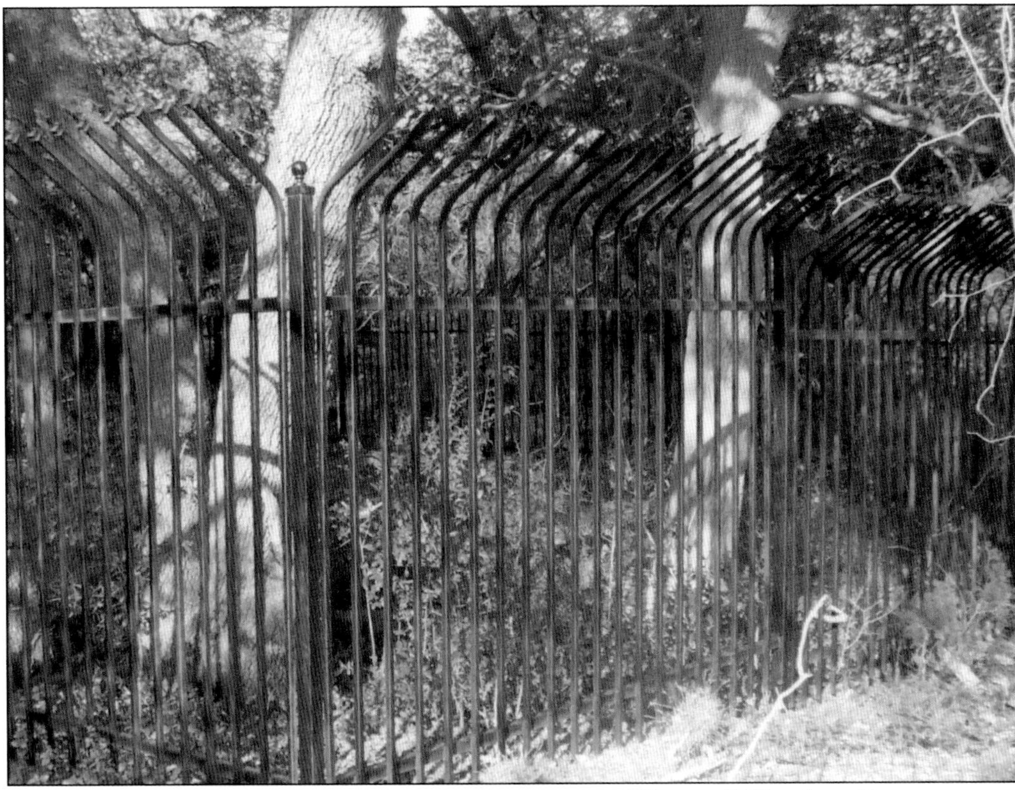

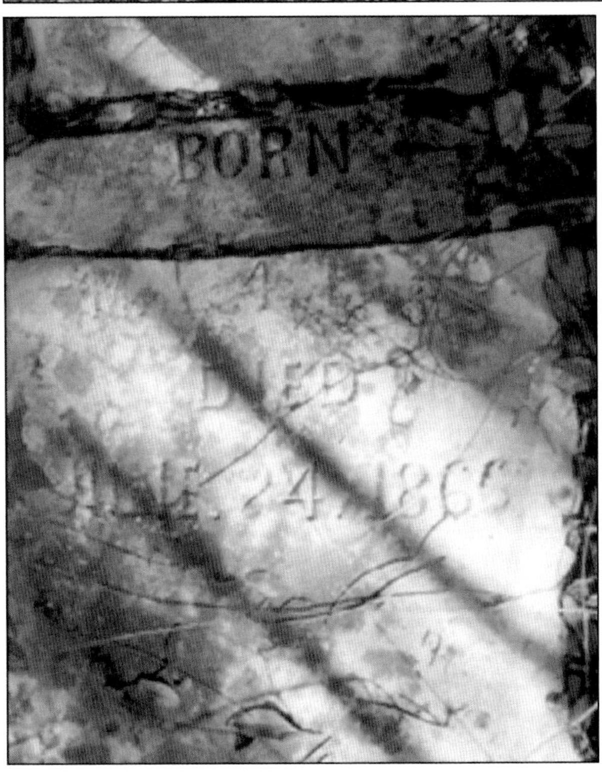


The small Slaughter Cemetery, located near Mary Moore Searight Park on Slaughter Lane, holds the remains of Augustine Slaughter and several of his relatives. His father was Kentuckian Stephen F. Slaughter, who received a league of land in 1835 that would later become part of Manchaca. Stephen named the creek that ran through his property Slaughter Creek, in honor of his son Augustine. (Courtesy Ann and Barry Trask.)

The Slaughter Cemetery has been ravaged by time, and few of the original headstones remain intact. What remains of the headstone belonging to Augustine Slaughter can be seen at left. He fought on the side of the north during the Civil War and was badly wounded. After he returned home, he succumbed to his war wounds. (Courtesy Fluttergirl.com.)

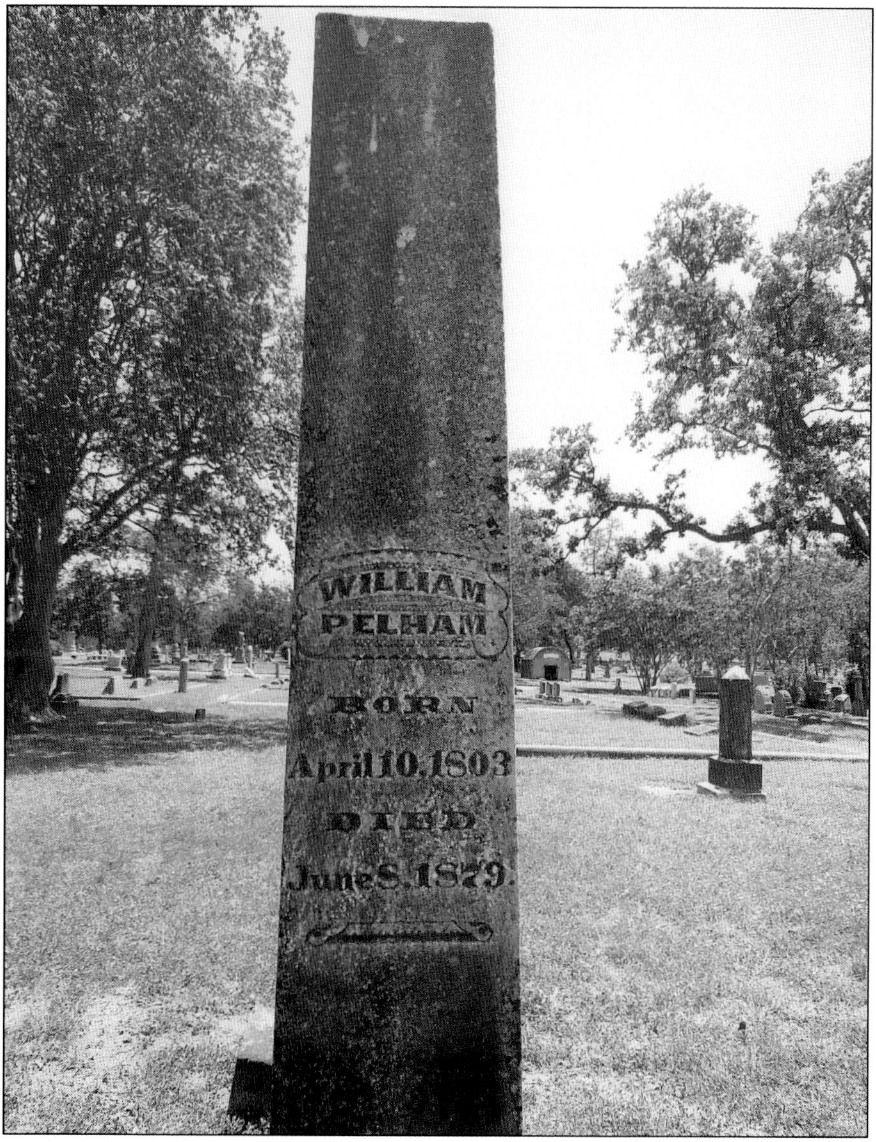


William Pelham; his wife, Mary Ann; and son Charles are buried in Oakwood Cemetery in downtown Austin. Pelham was the first postmaster at the Manchac House Post Office that operated from 1851 to 1852. Before 1880, *Manchac* was the accepted spelling of the springs and the area. The post office reflected that spelling in its name. Pelham had spent most of his life as a surveyor. In 1830, Pres. Andrew Jackson appointed him to survey the boundary between Arkansas and Louisiana. In 1841, President John Tyler appointed him surveyor general of Arkansas. His last presidential appointment came in 1854, when he was appointed by President Pierce to be surveyor general of the Territory of New Mexico. The Pelhams had three children, listed as follows: a son born in 1832 who died in 1834, a son named Charles Thomas, born 1839, and a daughter, Isabella, born in 1839. Charles was a noted Civil War hero who fought in Terry's Regiment, 8th Texas Cavalry, and was killed in 1864. William Pelham petitioned the Texas Legislature to rename his grandson Charles D. TenEyck, son of his daughter Isabella, to Charles Thomas Pelham, in honor of his fallen son. The petition was granted as noted in the *Weekly State Gazette* newspaper on November 16, 1864. (Courtesy Ann and Barry Trask.)

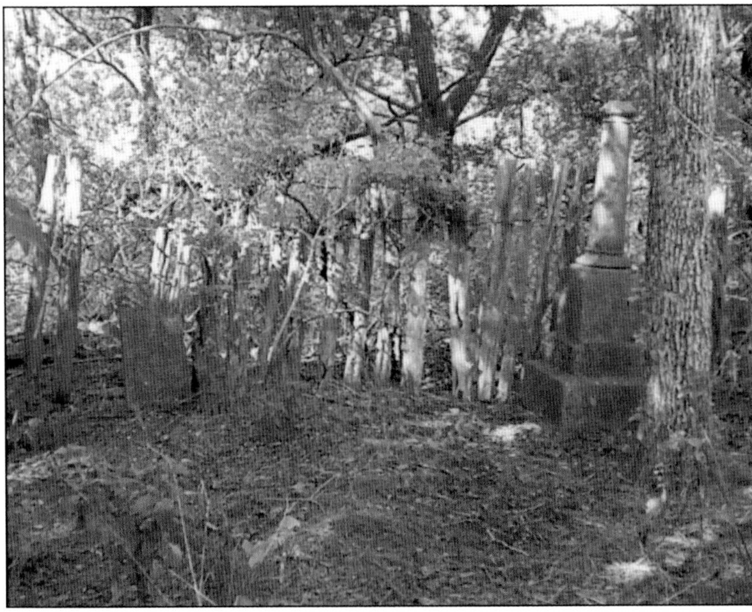

Deep in the woods behind Onion Creek Meadows subdivision, this cenotaph is testimony to the Shepperd family, who lived in the area in the 1800s. William and Thomas Shepperd died during the Civil War. It appears their mother, Sarah, also lost her husband Jay Shepperd, but remarried a John Runkle, who is buried here. (Courtesy Ann and Barry Trask.)

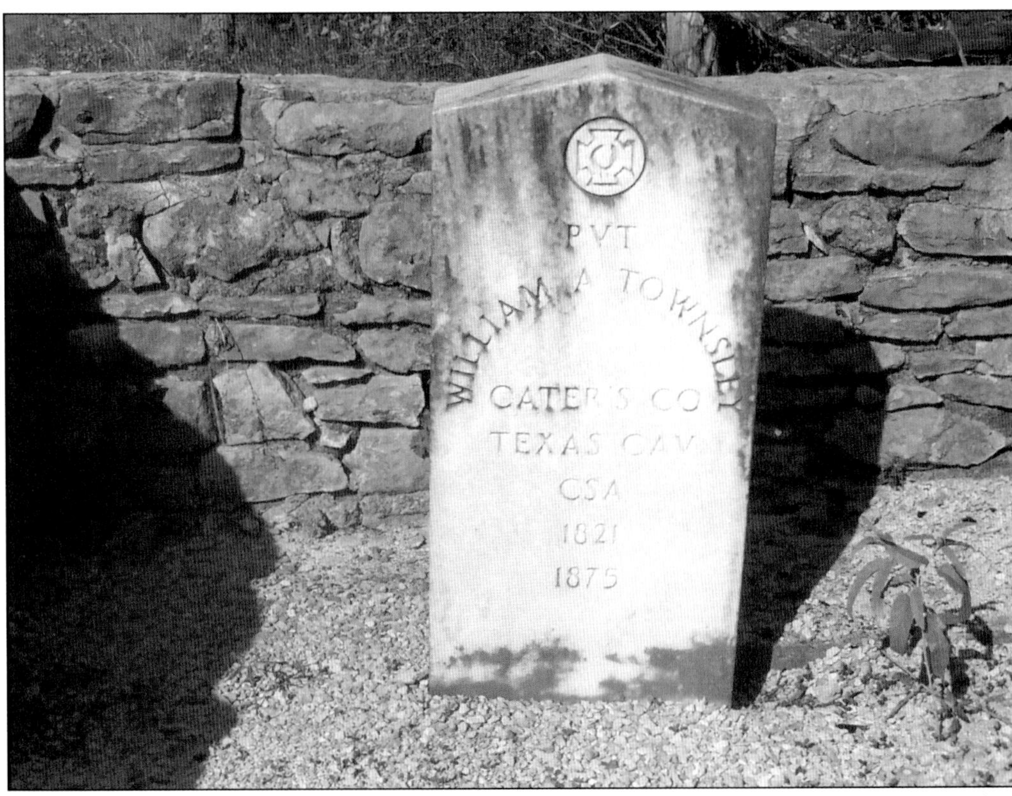


The Townsley Cemetery is located at the intersection of Johnson Road and FM 1626. Interred here is Civil War veteran William A. Townsley, who was born in Tennessee and came to Manchaca in 1856. Three other family members are buried next to him. Townsley was a justice of the peace. To signal the closing of the polls, he would shoot his gun. (Courtesy Ann and Barry Trask.)

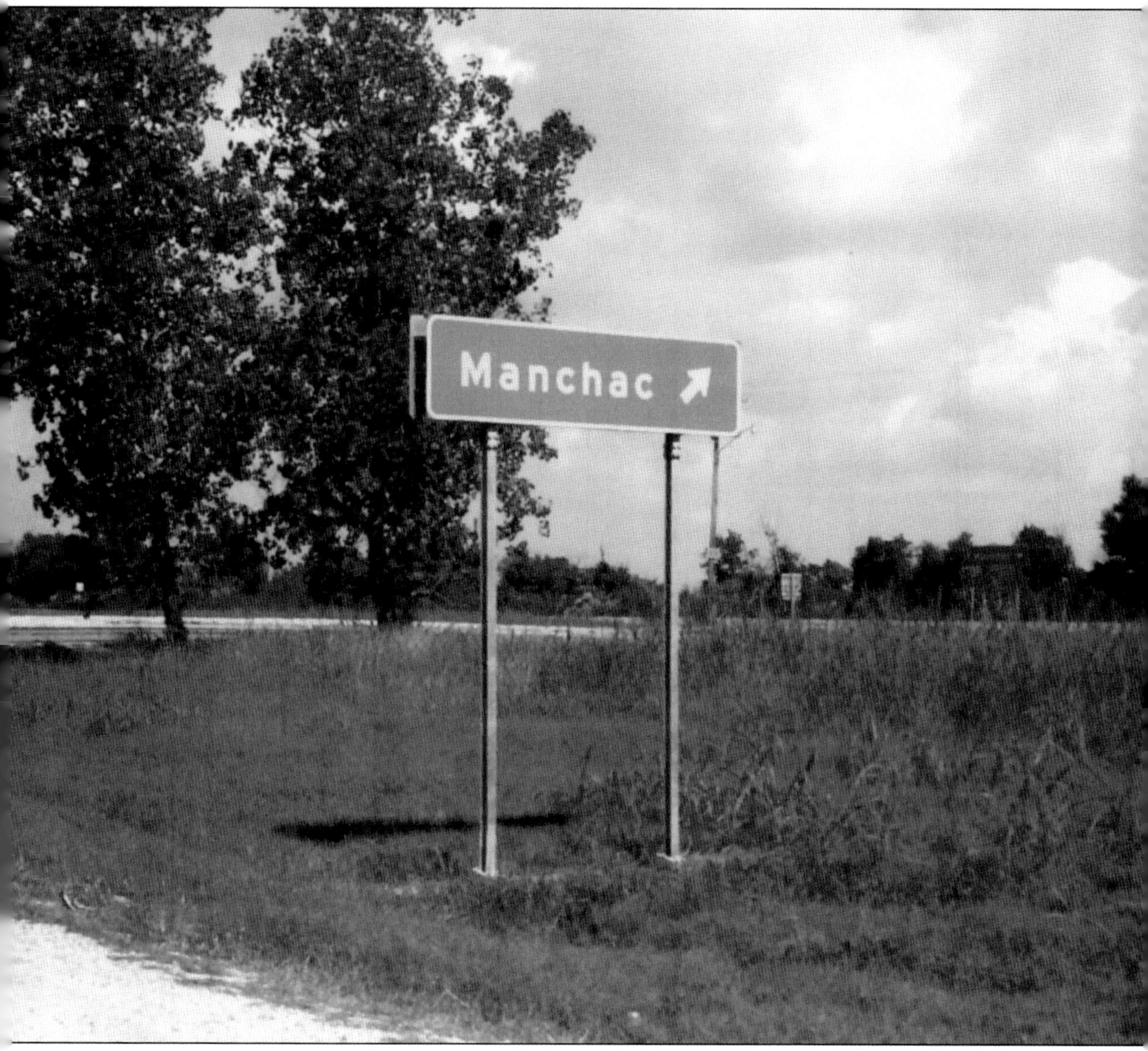


Old documents reveal that before the railroad came through Manchaca in 1880, the community of Manchaca and Manchaca Springs used the spelling of "Manchac". The origin of the name Manchaca or Manchac is a much debated subject and may never be proven. A possible explanation lies in the state of Louisiana where the name Manchac was first given to a military post established in 1763. Today in Louisiana, the community of Manchac, Pass Manchac, and Bayou Manchac all carry that name. The picture above was taken just outside the unincorporated community of Manchac, Louisiana which is situated on Lake Maurepas on the Pass Manchac waterway at the rear entrance to Lake Pontchartrain. Manchaca Springs, Manchaca, Texas, Pass Manchac, the community of Manchac, Louisiana, and Bayou Manchac are all located in the 30th parallel north of the equator. The word *Manchac* comes from the Choctaw language meaning "back door." Since Manchaca Springs is on the Old San Antonio Road that winds its way into the city of Austin from the south, could this be considered the "back door" to the capital of Texas? (Courtesy Kevin McCright.)

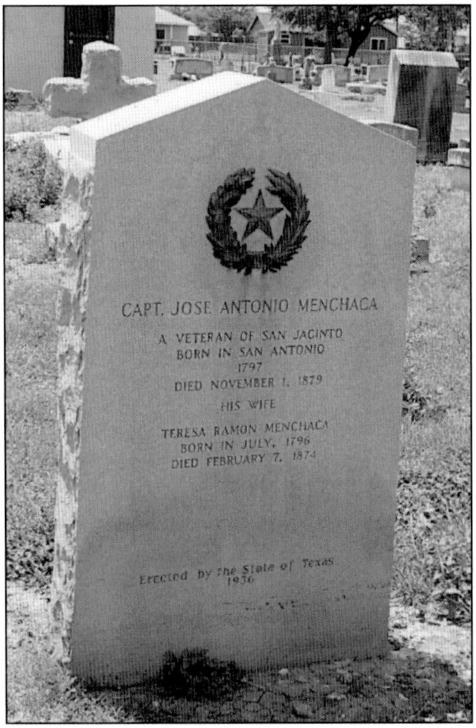


One oral tradition says Manchaca was named for Texas Revolutionary War hero Jose Antonio Menchaca, because he had camped at Manchaca Springs with his men to protect the settlers. Documentation has not been discovered that would support this story. According to the Texas State Historical Association, he commanded a company that patrolled the frontier from the San Antonio River to the Rio Grande. The "Ma" spelling of the name can be traced back to 1841. (Courtesy Ann and Barry Trask.)

In 1860, W.H. Jones, Mark Deloach, and Charles Harvey came to the area from Palestine, Texas, to establish themselves and buy stock. They were well armed and well financed. They called on resident Mr. Blocker and stopped a short time at Thomas Matthews's farm. Many days later, their bodies were discovered near the nine-mile post between Slaughter and Onion Creeks. The young men were buried in Oakwood Cemetery, and their burials were recorded on the ledger page below. (Courtesy Austin History Center, Austin Public Library.)

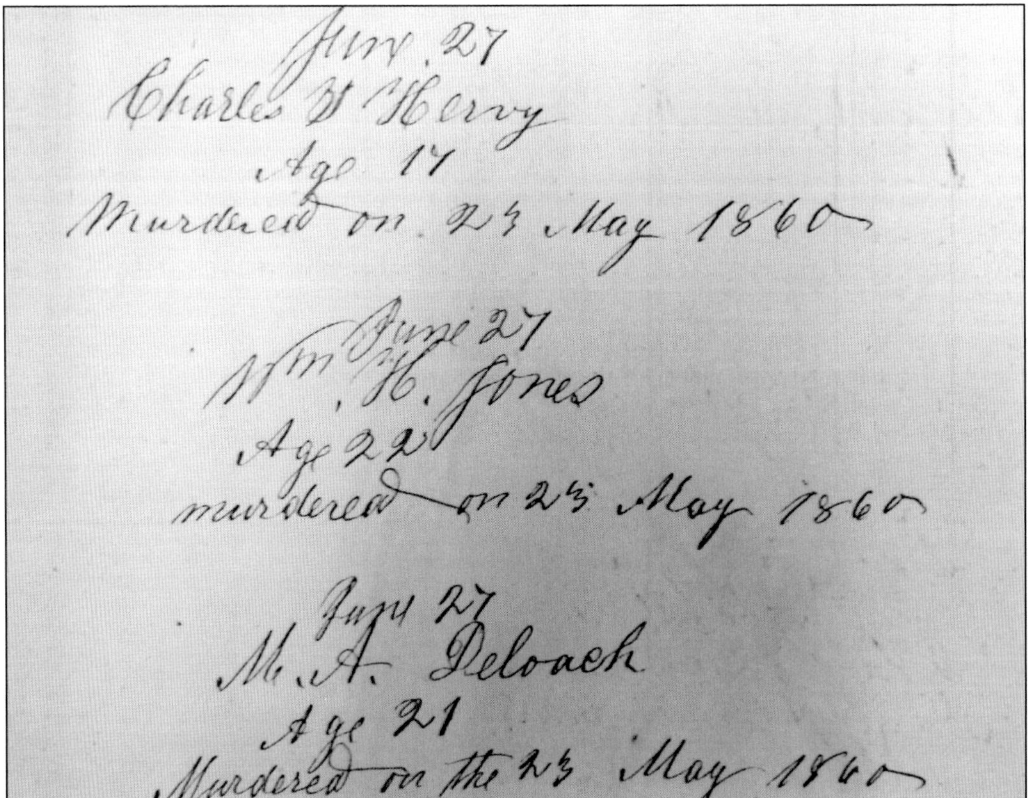
June 27
Charles H Hervy
Age 17
Murdered on 23 May 1860

June 27
Wm. H. Jones
Age 22
murdered on 23 May 1860

June 27
M. A. Deloach
Age 21
Murdered on the 23 May 1860

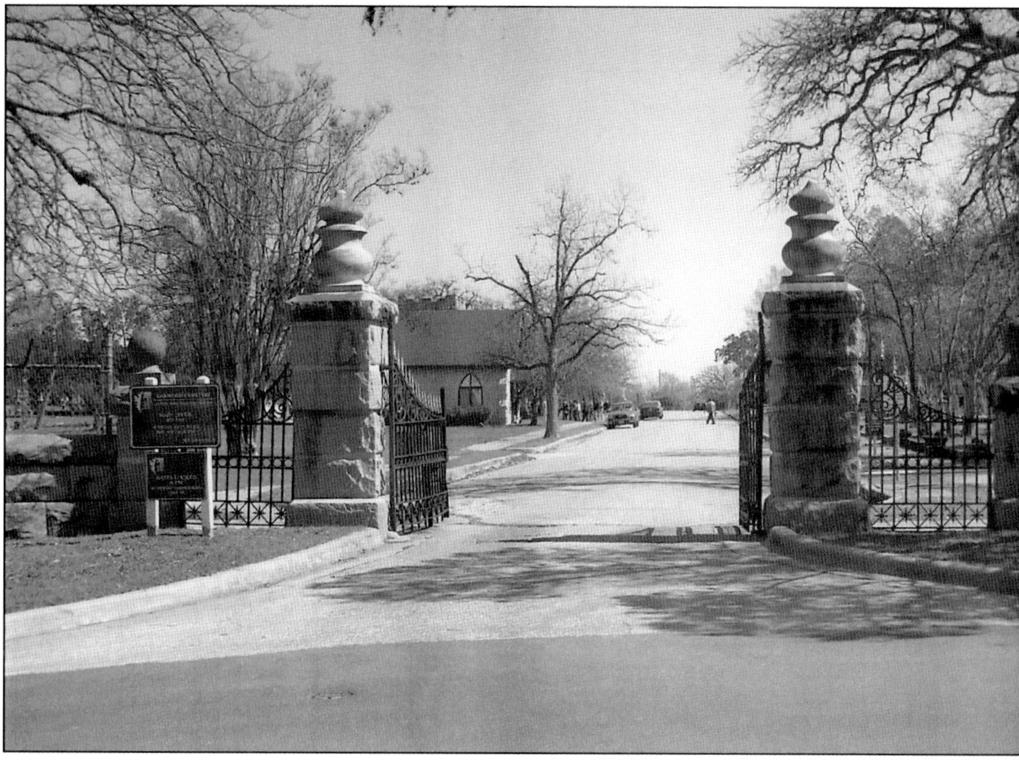

Two of the earliest recorded murders in the Manchaca area were perpetrated by Mier Expedition survivor John Taney, who settled on Bear Creek in the 1850s. These were also recorded in the *Annals of Frank Brown*, shelved at the Austin History Center. Paranoid and suffering from delusions, he shot two of his neighbors. On April 18, 1860, he was gunned down on the courthouse steps by friends of the men he killed. He is buried in an unmarked grave at Oakwood Cemetery, Austin, Texas. (Courtesy Ann and Barry Trask.)

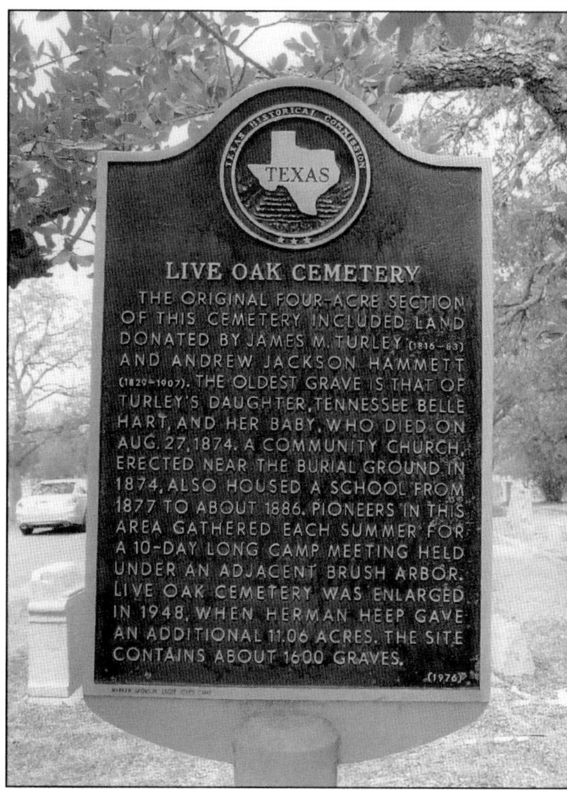


In 1874, Tennessee Belle Hart, daughter of James M. Turley, and her infant son were the first to be buried in historic Live Oak Cemetery. James Turley and Andrew Hammett donated the original four acres for the cemetery. Herman Heep donated an additional 11.06 acres in 1948. Live Oak is still an active cemetery. (Courtesy Ann and Barry Trask.)

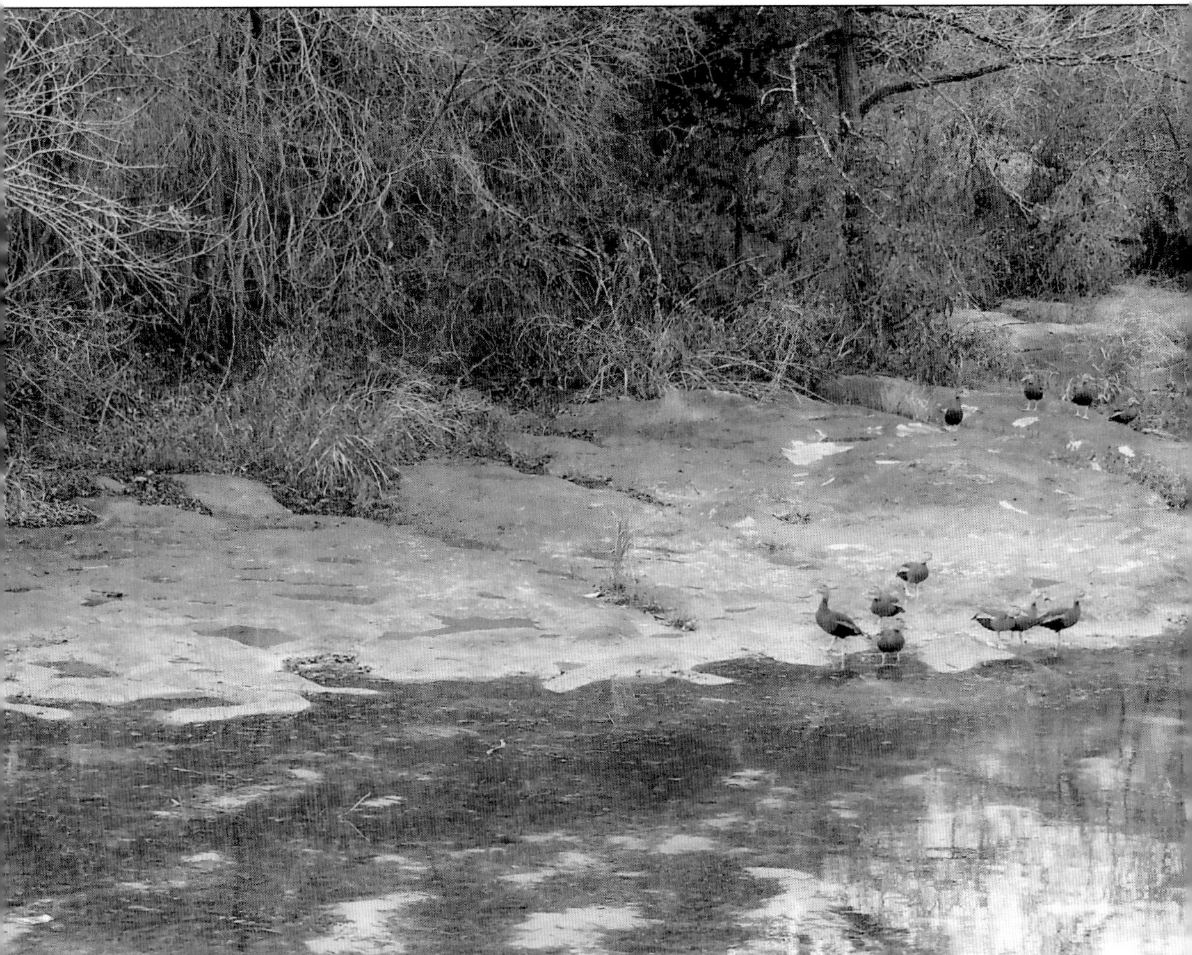

As pioneers moved west into Texas following the Old San Antonio Road, their wagons crossed a beautiful stream now called Onion Creek. Centuries of wagon wheels passing this way have left a permanent record in the limestone rock that covers the bottom of the creek. This crossing was mentioned in the *Annals of Frank Brown*. Back in 1841, a lone mail carrier crossed here on his way to Austin, but failed to arrive in town at the appointed time. A party of Indians had been seen along the creek at just the time the mail carrier would have made his crossing. The townspeople feared for the young man. Scouts were sent out to find him and, sadly, his body was discovered 12 miles from the city. He had been killed and scalped. (Courtesy Ann and Barry Trask.)

# *Two*

# Families and Friends

As people moved west to put down their roots, they were enticed to the Manchaca area by the rich farmland that is fed by several nearby creeks. When the railroad passed through town in 1880, it provided a means to get their crops to market. With these coveted resources available to them, farmers, ranchers, and businessmen liked what they found in Manchaca, and quickly made it their home.

The soul of Manchaca has always been the people who live there. It became a melting pot of hard working individuals with diverse personalities, nationalities, and talents. Blacksmiths, farmers, ranchers, merchants, butchers, teachers, constables, and doctors were all proud to call it home.

Several generations have passed since the original settlers of Manchaca purchased their land in the 19th century; however, they have certainly left their mark on the community. Driving through town, you will note that buildings and streets still carry such names as Blackwell, Johnson, Meredith, Deane, Turley, Wirth, and Polk. Descendants of some of those original families remain in the town today, living on cherished family land that has been passed down from generation to generation.

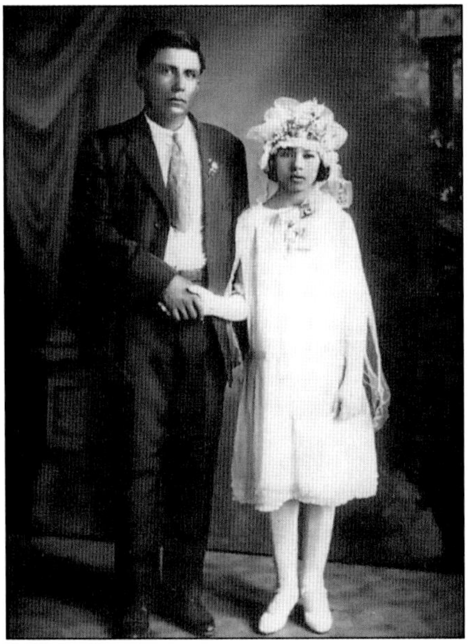

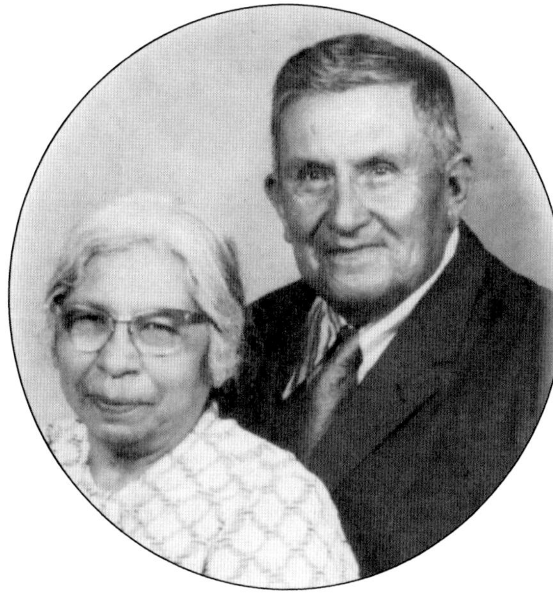

As the wedding day for Susie and Henry Acosta drew near in 1927, the excitement of the upcoming nuptials was infectious among their friends and family. The young couple is shown here on their wedding day, after reciting their solemn vows to each other. Susie and Henry moved to Manchaca in 1936, where they farmed cotton and raised hay on a piece of land just south of Onion Creek and east of Interstate Highway 35. Their son Frank remembers this land is just south of where Onion Creek Country Club is today. (Both photographs above courtesy Mary and Frank Acosta.)

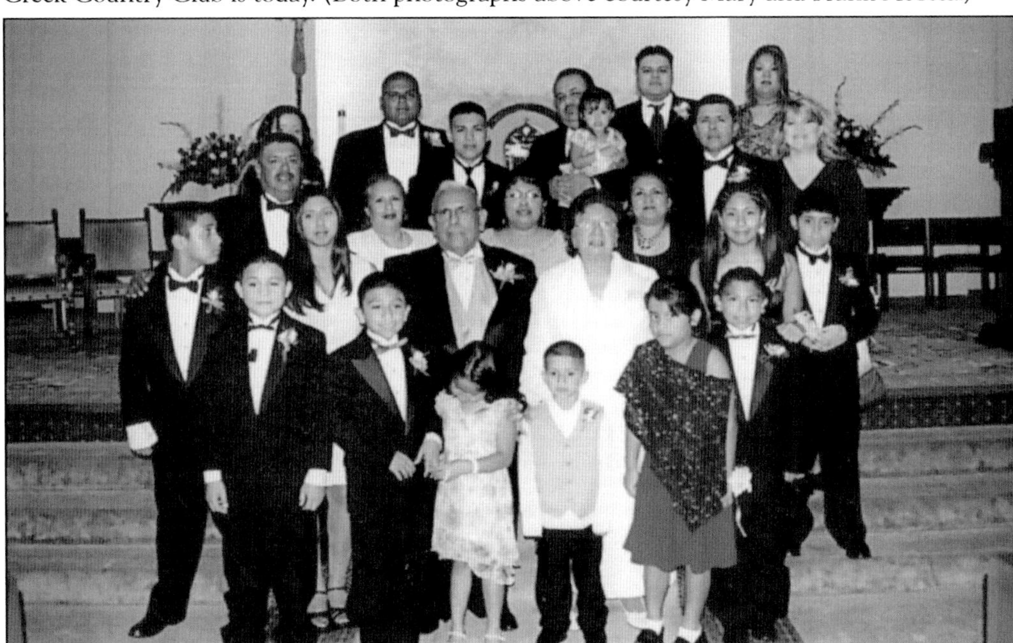

Few couples can claim 55 years of marriage, and fewer still can say they spent those years in one town. Mary and Frank Acosta can claim both of those achievements. Surrounded by family consisting of three daughters, three sons, many grandchildren, and several great-grandchildren, the Acostas gather to celebrate a memorable wedding anniversary. (Courtesy Mary and Frank Acosta.)

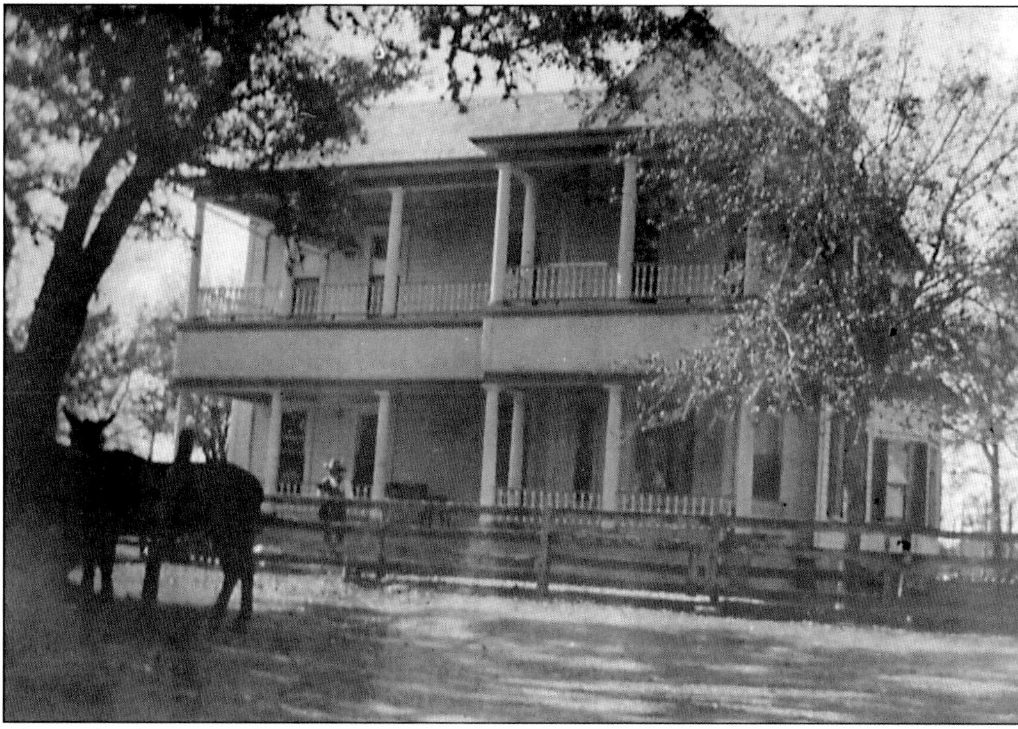

The Barker house was located on what is today called Frate Barker Road. It was the home of rancher Euphrates "Frate" Barker and his wife, Drusilla Johnson Barker. He and his wife ran a successful ranch. Drusilla's brother Bob Johnson and his wife, Ellen Bruce Blackwell Johnson, also lived in this home for several years after their marriage in 1917. (Courtesy Martha and Chester Johnson.)

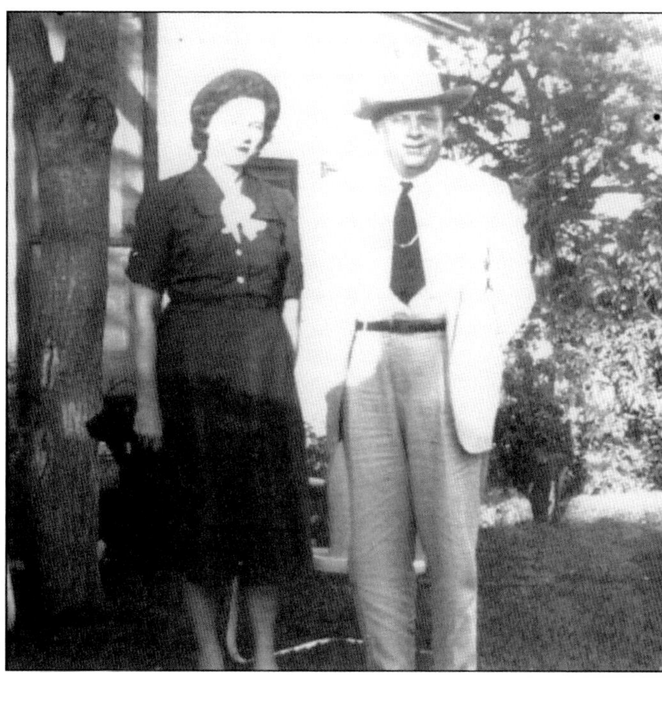

Maude and Robert Bauerle owned a successful grocery store located on south Lamar Boulevard. Enticed by the beautiful land just south of Austin, they sold their business and moved to Manchaca with their son, Leon, and daughter, Joyce. Once established in town, they took up ranching. (Courtesy Joy Simmons.)

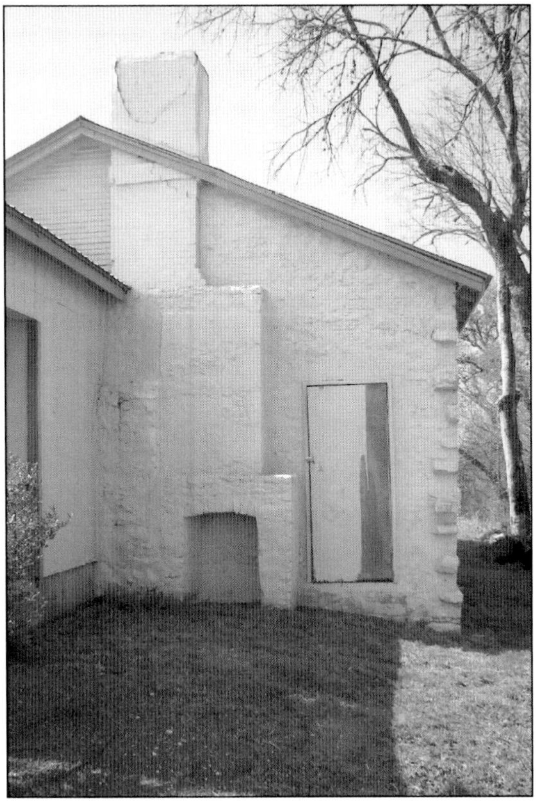

A portion of the Gottfried Birkner home, built along Bear Creek in 1876, can be seen at left. The home has been greatly modified and is now part of Marbridge. It is directly across FM 1626 from the home Gottfried's son William built, located on the Johnson property. The homes are within waving distance of each other. (Courtesy Betty Korts.)

Built between 1898 and 1900 by William H. Birkner for his family, this home is located on property owned by Martha and Chester Johnson. Sadly, it is scheduled for demolition the summer of 2013 to make way for a new housing development. Martha's parents, Ellen Bruce Blackwell Johnson and Bob Johnson, lived in this home, and Martha grew up here. It sits directly across FM 1626 from the Gottfried Birkner home that is now part of the Marbridge property. (Courtesy Martha and Chester Johnson.)

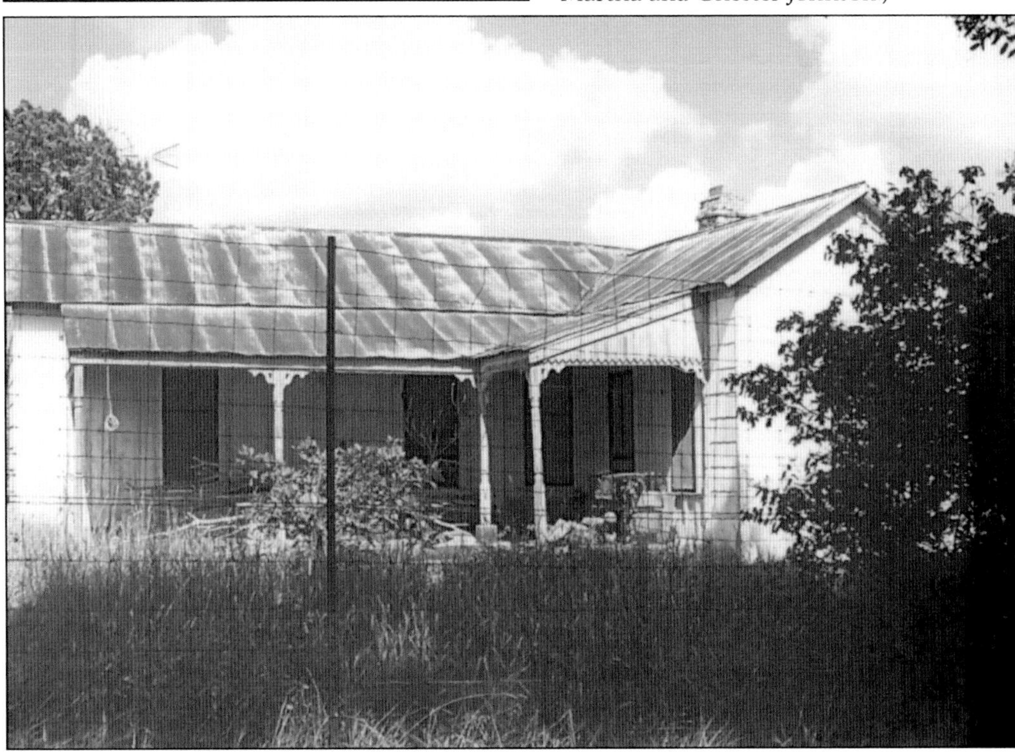

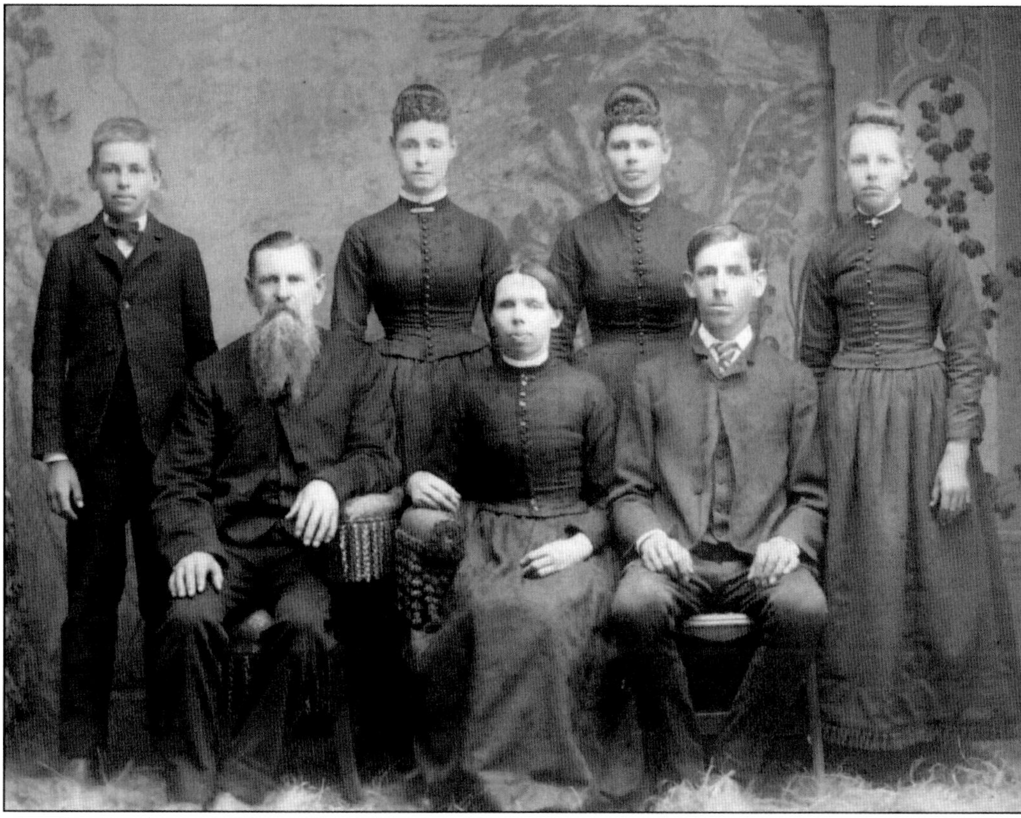

Gottfried Birkner and his wife, Helena Stoffers Birkner, came from Germany. Gottfried was a CSA Civil War veteran who fought at Galveston in the 1st Texas Heavy Artillery. He is shown here around 1888 in Austin with five of his six children. From left to right are (seated) Gottfried Birkner, Helene Stoffers Birkner, and son Otto Birkner; (standing) William H. Birkner, Minnie Birkner (Huff), Mollie Birkner (Brown), and Callie Birkner (Elliott). They were expert stone masons, grain millers, and farmers. (Courtesy Alan Owens, Clif Ladd, and Betsy Wilkinson.)

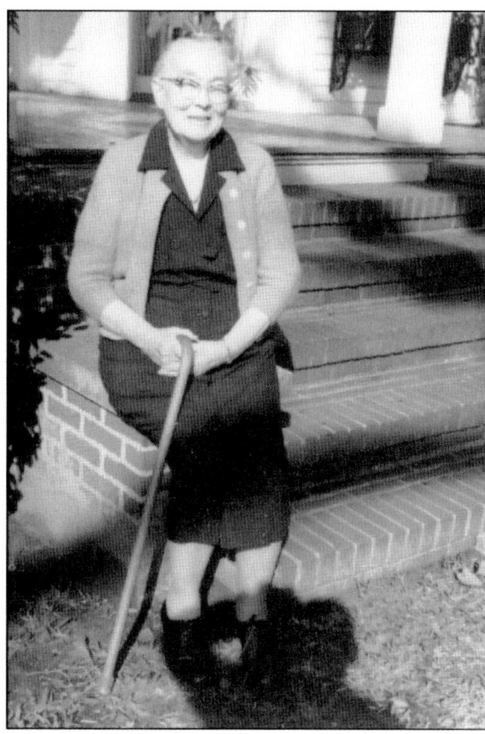

In 1965, when fifth grader Christine Allen was assigned a school project to research someone in Texas history, she chose Edna Carpenter. She contacted the Hogans, who authored *Tales from the Manchaca Hills*, which contains Edna's memoirs. The Hogans sent her a copy of the book, plus this wonderful photograph of Edna taken in 1965, the last year of her life. (Courtesy Christine A. Moseley, PhD.)

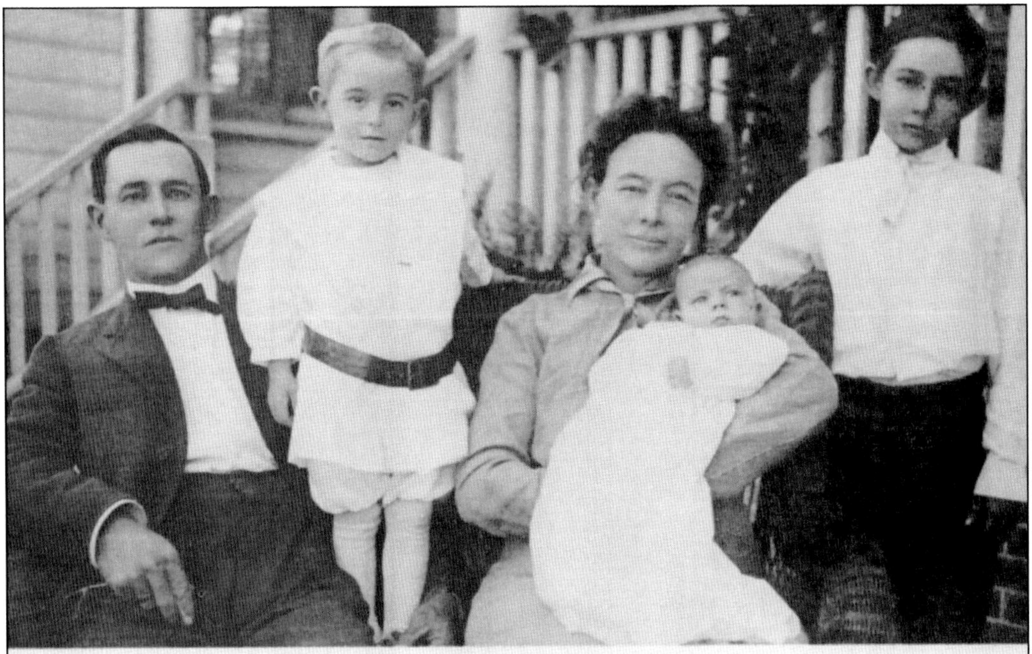

*Family portrait, 1914*

In 1914, the Carpenter family of Manchaca gathered for a photograph. Shown from left to right are Shawnee Thomas, Thomas Wheeler, Edna, baby Jane Sue, and Shawnee Turley, their oldest who went by "Buck." Their daughter, Jane Carpenter Hogan, and her husband, William Ransom Hogan, recorded Edna's life story in the delightful book, *Tales of the Manchaca Hills an Unvarnished Memoir.* The family moved into the Victorian home shown below in 1909. It still stands today on the south side of FM 1626, in the heart of Manchaca, and is known as The Carpenter House. (Above, courtesy *Tales of the Manchaca Hills: An Unvarnished Memoir*; below, courtesy PICA 29119, Austin History Center, Austin Public Library.)

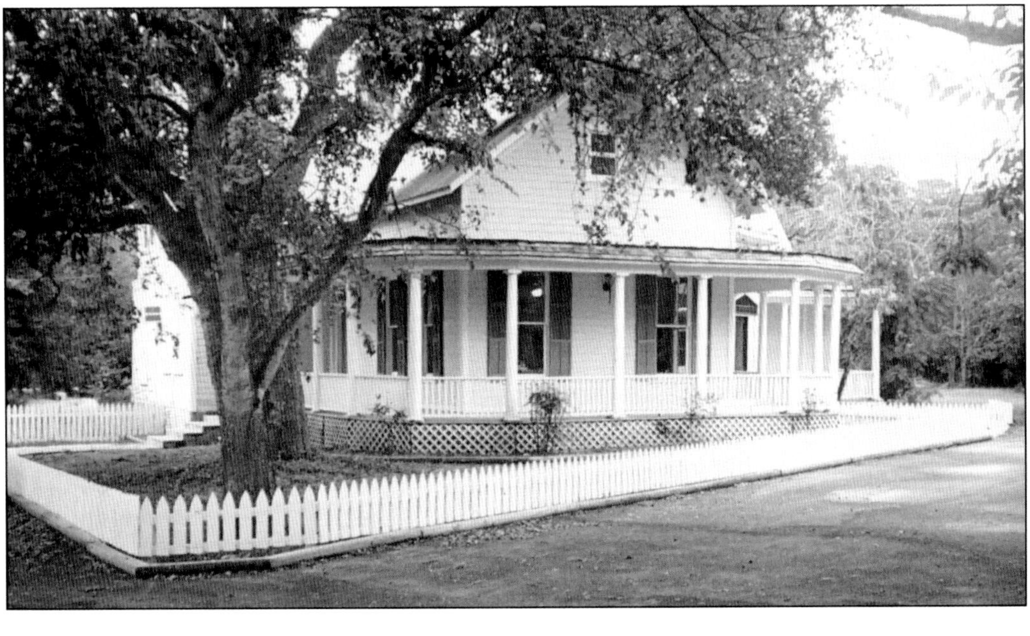

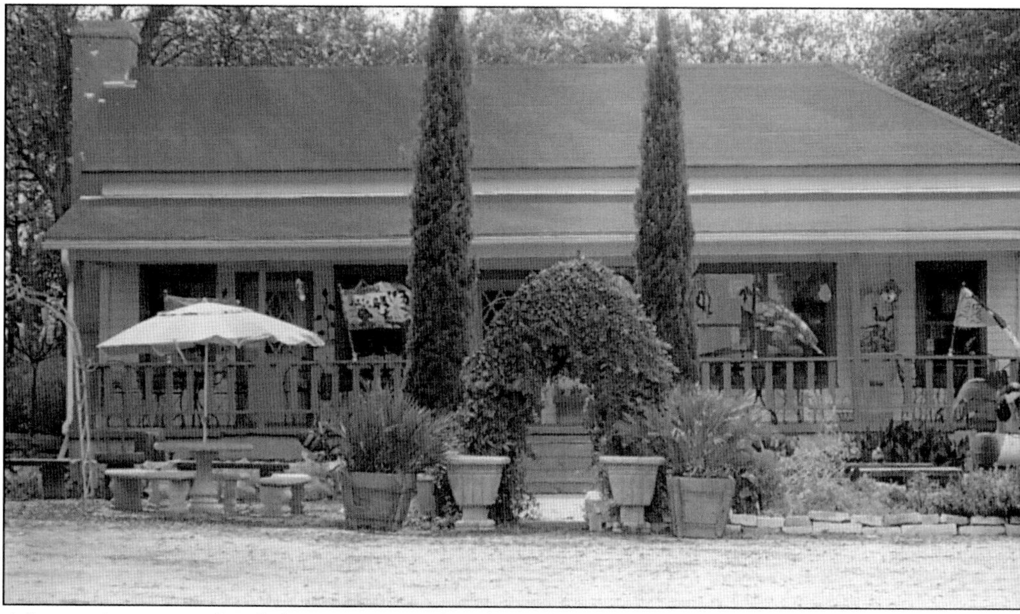

African American freed slaves Mary and Jack Dodson had both belonged to a man named Jim Dodson while enslaved. They fell in love and married in 1870, when Mary was just 21 years old. They moved to Manchaca by 1900 and built this home, which we know today as the neighborhood nursery "Its About Thyme." Mary and Jack raised nine children, three girls and six boys. Dodson excelled as a businessman in the community, owning a meat market and a molasses mill. The handsome headstone below for Mary and Jack is located in historic Bethany Cemetery in east Austin. (Both, courtesy Ann and Barry Trask.)

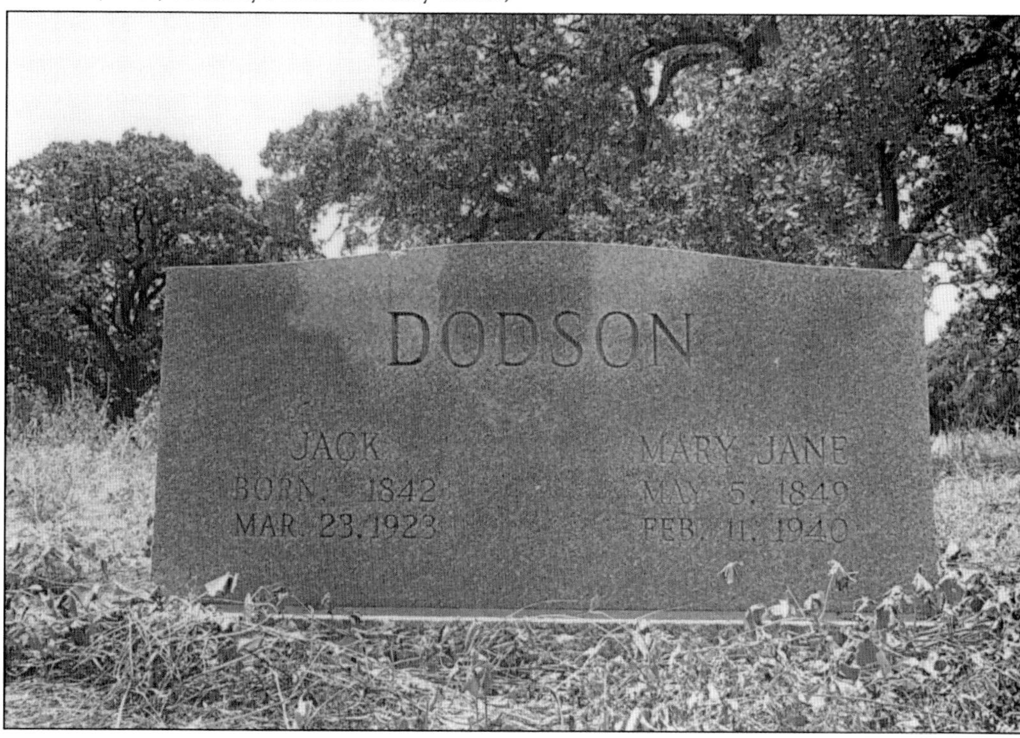

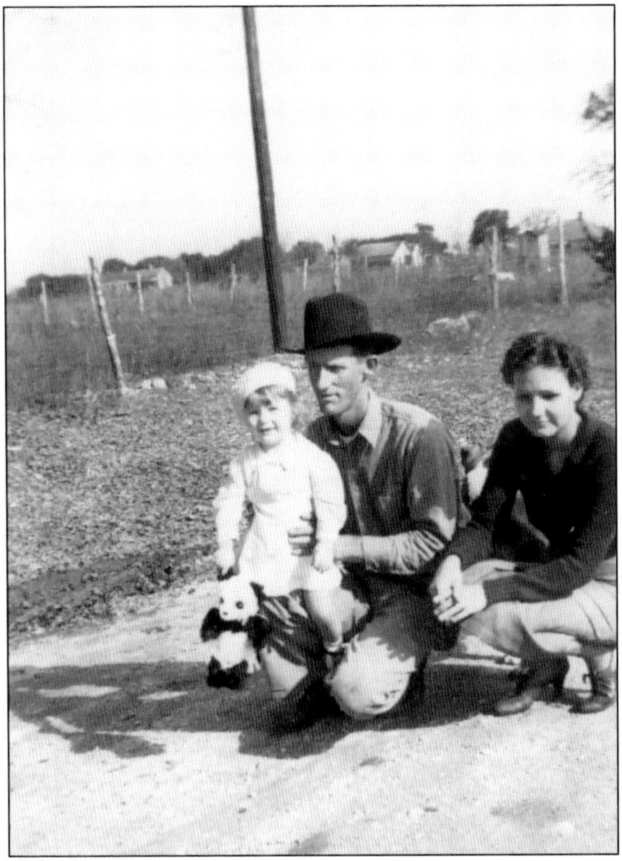

John Blanton Deane, born in 1910, and Rowena Cruze Deane, born in 1919, knew each other all their lives. It was no surprise to friends in Manchaca when they fell in love and married. They are shown here in the late 1930s with their daughter Joanne. (Courtesy Joanne Deane.)

Photographed in front of a weathered old board-and-batten building are members of three related families who called the Manchaca area home. Shown from left to right are Ed Boyles, Addie Boyles, Claude Deane, Nolen Murry Cruze, Clyde Deane, and Joe Forrest Deane. (Courtesy Lillie M. Moreland.)

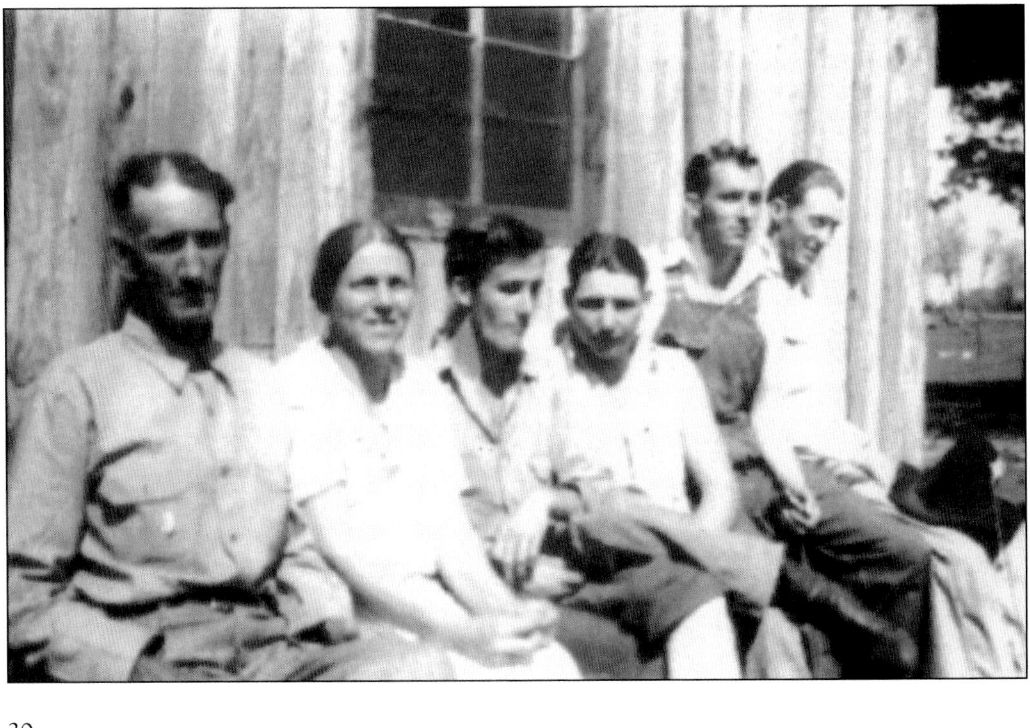

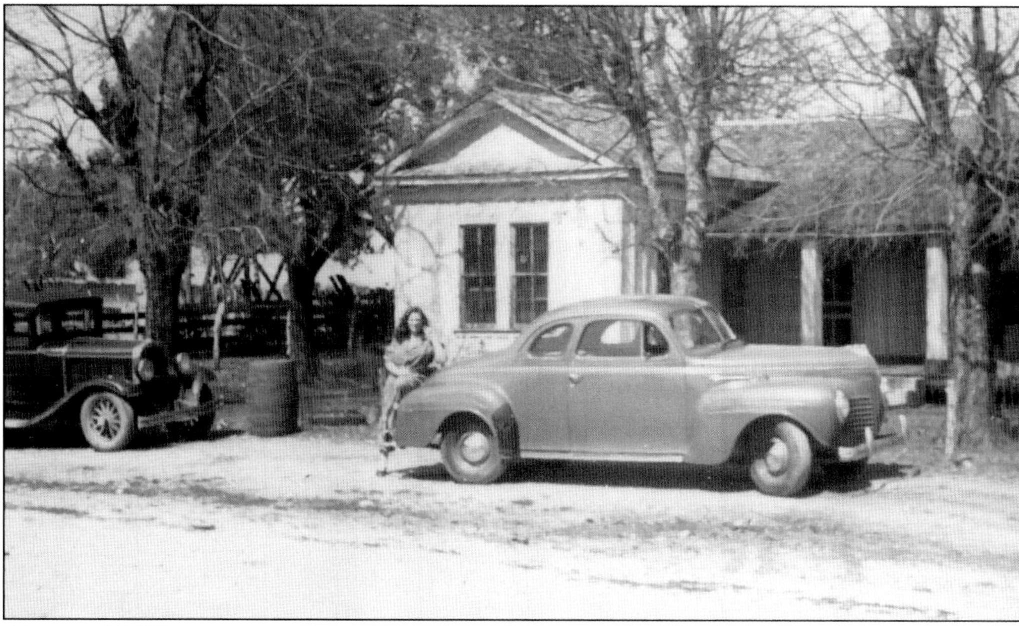

Alice and William Peyton Cruze moved into this home in 1922, where they raised their three children, Rowena Christine, Elle Rae (shown here), and Nolan Murphy. William was a skilled butcher, and Alice was known for the wonderful meat dishes she cooked. The home had a deep well that provided much-needed water for several Manchaca residents. (Courtesy Joanne Deane.)

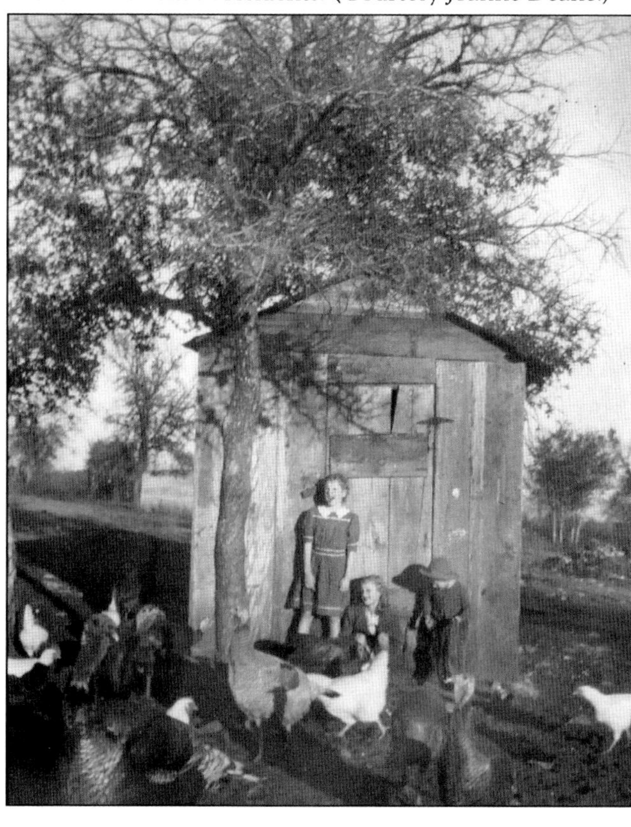

Every home had an outhouse in the old days. Much to the chagrin of their owners, sometimes the older neighborhood boys thought it was great fun to turn them over. Playing in front of the outhouse at their Grandma Deane's home are, from left to right, Claudette, Joanne, and Will Scott Deane. (Courtesy Joanne Deane.)

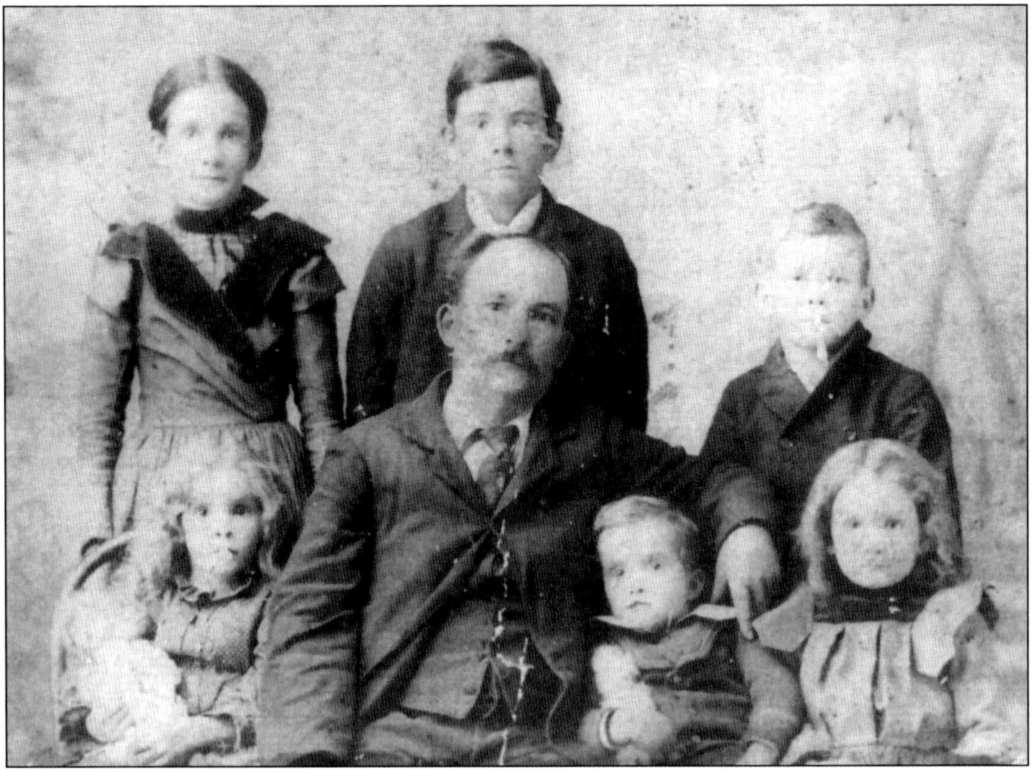

Blacksmith Joseph Lamb lost his wife, Mary Dunnahoo, to typhoid fever in 1899. This portrait shows the young family a few short years after Mary's death. Shown here from left to right are (first row) Vivian, Joe, Walter, and Mattie; (second row) Virginia, Jesse, and Edgar. (Courtesy Caroline O'Brien.)

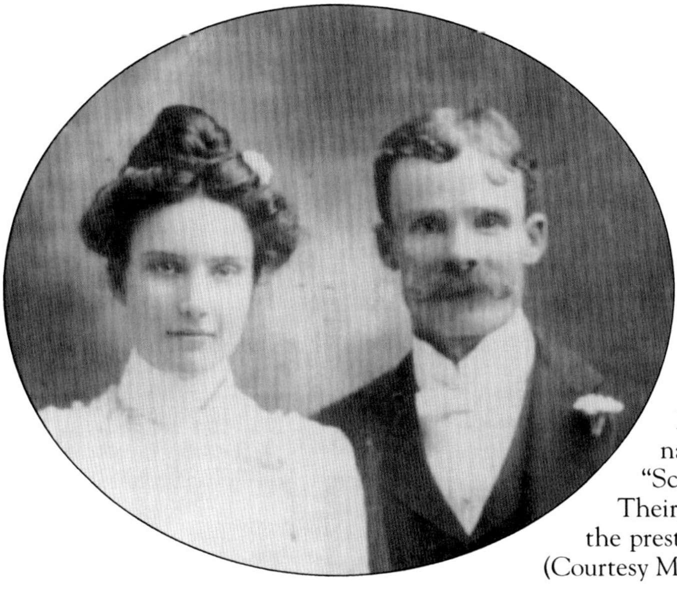

On May 16, 1901, Cordie N. Labenske and Thomas Matthews Dunnahoo married at Manchaca Methodist church. The two had both been correspondents for the *Texas State Democrat Farm and Home* newspaper using the pen names "Antoinette" for Cordie and "Scarlet" for Tom, who had red hair. Their first night together was spent at the prestigious Driskill Hotel in Austin. (Courtesy Marilyn Dunnahoo McLeod.)

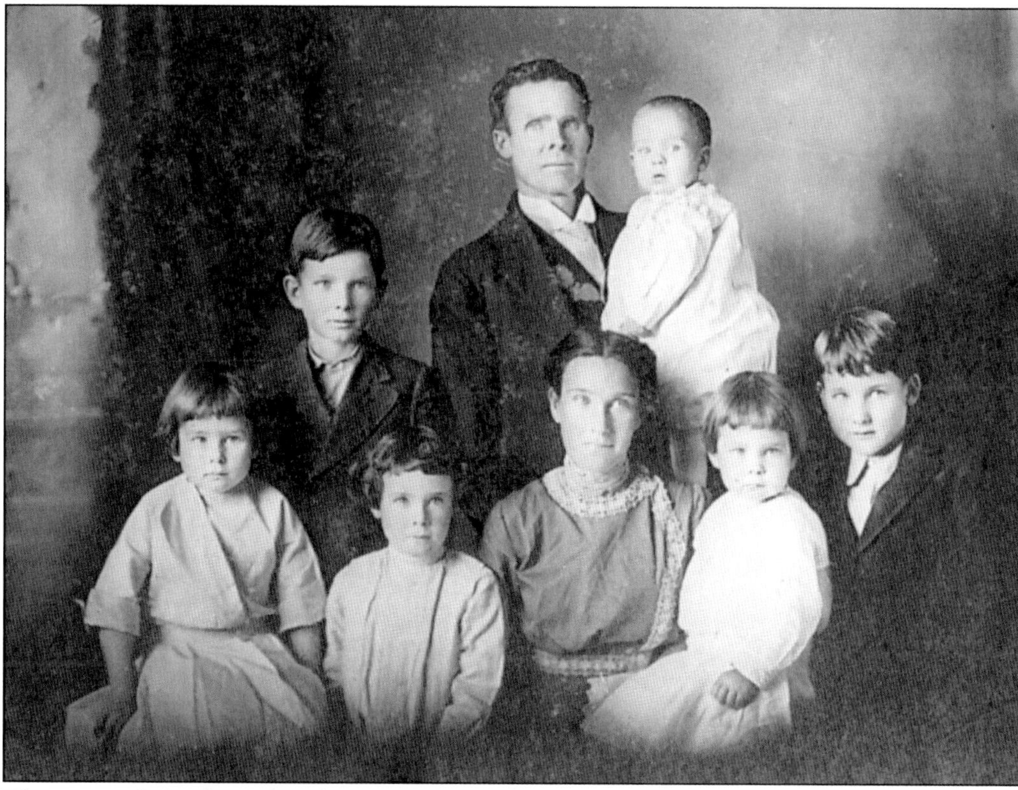

Thomas and Cordie Labenske Dunnahoo raised a family of nine in Manchaca. This 1913 photograph shows the young growing family posing for the camera in their Sunday best. Shown from left to right are (first row) Genevieve, Lillian, Cordie, Cordelia and Timothy; (second row) Chester, Thomas, and baby Daniel. (Courtesy Marilyn Dunnahoo McLeod.)

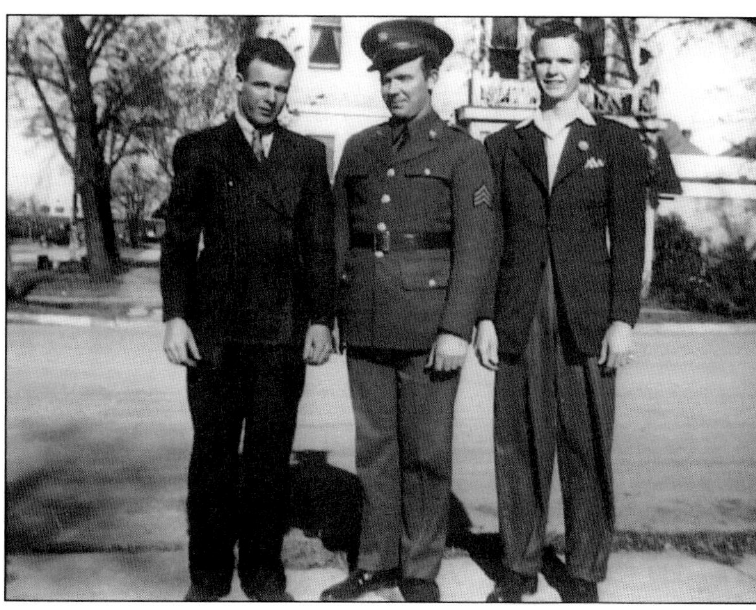

A family gathering in December 1942 brought these Dunnahoo brothers together for some family time. Shown from left to right are Seth, Daniel, and James. Coming from a large family of nine children, it was always nice to get together for the holidays. (Courtesy Marilyn Dunnahoo McLeod.)

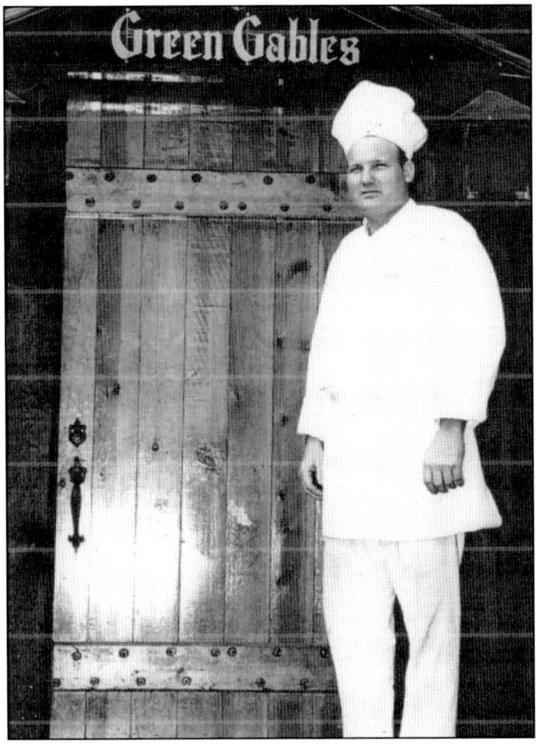


Timothy "Red" Dunnahoo was born in Manchaca in 1904. He started his cooking career in the oil fields of west Texas. In 1940, he became the head chef at the Green Gables Restaurant in Phoenix, Arizona, and held that position for 20 years. The Green Gables was a legendary restaurant in Phoenix during that time, catering to the rich and famous, such as Duncan Hines and Henry Fonda. (Courtesy Virginia Dunnahoo.)

Roy Felps was the son of Newton Felps. Roy and his wife, Vera, had five children, pictured below. Shown from left to right are (first row) Joan Joy, Jimmie Wesley, and John Roy (John Roy and Joan Joy are twins); (second row) Loretta Mae and Margie Elaine. Roy passed away shortly after the twins were born. (Courtesy Shirley DeBerry.)

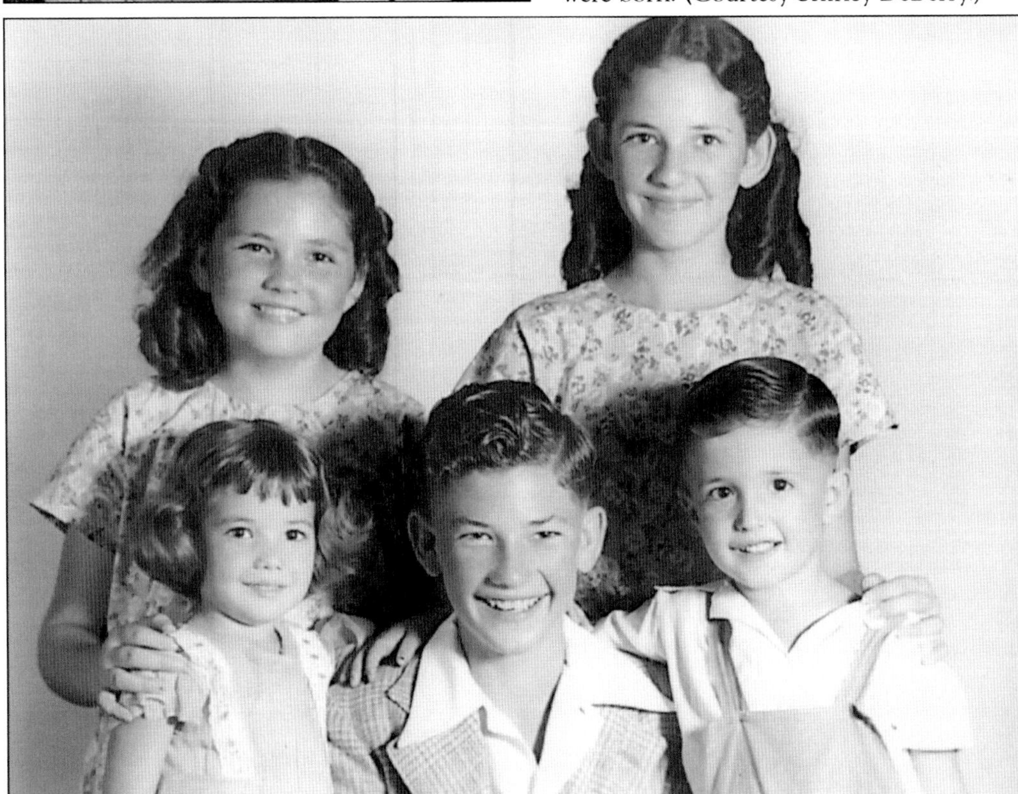

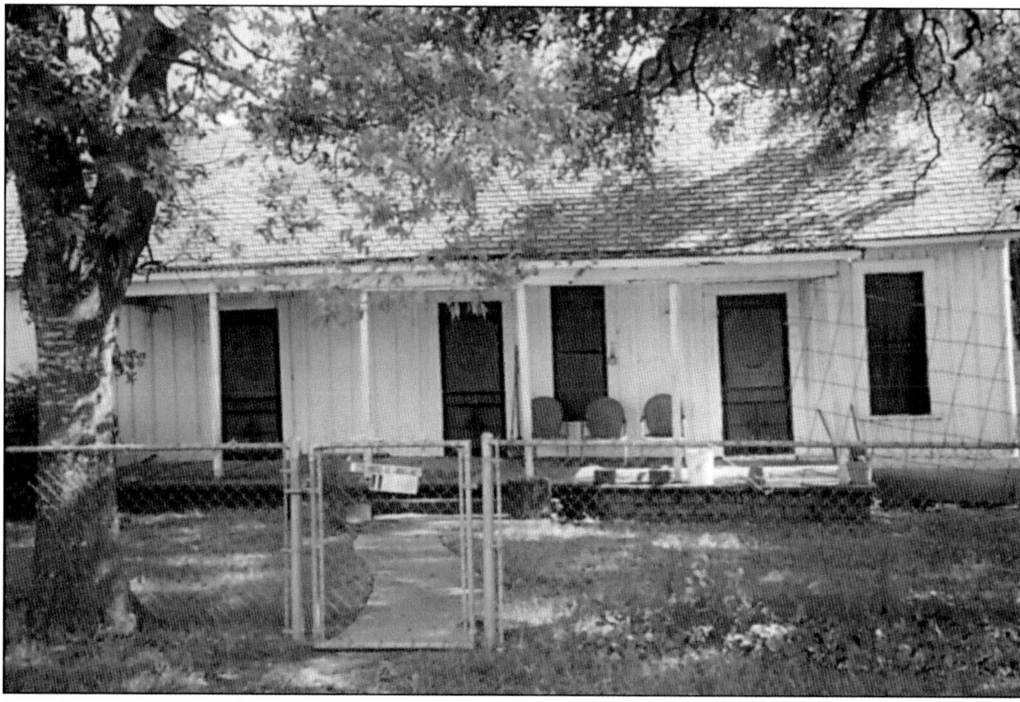

Standing on the southwest corner of FM 1626 and Twin Creeks Road, the Felps home was a familiar sight to Manchaca residents. This home takes its name from Newton Henry Felps Sr. and his wife, Louise Ellen Felps, who lived there for more than 60 years. It was built by Thomas Carpenter. After falling into disrepair, it was recently demolished to make way for new construction in town. (Courtesy Shirley DeBerry.)

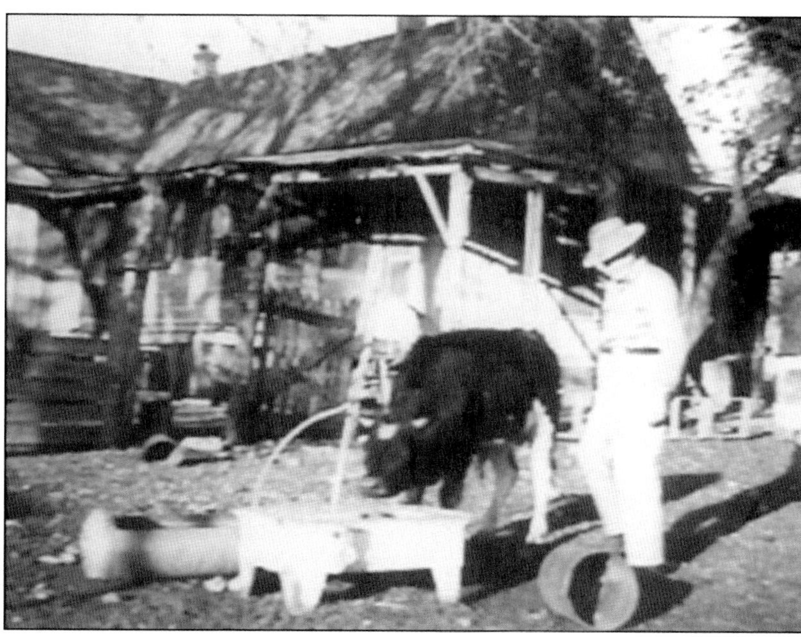

Newton Henry Felps, Sr. is seen here feeding one of his cows. He usually kept two to three cows, a hog or two, chickens, and a horse. He also kept a large garden that provided his family with fresh, hand-picked produce. Felps was a blacksmith by trade. (Courtesy Shirley DeBerry.)

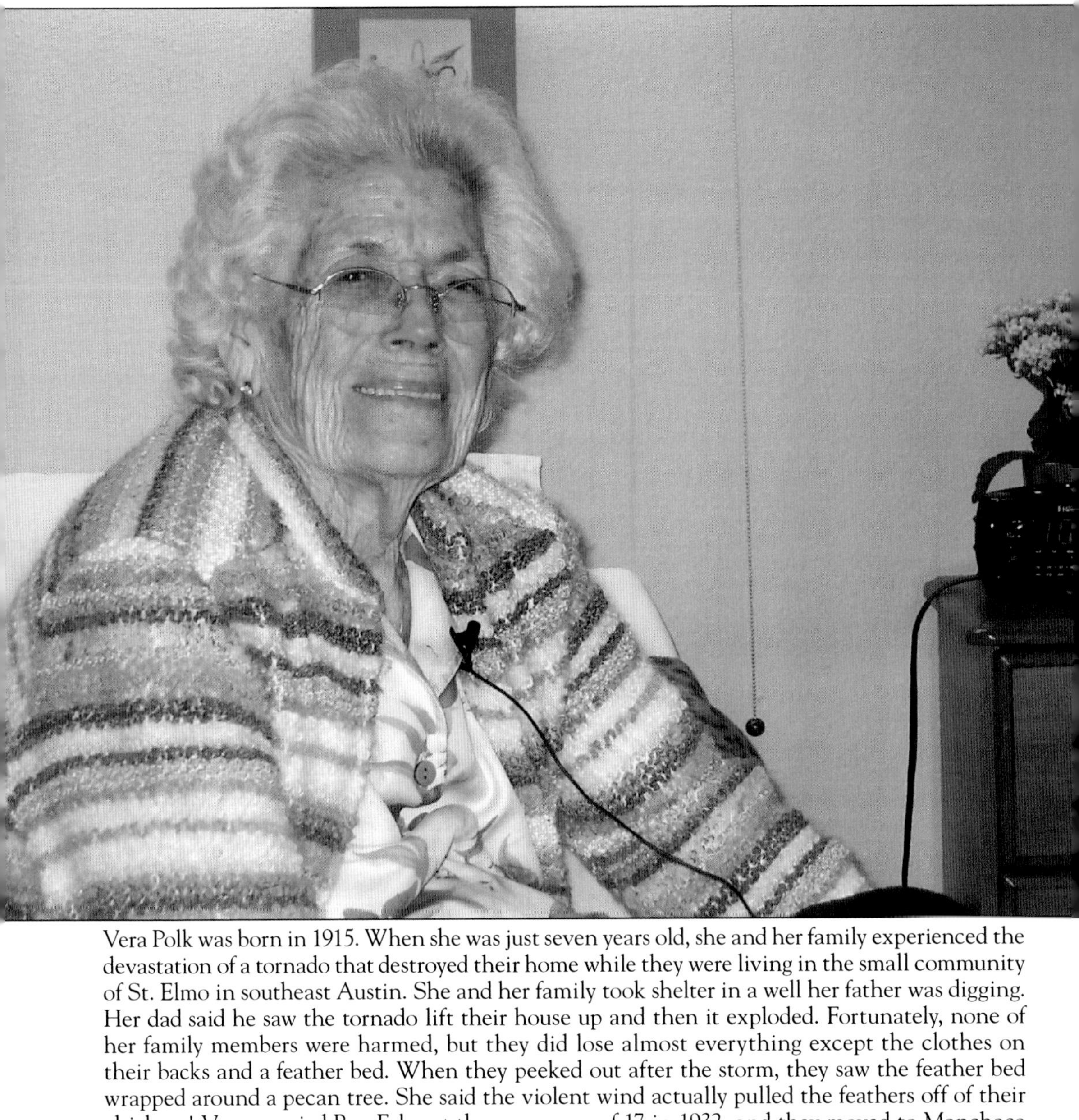

Vera Polk was born in 1915. When she was just seven years old, she and her family experienced the devastation of a tornado that destroyed their home while they were living in the small community of St. Elmo in southeast Austin. She and her family took shelter in a well her father was digging. Her dad said he saw the tornado lift their house up and then it exploded. Fortunately, none of her family members were harmed, but they did lose almost everything except the clothes on their backs and a feather bed. When they peeked out after the storm, they saw the feather bed wrapped around a pecan tree. She said the violent wind actually pulled the feathers off of their chickens! Vera married Roy Felps at the young age of 17 in 1932, and they moved to Manchaca in 1938 with their three children. They saved their money and were able to purchase two acres and build a one-room house. Roy passed on in 1944. Vera then married Alton Polk in 1947, and they moved into a home on Polk Road. (Courtesy Ann and Barry Trask.)

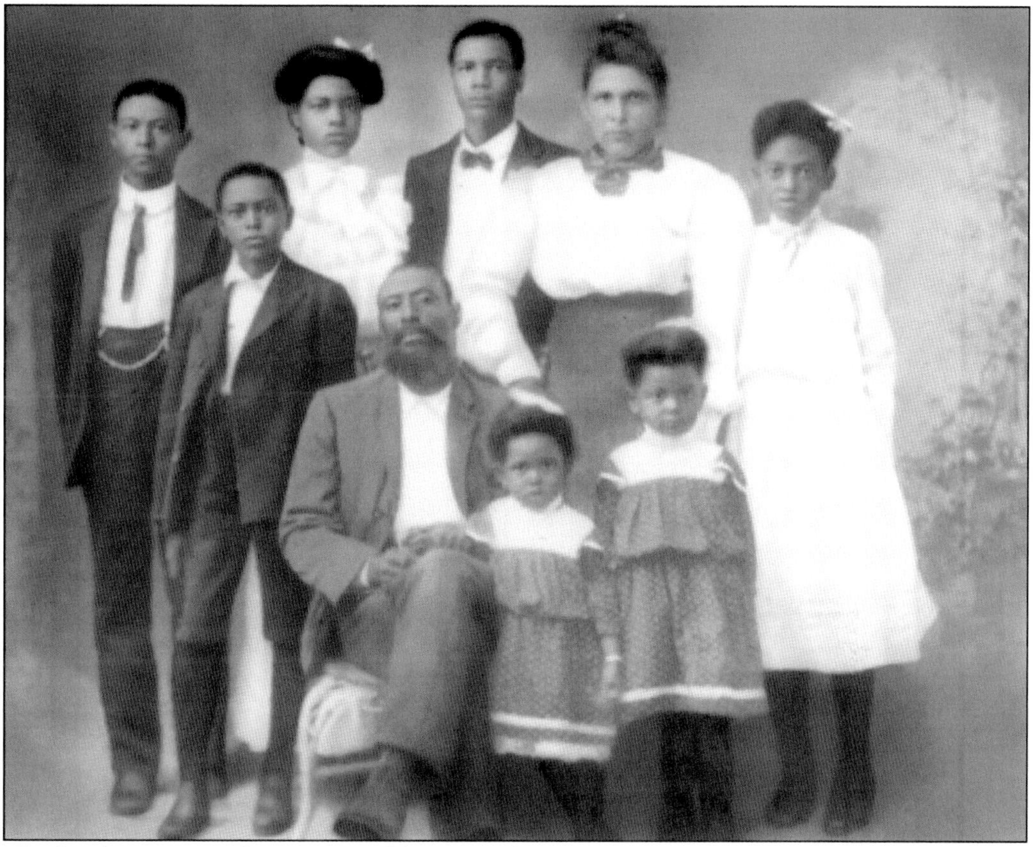

The family surname of Hargis is well known to longtime Manchaca residents. Willie Hargis was born in 1883 to Aaron and Roxie Ann Bailey Hargis. He and his bride, Maggie Perry, settled in Manchaca. They raised eight children, Estella, Lonnie, Odean, Bertha, Willie Jr., Otis, Corrine, and Chatam. Their son Chatam was named for Chatam Perry, who came to the Manchaca area some time after 1865 with his wife Ann. The Perry Cemetery was founded in 1896 when Chatam Perry died and was buried there. Willie and Maggie are also buried in this historic cemetery. Willie's parents are shown above with some of their children. Shown from left to right are (first row) Leslie, Aaron, Ethel, and unidentified; (second row) James Green, unidentified, Otto, Roxie Ann, and unidentified. (Above, courtesy Willie Hargis; below, courtesy Ann and Barry Trask.)

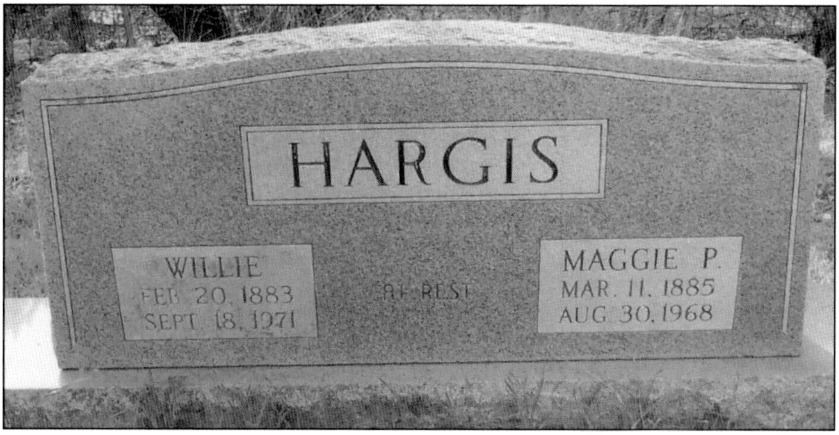

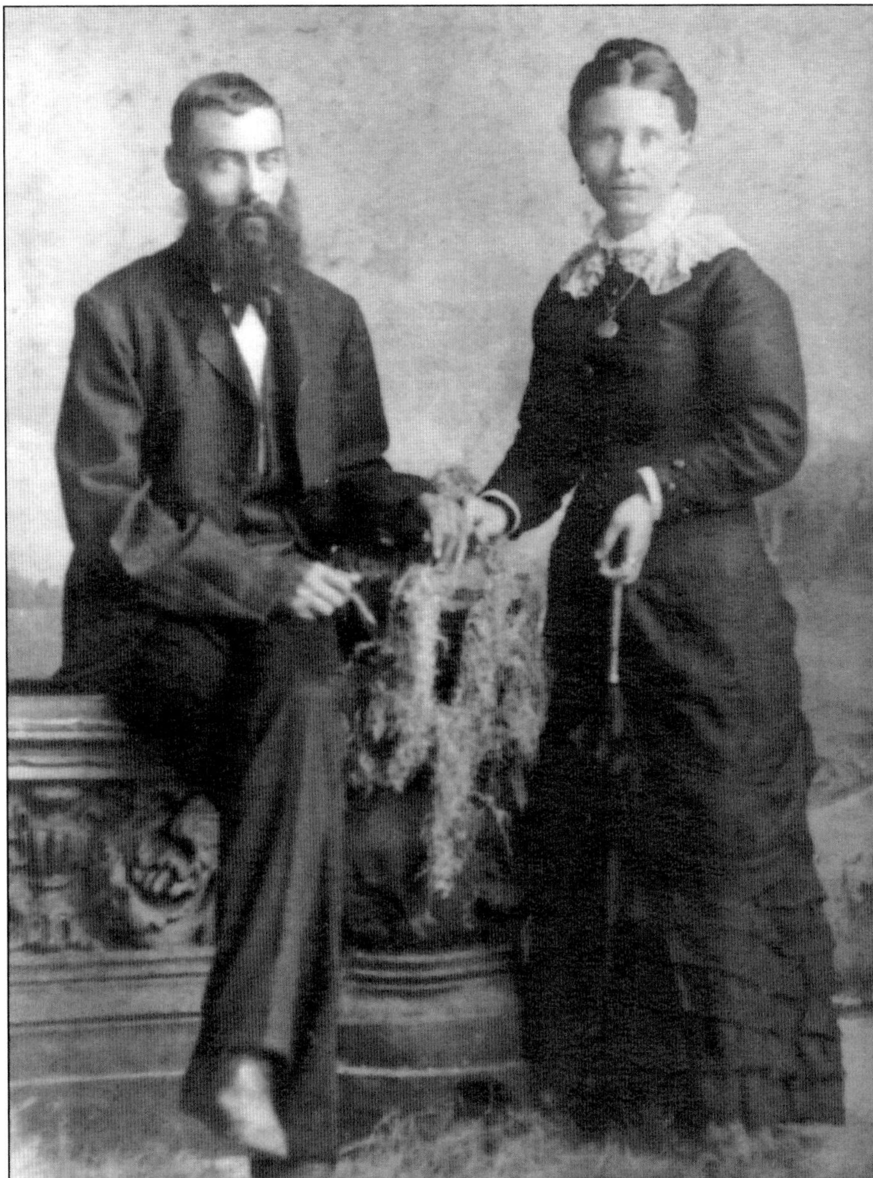

The Hector name in Manchaca dates back to 1859, when James Priam Hector II and his wife, Ann Elizabeth Logan Hector, purchased 1009 acres that spread from Live Oak Cemetery to Slaughter Creek. Originally from Scotland, James was an executive draughtsman and mapmaker for the Republic of Texas. James and Ann's son Alonzo Hector and his wife, Emma Pichot Hector, (shown above) spent many years living in Castroville, but moved to Alonzo's parents' property in Manchaca by 1900. Alonzo and Emma's son Jett married Amy Elvina Milam in 1909. They set up house in Jett's parents home, situated on the lush banks of Onion Creek. Amy's father was James Brice Milam. His great-great-grandfather Samuel Milam was the first cousin of Benjamin Rush Milam's father, Moses Milam. Noted Texas hero Benjamin Rush Milam received an Empresario Grant from the Mexican government in 1826 to settle families in Texas. Part of the land he was granted would later become Manchaca. Jett and Amy's son Walter Bremond Hector and his wife, Willie Mae, live in their home of 66 years in Manchaca today. (Courtesy Jackie Vaughn.)

Reminiscent of Marty Robbins's song "She Was Only 17," 18-year-old Manchaca resident Walter Hector fell in love with Willie Mae Marks when she was but 17 years old. The couple is shown here in 1941 in downtown Austin. They married in 1942 during World War II and, like so many of that time, Walter served his country in the Navy. They are still together today, 70 years later. (Courtesy Walter and Willie Mae Hector.)

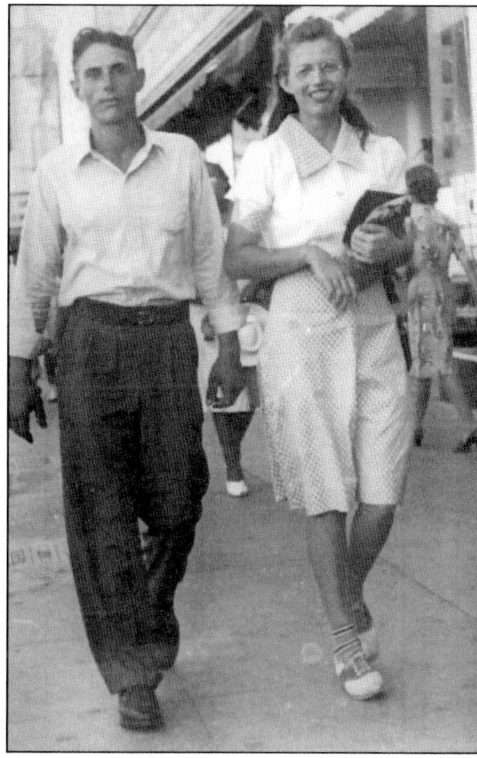

Walter and Willie Mae Hector are shown here celebrating their 70th wedding anniversary at a party given by their daughter and son-in-law Edie and Robert Bentley Tyler. Edie says, "Walter still hauls water and hay to his cattle every day, enjoys hunting, and watching sports on TV. Willie Mae enjoys cooking and sewing for her family. They love their home, and living in Manchaca." (Courtesy Edie Tyler.)

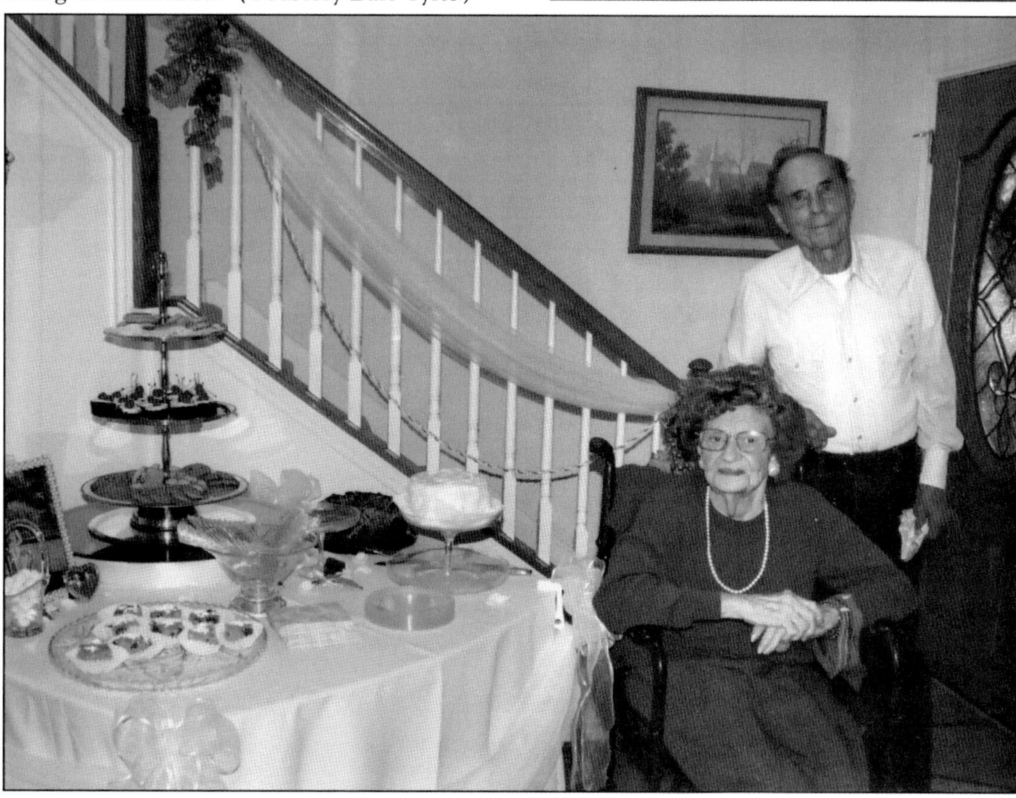

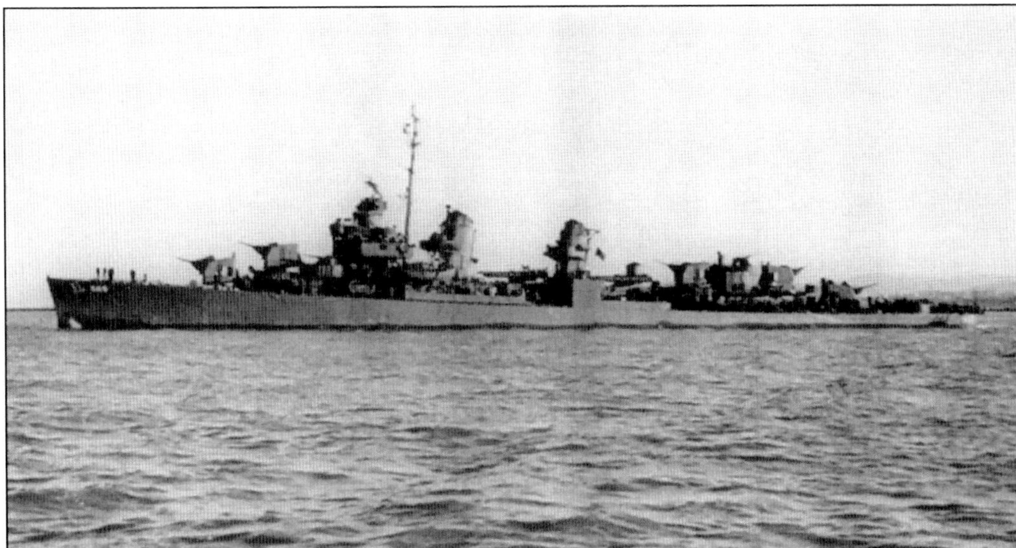

**Walter Bremond Hector**
Worked as a Civil Engineer from 1942-1946
He worked on the U.S.S. Aulick-D.D. 569,
and repaired it during test runs out at sea.

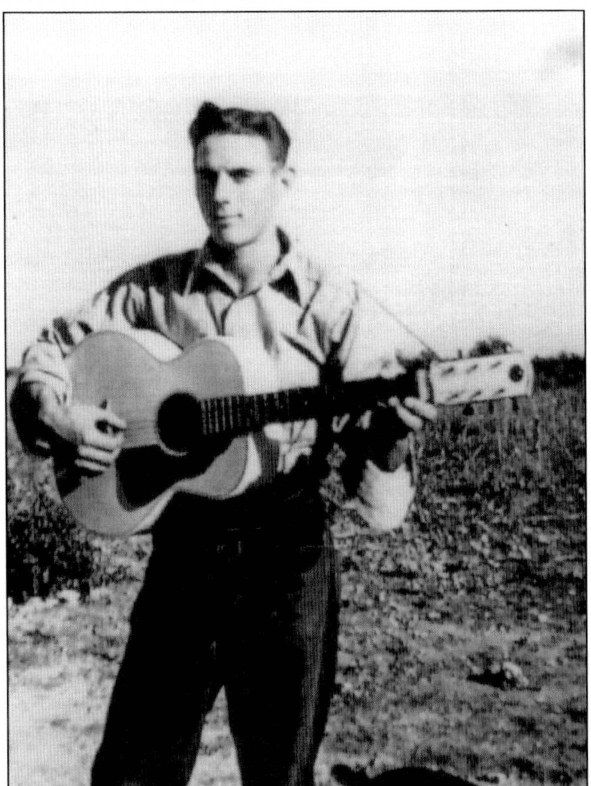

When Walter Hector served his country during World War II, he worked as a civil engineer on the USS *Aulick-DD 569*. After the ship was retired, the steel was sold to Japan for scrap. That fact still upsets Walter. Walter's great-grandfather James Priam Hector II was also a civil engineer, as was his father. James served as draughtsman in the executive branch of the Republic of Texas during the 1840s, under Texas president Anson Jones. (Courtesy Willie Mae and Walter Hector.)

Walter Hector is a man of many talents. Shown here playing his guitar as a young man, he also enjoys playing his harmonica and has been known to write some poetry. His greatest joy in life is his family. His daughter Edie says he loves nothing more than slicing open a red ripe watermelon to enjoy with his family at one of their gatherings under the oaks at their home in Manchaca. (Courtesy Edie Tyler.)

Herman F. Heep was a successful businessman, oilman, and rancher, well known in the Manchaca area and around Texas in general. His early success in the Conroe Oil Field led to the formation of the Heep Oil Corporation, Heep Energy, and the Heep Dairy. Always willing to give back to the community, Heep was well known for his generous philanthropy. (Courtesy Elizabeth H. Urban.)

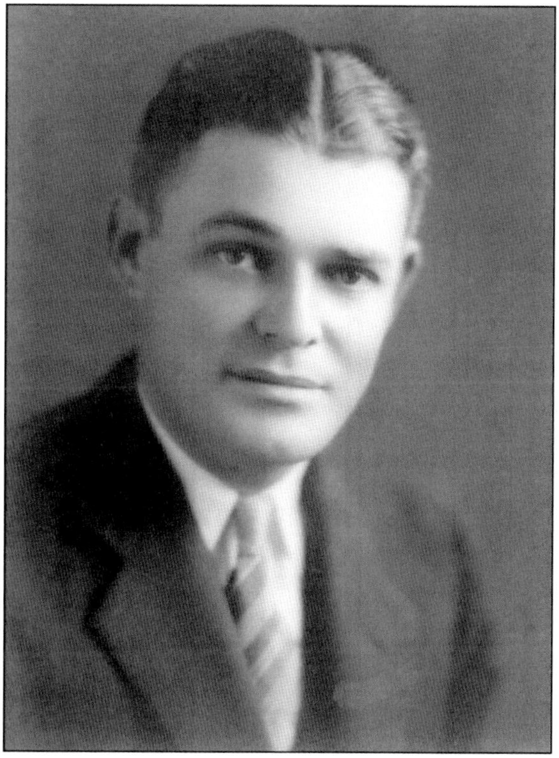

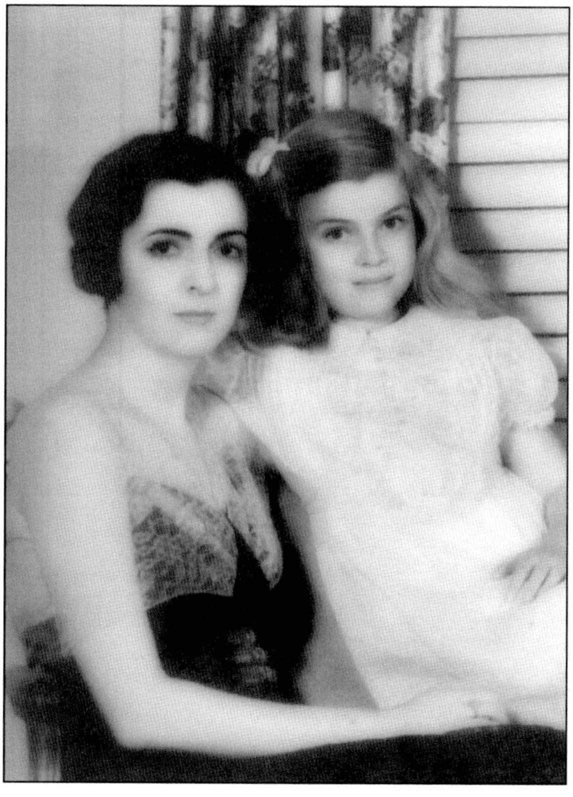

When the up-and-coming young oilman Herman Heep locked eyes with the beautiful Harriette Lopez, the attraction was strong and mutually felt. Love blossomed, and the young couple married with the promise of a wonderful future together. Harriette is shown here with their only child, Mary Lou, who was born in 1927. (Courtesy Elizabeth H. Urban.)

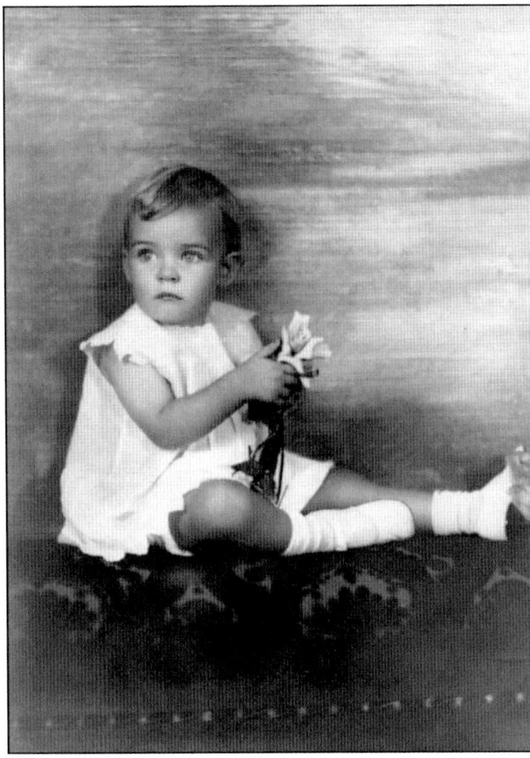

Mary Lou Heep is shown here on her second birthday. As with all children, birthdays were always looked forward to with great anticipation by Mary Lou. She had very fond memories of a playhouse her father surprised her with one year. She and her friends spent endless hours playing tea party and dress up under its roof. (Courtesy Elizabeth H. Urban.)

A fun day riding at the Heep Ranch is recorded in this photograph of teenager Mary Lou Heep. The image was taken in 1945 as she rode her favorite horse, Johnny. Herman Heep bought the gentle quarter horse specifically for his daughter to ride. (Courtesy Elizabeth H. Urban.)

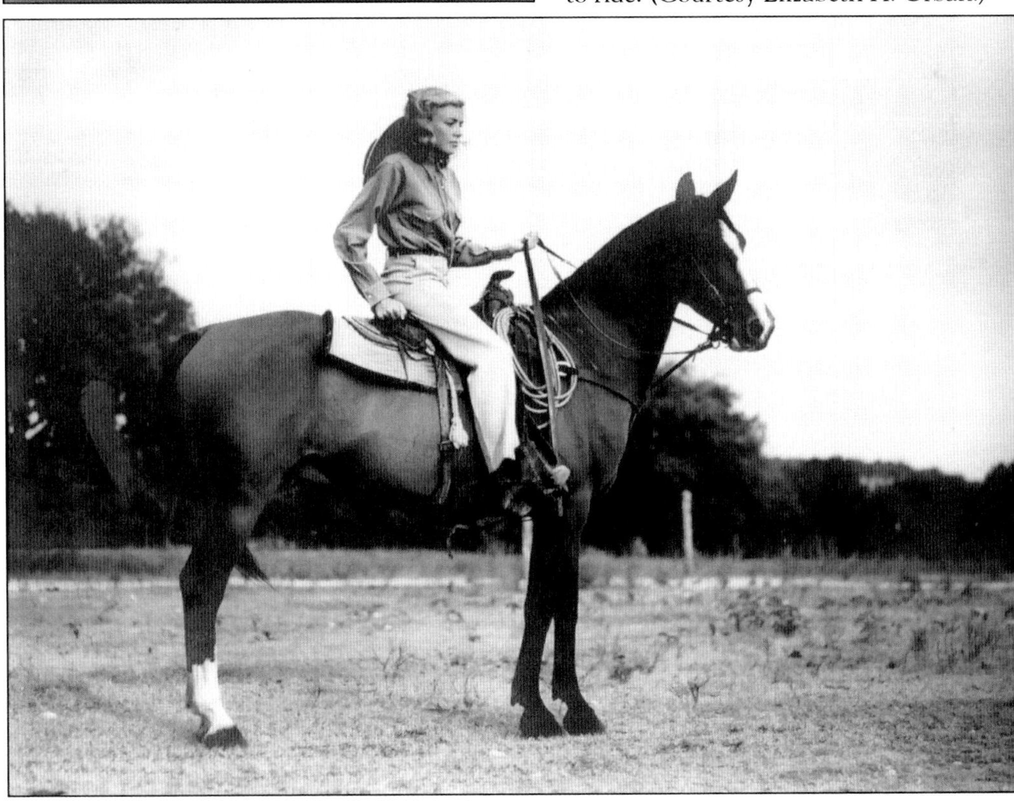

Martha Johnson remembers that her father, Bob Johnson, had several automobiles. He started out with a Model T and subsequently owned several Model A's. She called these automobiles a "Hoopie." In the fall of 1916, Bob Johnson had this photograph taken in one of his automobiles. (Courtesy Martha and Chester Johnson.)

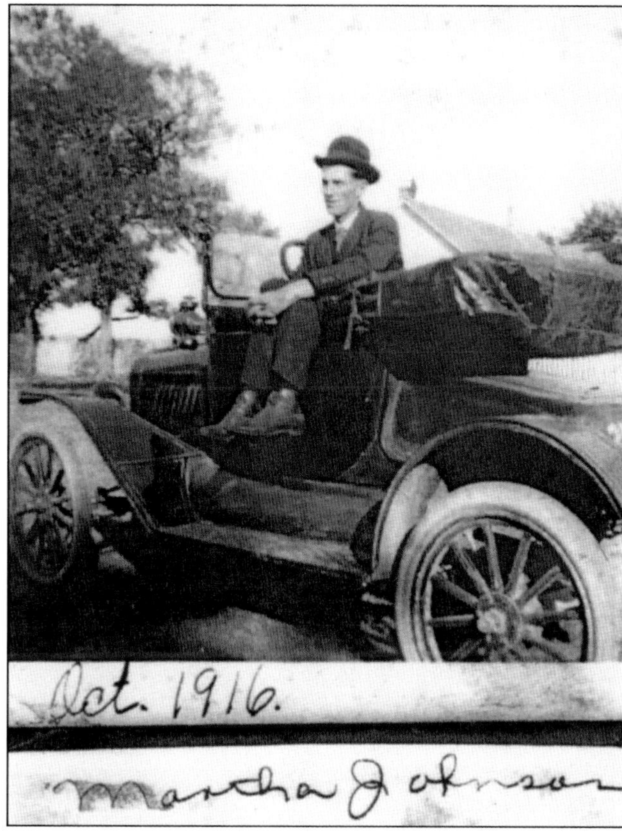


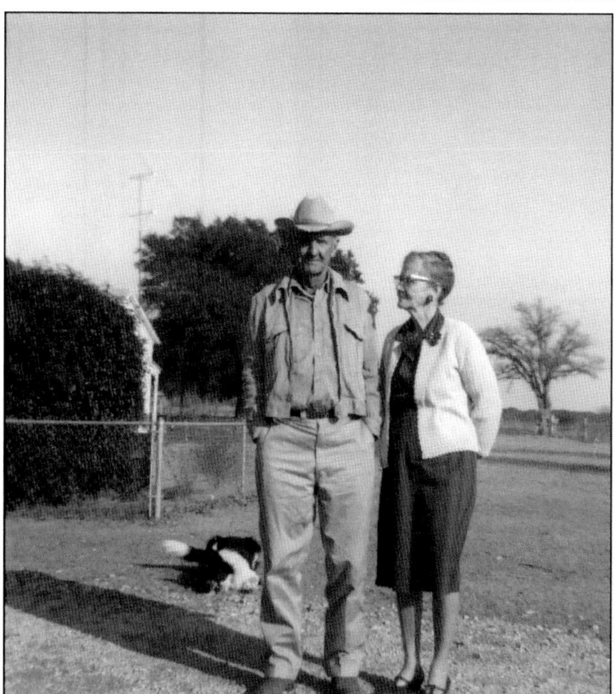

The oldest daughter of local store owners Hannah and Thomas Blackwell was Ellen Bruce Blackwell, who always went by her middle name of Bruce. She and Bob Johnson, shown here, fell in love and were married in 1917. After their wedding, they took up residence in Manchaca. Rowena and John Dean's daughter Joanne loved dogs, and she cherishes the childhood memory of receiving her very first puppy from the Johnsons. (Courtesy Joanne Deane.)

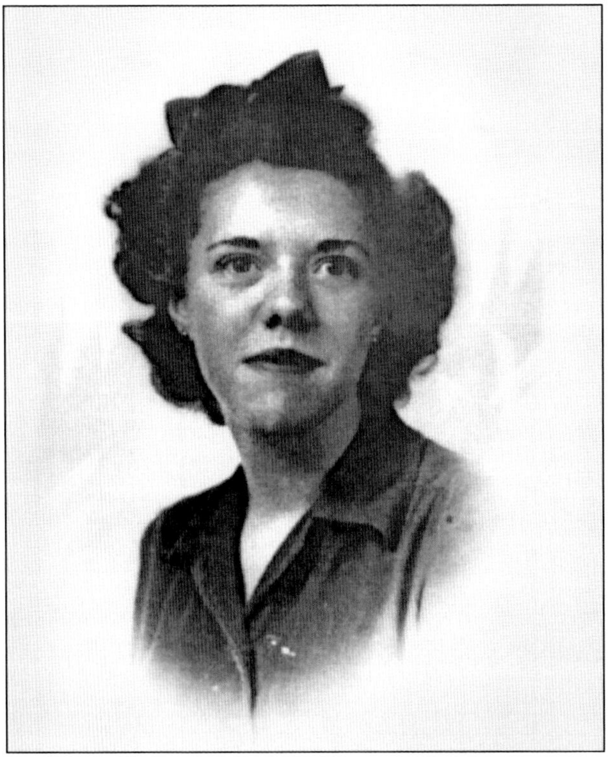

Martha Ellen Johnson is shown here at the age of 16. She was born in 1926 and is the daughter of Ellen Bruce Blackwell Johnson and Bob Johnson. Martha grew up in Manchaca. Chester Johnson is shown below at the age of 19. Chester comes from a separate Johnson family that lived in west Austin. He grew up in the Eanes area. Martha and Chester met when she was a chaperone with a group of children. Love was kindled when they noticed each other again at a barn dance held at a dairy farm located on South First Street and Ben White. They married on June 3, 1946. (Both, courtesy Martha and Chester Johnson.)

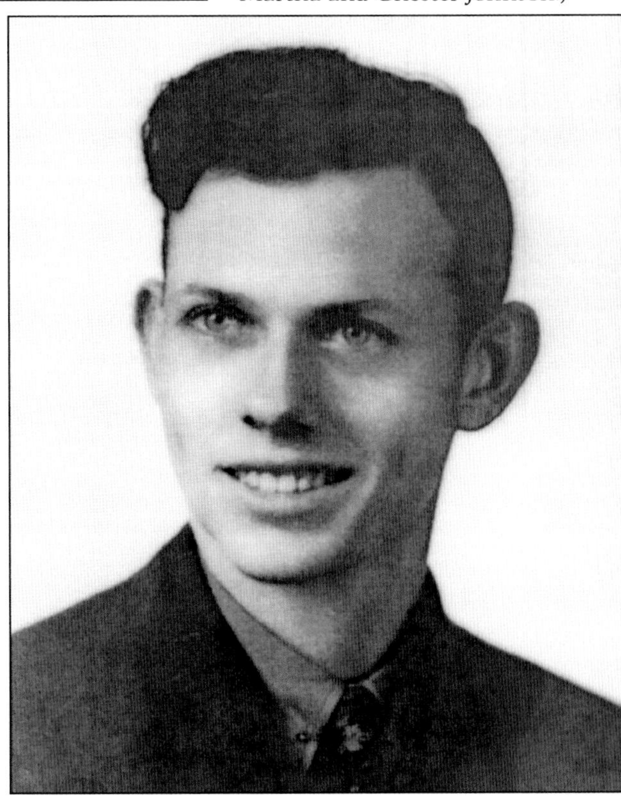

When Martha and Chester Johnson married, they each brought talents into the relationship. Martha is an exceptional cook who learned her skills from her mother cooking on a wood stove. She is also an excellent shot and a trophy deer displayed in their home is witness to that. Chester was a very talented craftsman. He and his brother made the beautifully crafted furniture used in their home. (Courtesy Martha and Chester Johnson.)

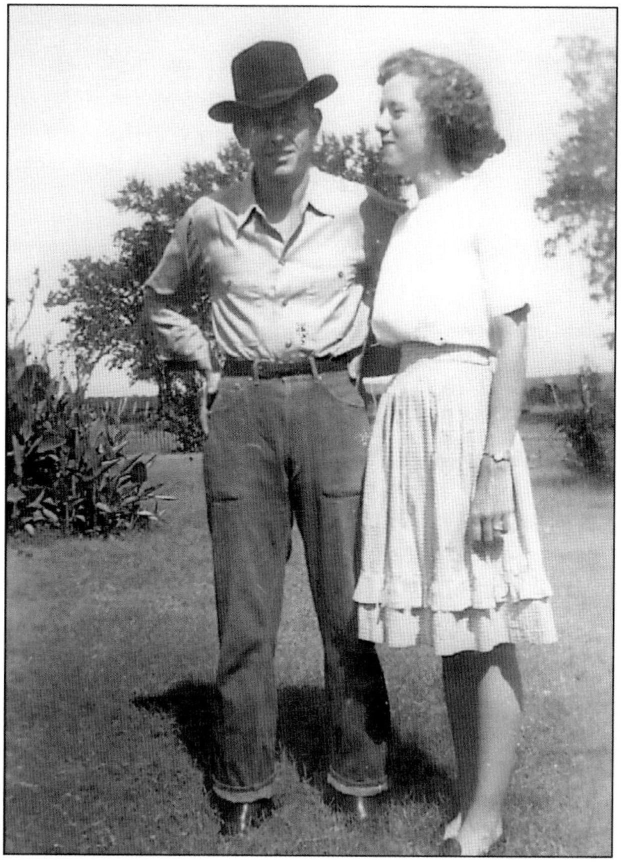

The home of Martha and Chester Johnson is located on FM 1626 and Johnson Road. It is covered in native stone and sits atop a hill on property that has been passed down in Martha's family. A generous porch affords a shady place to sit, visit, and take in the panoramic view. (Courtesy Martha and Chester Johnson.)

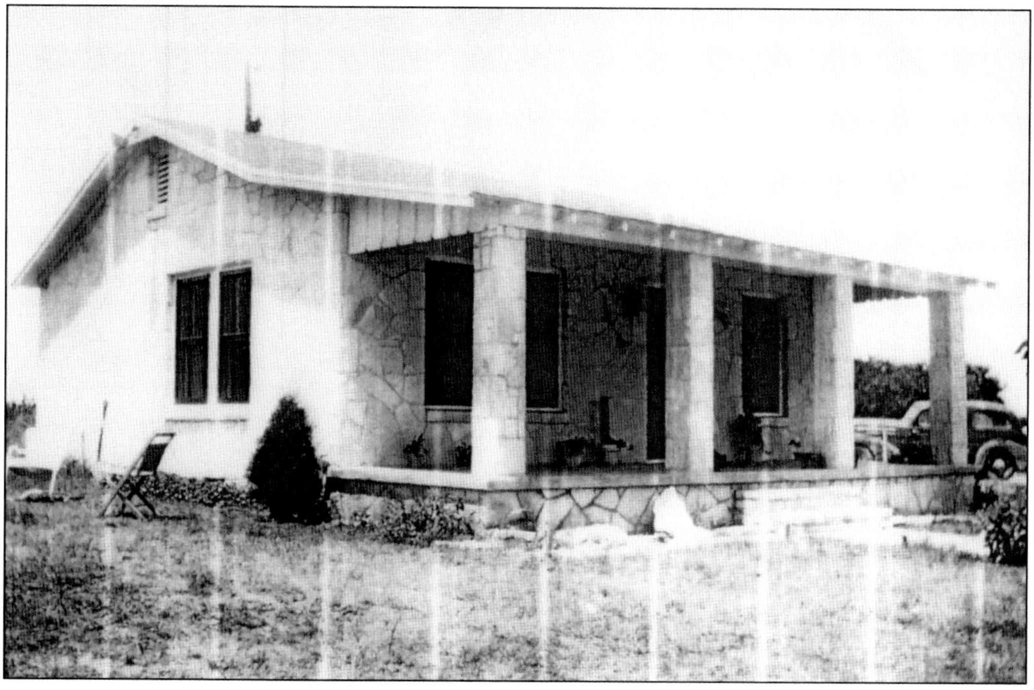

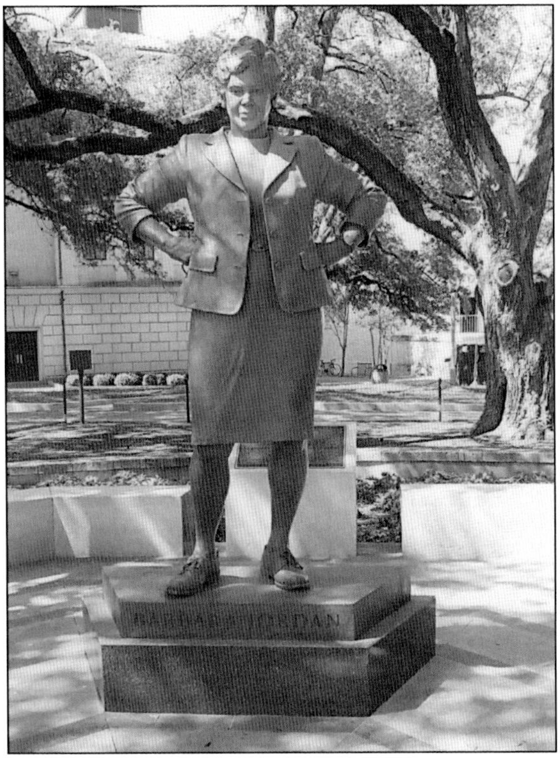

Congresswoman Barbara Jordan chose to make her home in Manchaca. This statue of her was the first statue of a female placed on the campus of the University of Texas. In 1966, Jordan was elected to serve as senator in the Texas Legislature. In 1972, she was elected to serve in the United States House of Representatives. (Courtesy Ann and Barry Trask.)

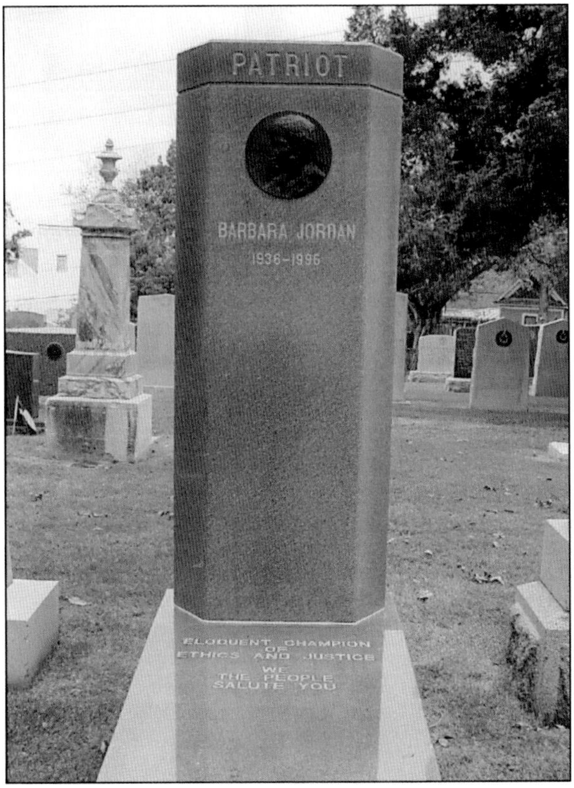


When Barbara Jordan was elected to the United States House of Representatives, she was the first southern African American female elected to that position. She received many honors during her lifetime, including the coveted Presidential Medal of Freedom. Upon her death in 1996, she was interred in the Texas State Cemetery. (Courtesy Ann and Barry Trask.)

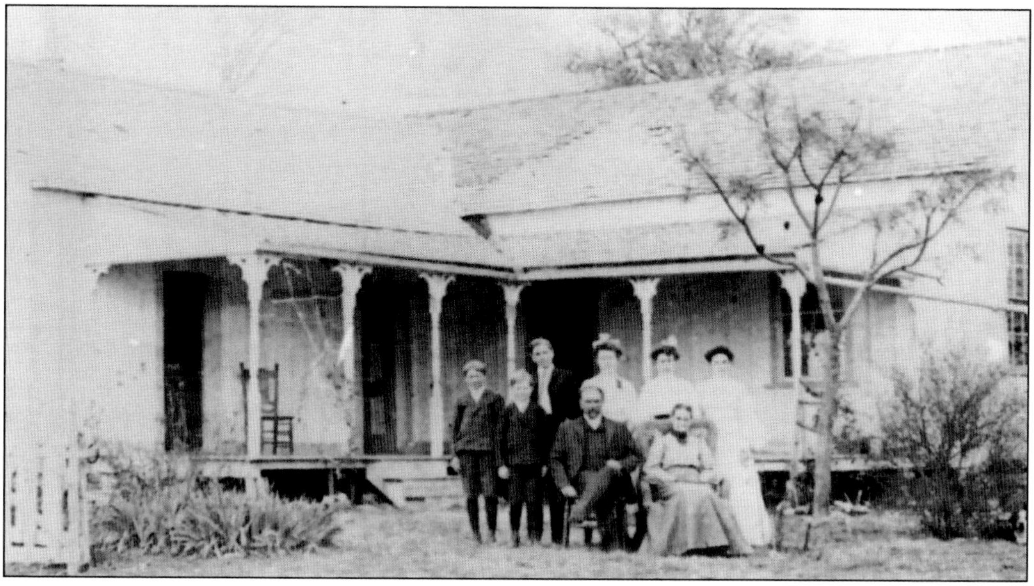

In 1872, Daniel and Mary Ann Labenske purchased 120 acres of land on Bear Creek, where this home was later erected. Photographed here are 6 of their 10 children, standing behind Daniel and Mary Ann. The family ran a successful dairy farm that produced 1,300 pounds of butter in 1879 from their 17 milk cows. (Courtesy Victoria Dunnahoo Daywood.)

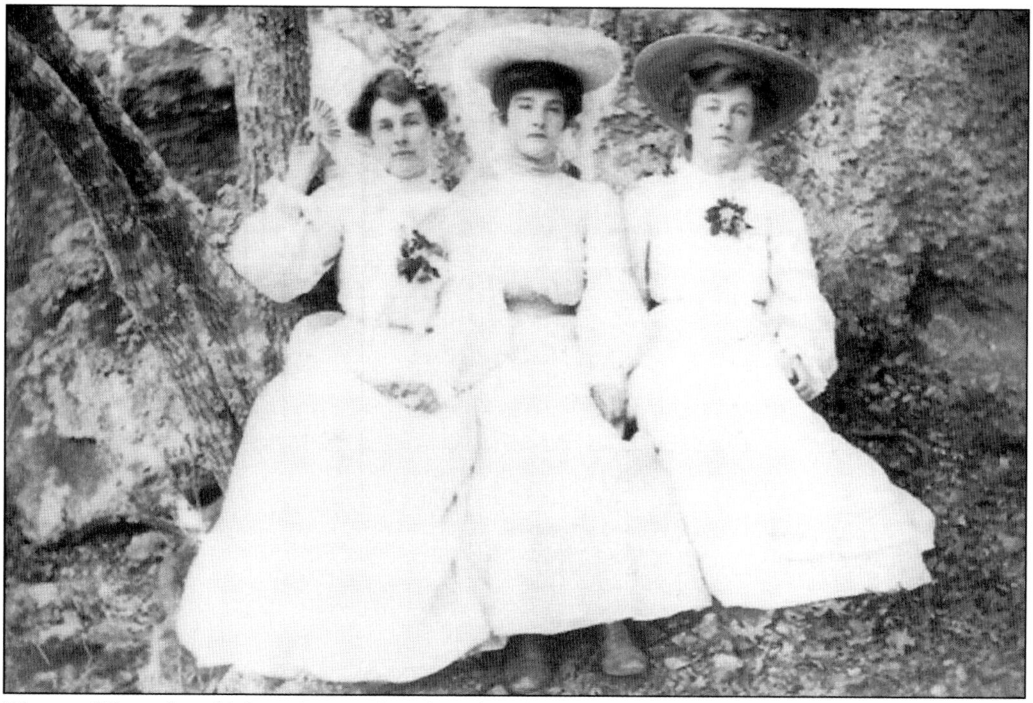

Three of Daniel and Mary Ann Labenske's daughters posed for this Kodak moment in the early 1900s. Shown from left to right are Rebecca Labenske Driskill, Velma Labenske, and Edna Labenske. The girls were born between 1880 and 1886 at the Labenske homestead on Bear Creek. Their part of the creek boasted the best rock bottom swimming hole in the area. (Courtesy La Vern Fields Johnson and Joe W. Fields.)

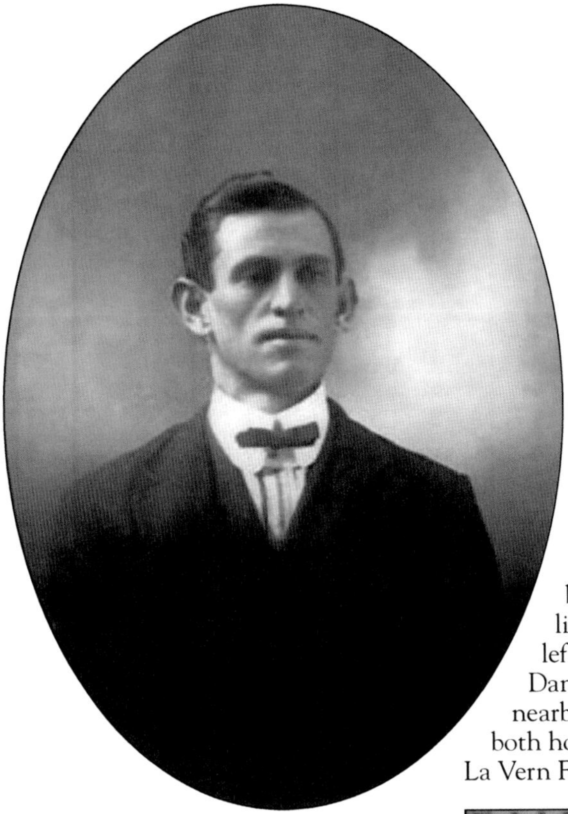

Samuel Newton Driskill's uncle, Jesse Driskill, built the Driskill Hotel in downtown Austin. Samuel married Rebecca Labenske in 1906. Their daughter Margaret, shown below, was born in 1909 while they lived in a home located just to the left of Manchaca Methodist Church. Daniel Labenske's house in town was nearby. When the new church was built, both homes were torn down. (Both, courtesy La Vern Fields Johnson and Joe W. Fields.)

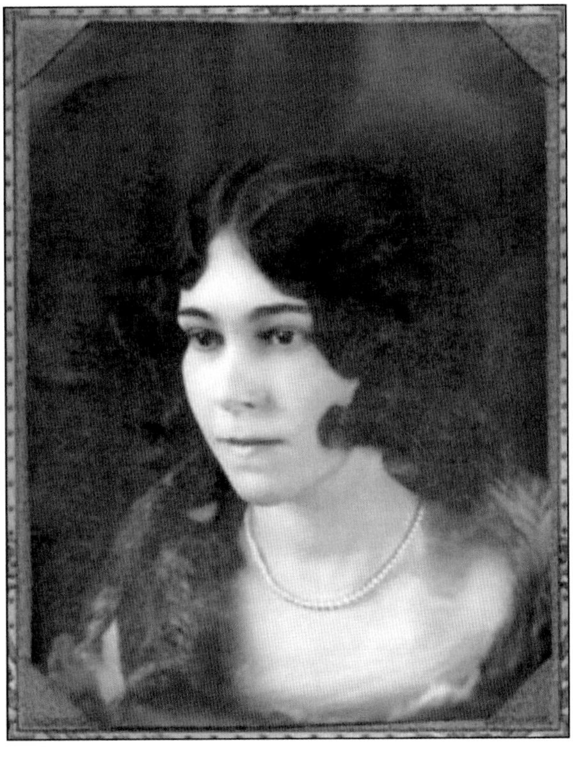

The luxurious hair of the Maples sisters Vita, on the left, and Rebecca was truly their "crowning glory." After the death of their parents, the children were divided between their various Labenski relatives, coming back together for brief visits when time and the opportunity would allow. Thoughts of their young family and their home on Bear Creek became a distant memory. (Courtesy Vita Pressburg Clement.)

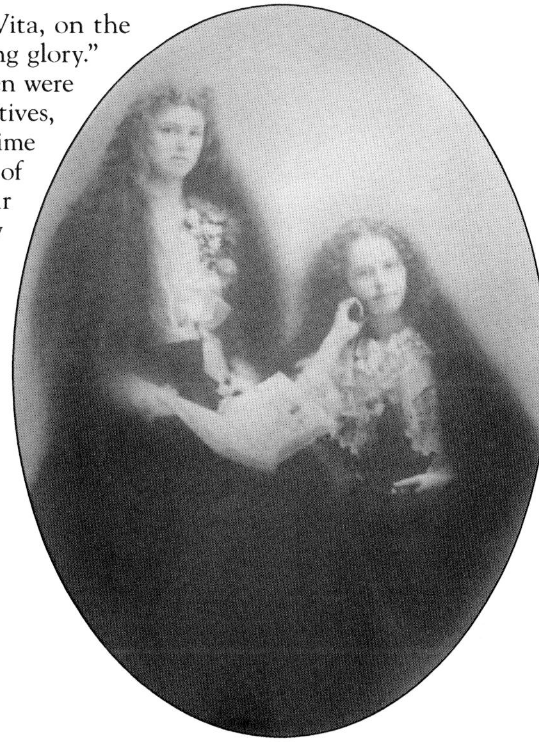

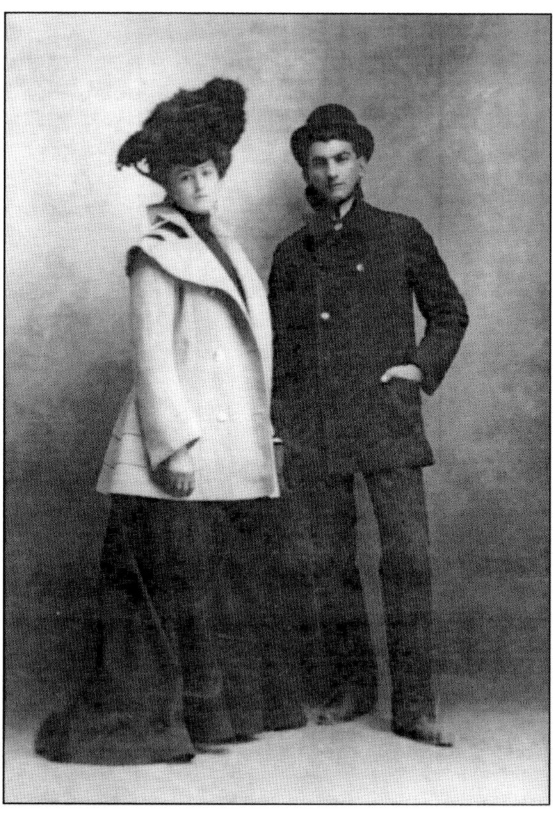

Melissa "Jenny" Labenski Maples and her husband, John, lived a short distance from her brother Daniel on Bear Creek in 1880. Vita Maples, daughter of Melissa and John, is shown here with her husband, Israel Pressburg, in the early 1900s. (Courtesy Benjamin David Pressburg.)

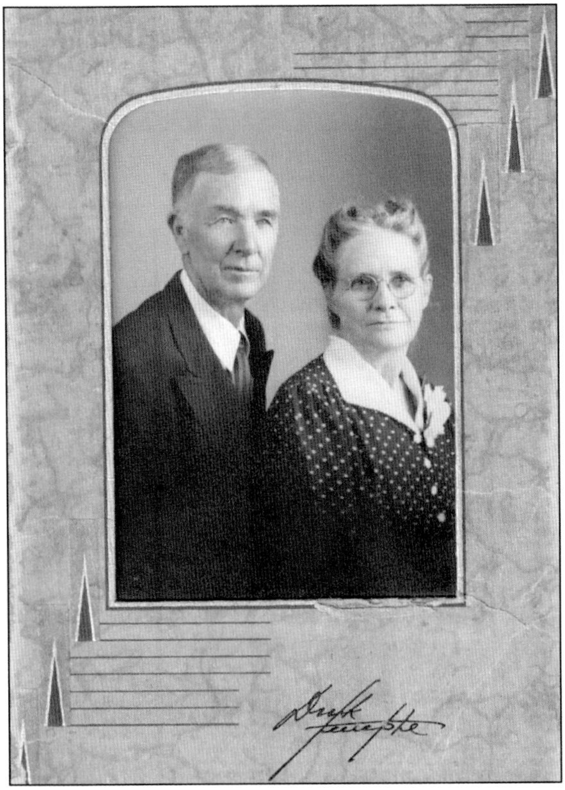

George Labenske was born at the family homestead along Bear Creek in 1872. He and his wife, Loretta Ennis Labenske, are noted there in the 1910 census, living close to the Deane and Birkner families. When one of their six children did something mischievous, George would tell them, "It's just the Felix coming out in you!" Felix Labenske was George's uncle who enjoyed playing practical jokes. (Courtesy Victor Labenske.)

Dr. Claud A. Martin was born in Manchaca, not far from Onion Creek, in 1904. After receiving his medical degree from the University of Texas Medical Branch at Galveston, he practiced medicine for 50 years. His patients were not just patients; they were his friends. (Courtesy Lillie M. Moreland.)

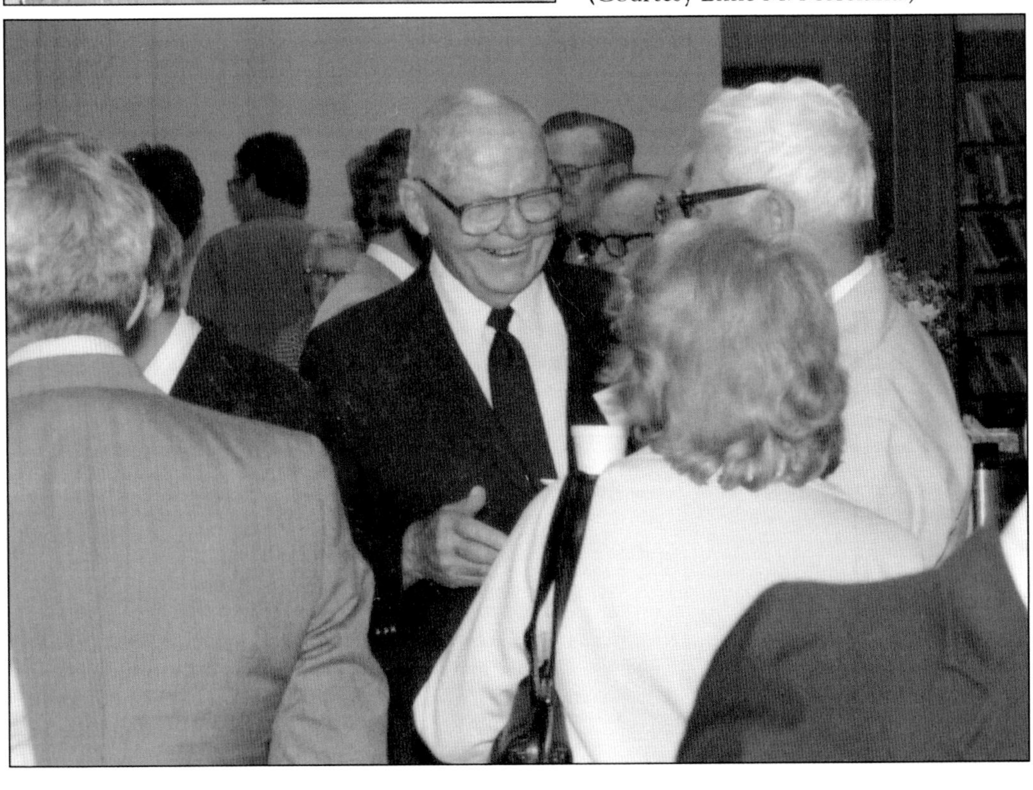

The founders of the Marbridge Foundation were Ed and Marge Bridges, shown here with their son Jim, who suffered a brain injury at birth. Seeing the challenges ahead for their son, the Bridges conceived the Marbridge Plan, a place where Jim and others like him could grow and learn. (Courtesy Marbridge Foundation.)

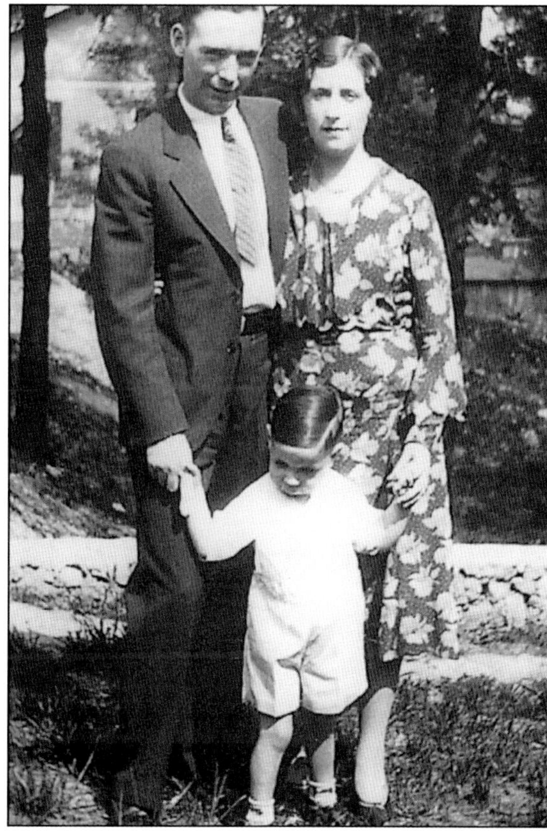

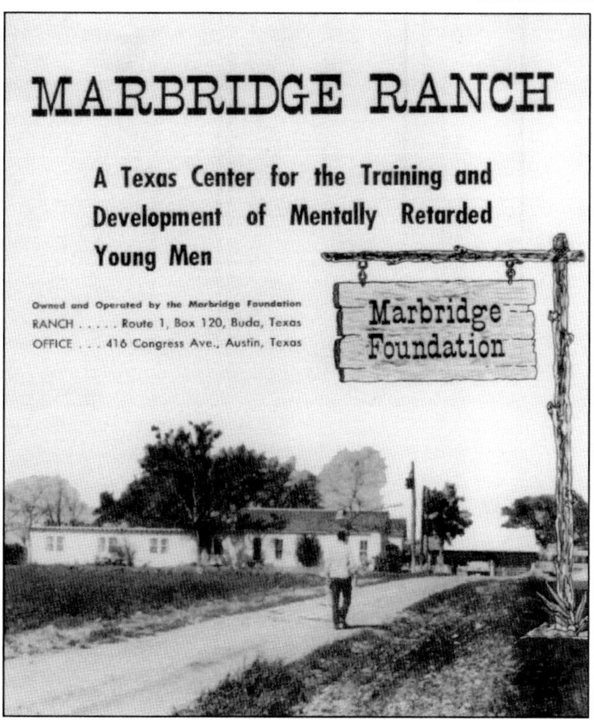


Nestled in the meadows and oak tree covered acres of Manchaca, the Marbridge Plan, conceived by Ed and Marge Bridges, blossomed into Marbridge Ranch, which opened its doors on June 1, 1953. Within six months, their son Jim was joined by six other boys. The 80 acres at Marbridge would provide a farm environment for special needs men to learn a trade. (Courtesy Marbridge Foundation.)

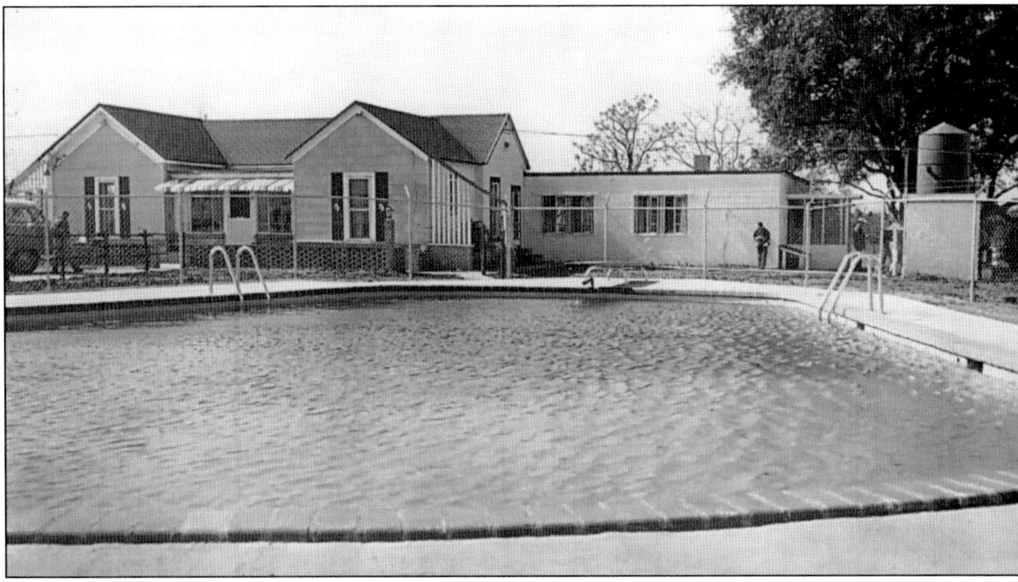

Shown above is the original ranch house at Marbridge and the large swimming pool that was constructed in 1960 for the residents. Taking a dip in its cool water during the hot Texas summers was a welcome relief from the heat. The boys enjoyed countless hours of fun here. (Courtesy Marbridge Foundation.)

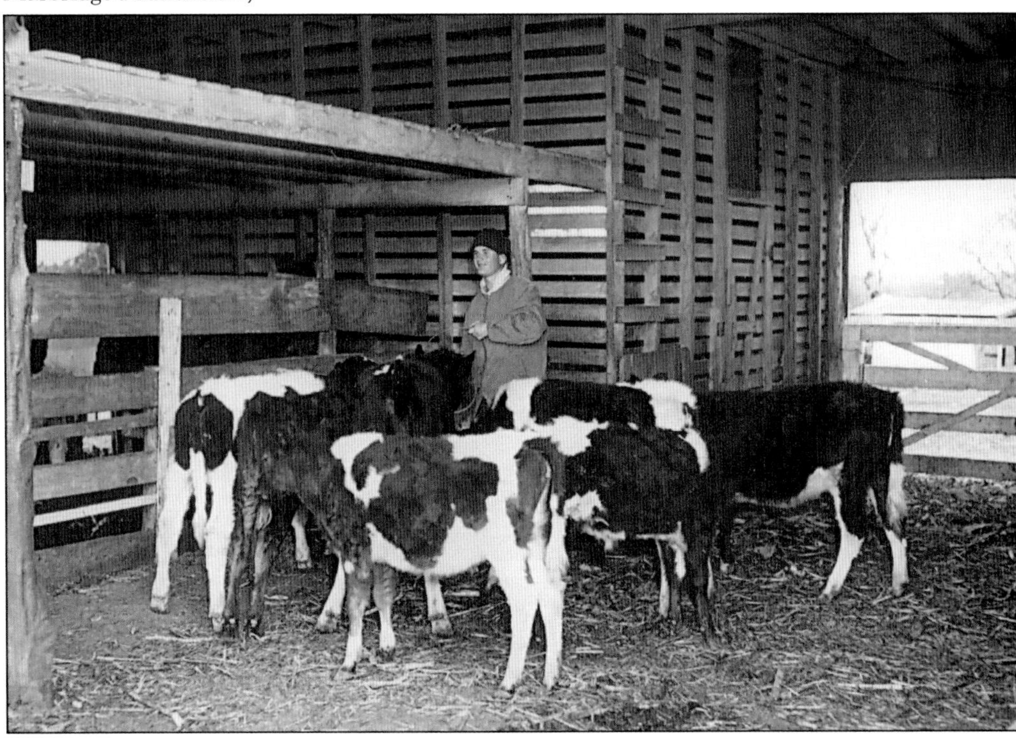

The Marbridge boys were busy and happy learning a trade. Some of the skills taught in 1960 included working with cows at the ranch dairy, carpentry at the woodwork shop, and working at the pen and hatcheries for raising game birds. Halfway houses were built throughout Texas for graduates from the program at Marbridge. (Courtesy Marbridge Foundation.)

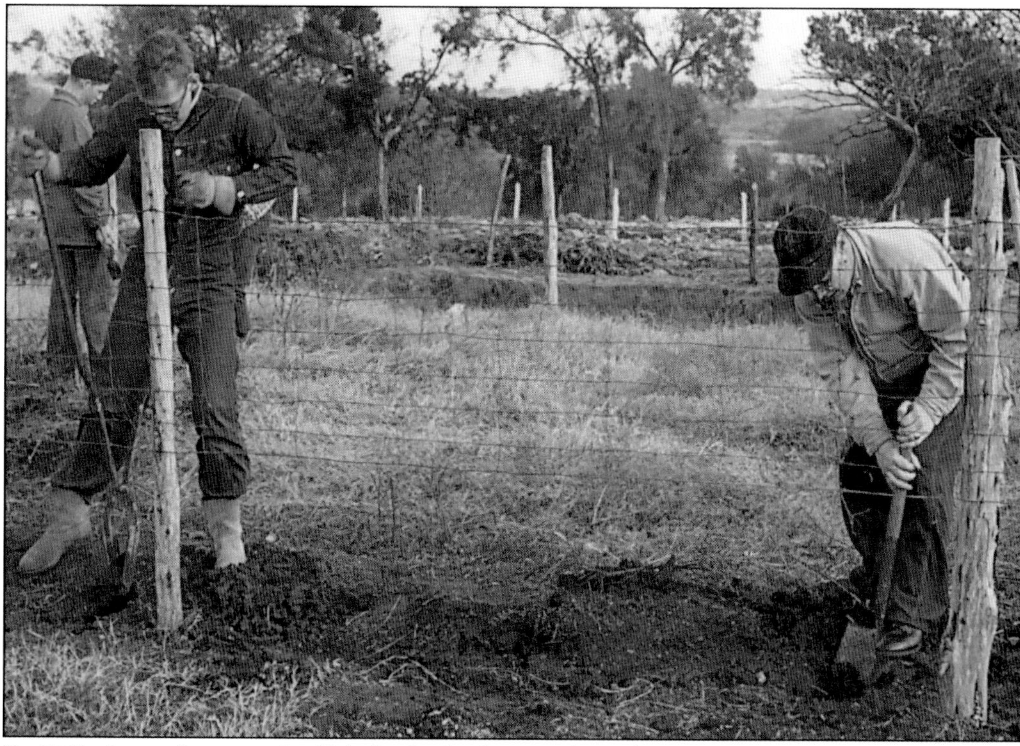

By 1969, the working ranch of Marbridge had grown from the original 80 acres purchased by the Bridges, to 440 acres. The focus at the ranch is on the ability of each boy, and not the disability. Today, the campus serves as home and workplace for more than 220 adults with various cognitive disorders. (Courtesy Marbridge Foundation.)

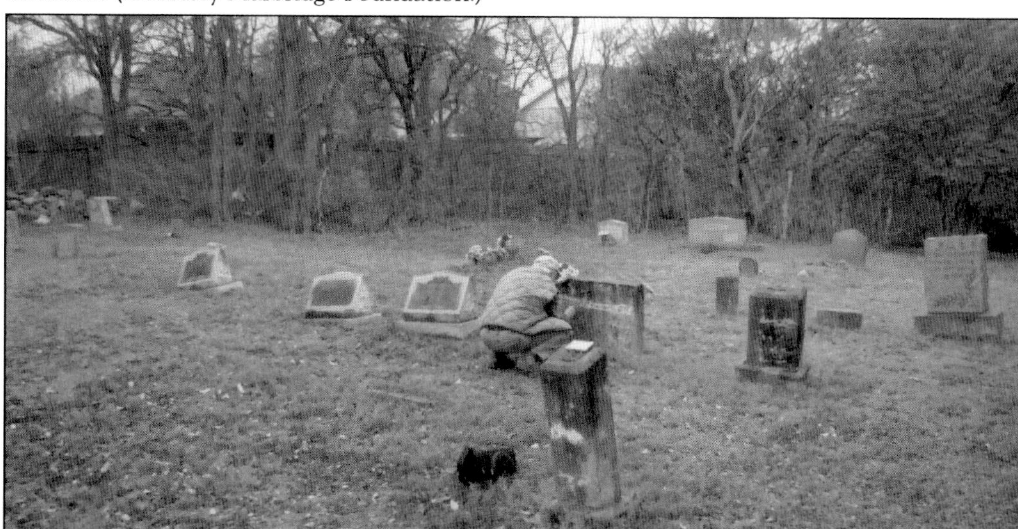

The Perry Cemetery is located on land that was owned by African Americans Chatam Perry and his wife, Ann Moss Perry. They moved to Manchaca by 1880, and purchased 400 acres of land. The Perry Cemetery is located on private property west of Manchaca Road and about a mile north of Manchaca. In the 1900 census, Ann Perry declared they had 15 children. (Courtesy Ann and Barry Trask.)

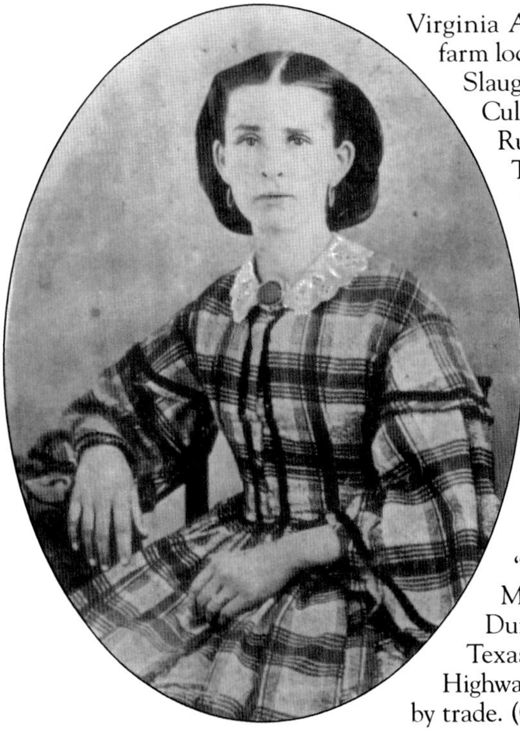

Virginia Ann Matthews Cullen Dunnahoo lived on a farm located where Southpark Meadows is today, off of Slaughter Lane and I35. Her first husband, George Cullen, was killed in the Civil War. She next married Rufus P. Dunnahoo, and they had five children. Thomas Dunnahoo, constable of Manchaca for 23 years, was their oldest child. (Courtesy Marilyn Dunnahoo McLeod.)

On the day before Valentine's Day in 1868, Virginia Ann Matthews Cullen married R.P. "Rufus" Dunnahoo at her parents' home in Manchaca. After the wedding, they settled on Dunnahoo's farm in Mendoza, Caldwell County, Texas. Today, this land sits at the southwest corner of Highways 21 and 183. He was a blacksmith and mechanic by trade. (Courtesy Diana Dunnahoo.)

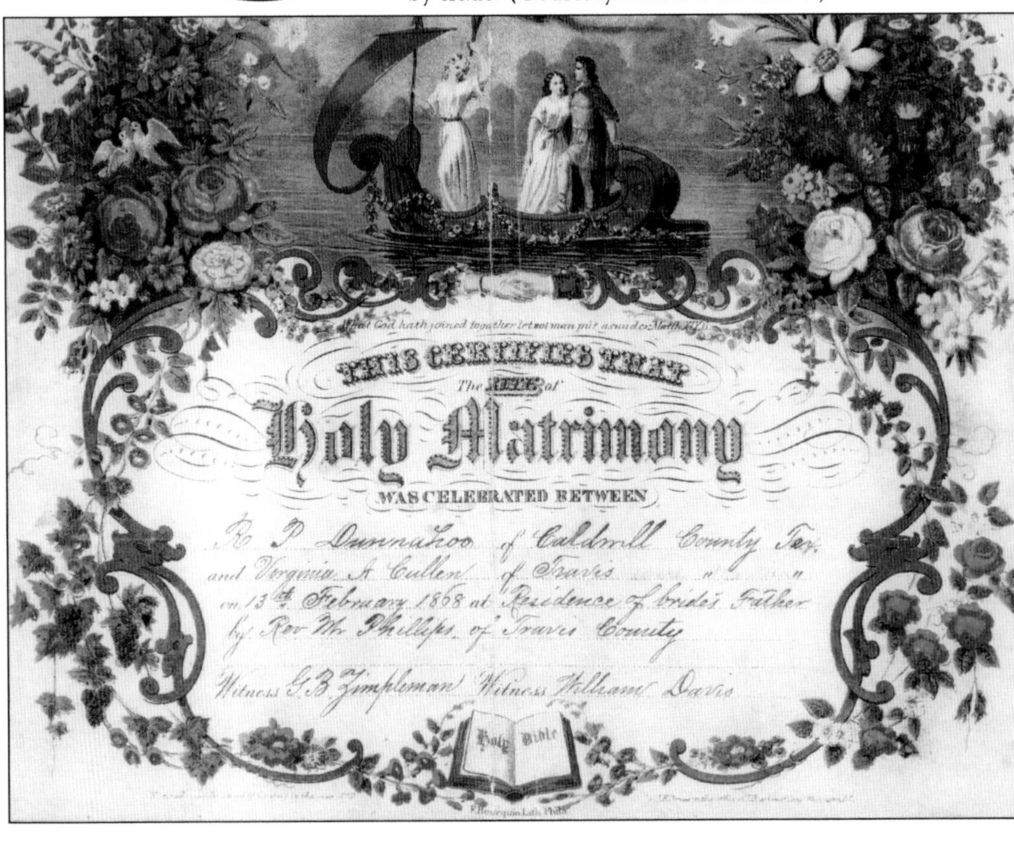

What God hath joined together let not man put asunder. Matth. XIX.6

THIS CERTIFIES THAT
The RITE of
Holy Matrimony
WAS CELEBRATED BETWEEN

R. P. Dunnahoo of Caldwell County Tex.
and Virginia A Cullen of Travis " "
on 13th February 1868 at Residence of bride's Father
by Rev Mr Phillips of Travis County

Witness G. B. Zimpleman Witness William Davis

Holy Bible

The McCuistian Cemetery is located on private property next to Live Oak Cemetery. In 1879, John J. McCuistian buried his wife, Rebecca, there. Later, their daughters Mary Emily and Sue were also buried here. Sue McCuistian married four times. She was quoted as saying, "Life is just one devilment after another." (Courtesy Ann and Barry Trask.)

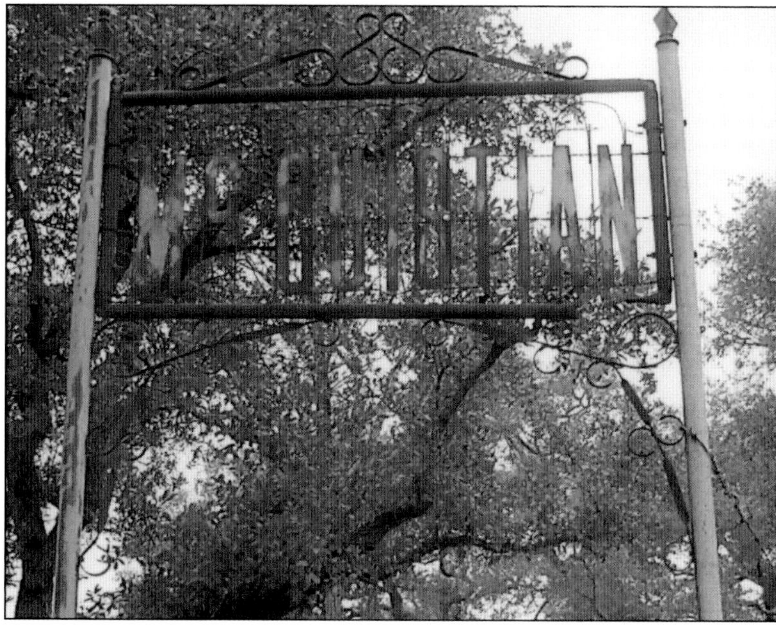

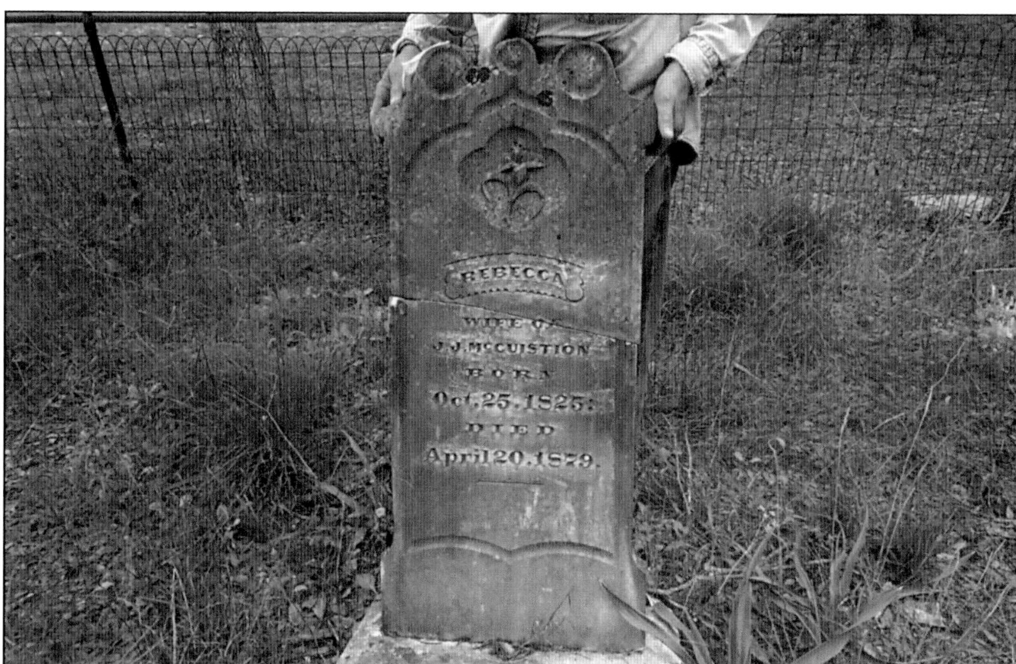


Virginia native Rebecca Thompson married Tennessean John Jordan McCuistian. They traveled west and settled in Manchaca. Rebecca died at the age of 54 and is buried in the McCuistian Cemetery, close to her daughters Mary Emily and Sue. (Courtesy Ann and Barry Trask.)

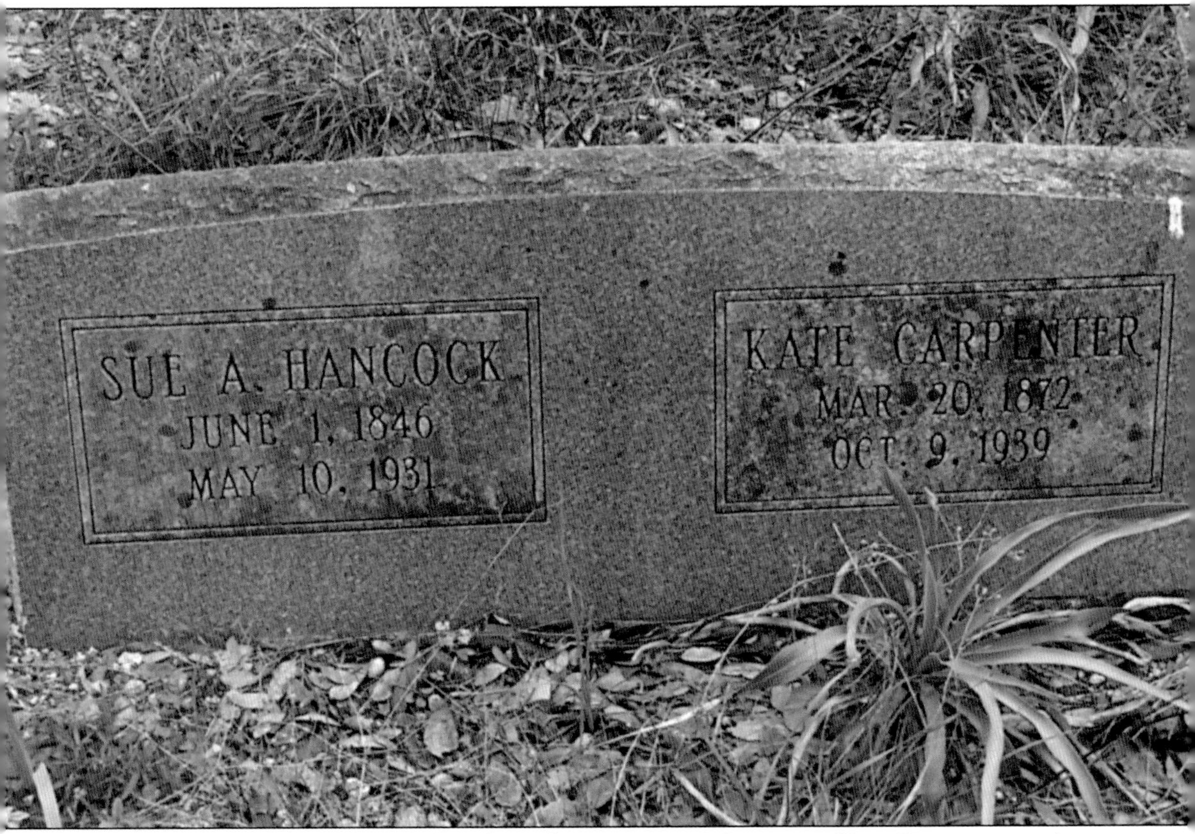


Mother and daughter lay side by side in the McCuistian Cemetery. Kate Carpenter was born to Sue McCuistian after she married W.G. Carpenter in 1871. Mr. Carpenter was the third of four husbands that Sue would unite with. Following his death in 1876, Sue married William Hancock. Kate Carpenter was known in Manchaca as "Katie." She was appointed postmistress for Manchaca in 1910, when the post office was located in the Blackwell Store. Katie served the community in that position for many years. As a stark contrast to her mother's four marriages, Katie remained single her entire life. (Courtesy Ann and Barry Trask.)

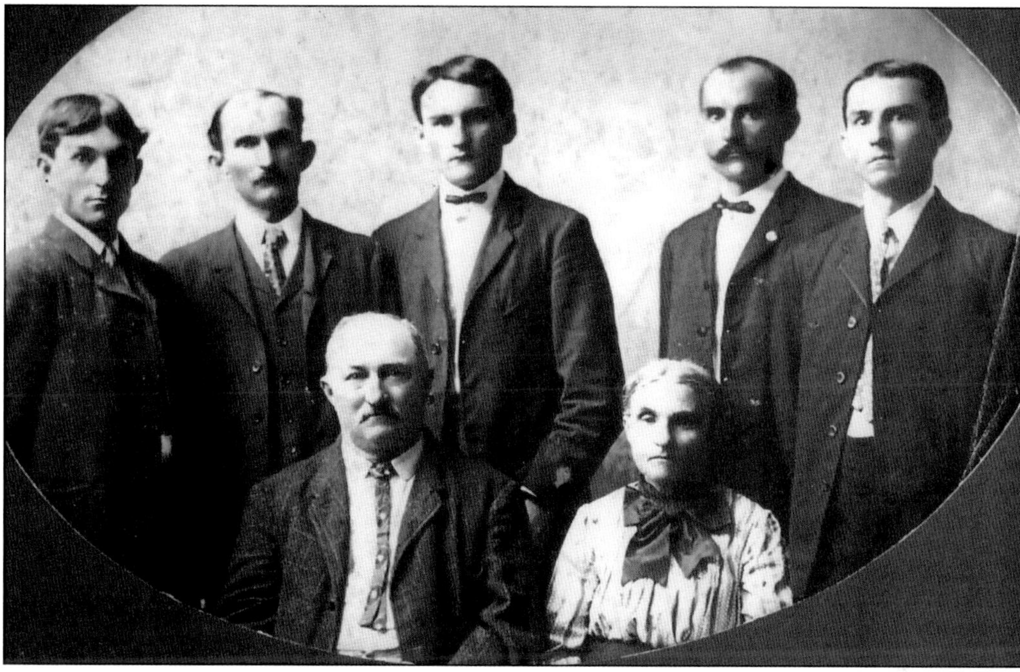

Travis County Prison jailer John I. Meredith and his wife, Lydia, are seated here with their sons behind them. Shown from left to right are Will, James, Neal, Lee, and John M. In 1904, John Meredith was quoted in the *Southern Mercury* paper, reporting that crime in Travis County was on the decline as only 24 prisoners were in jail. (Courtesy Lillie M. Moreland.)

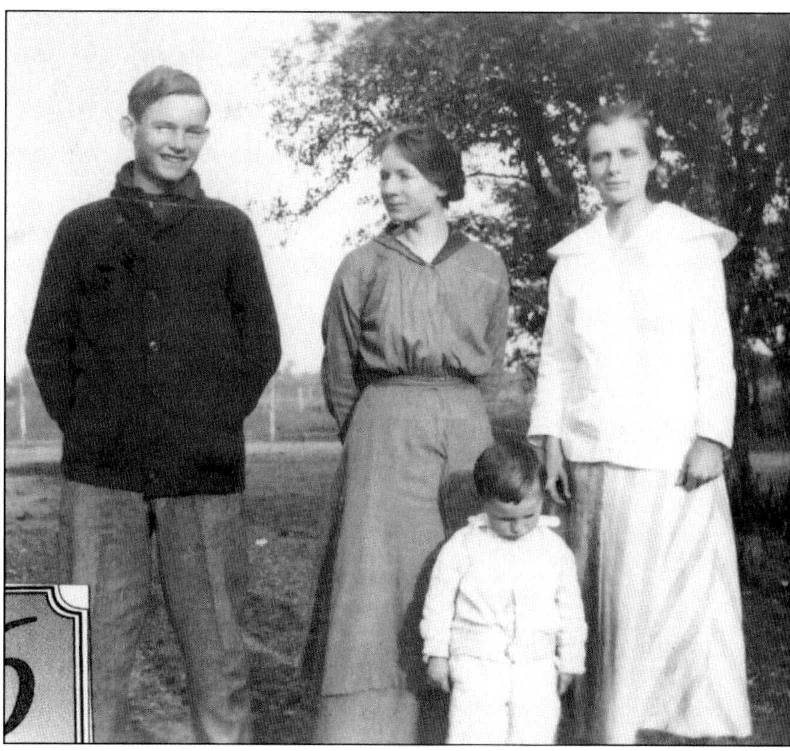

The Meredith and Wirth families enjoyed some visiting in this 1916 photograph. Shown from left to right are Albert Wirth, Ella W. Meredith, and Nora Wirth. Standing in front of the adults is young John Fred Meredith, the oldest child of Ella W. Meredith and her husband Neal Meredith. (Courtesy Lillie M. Moreland.)

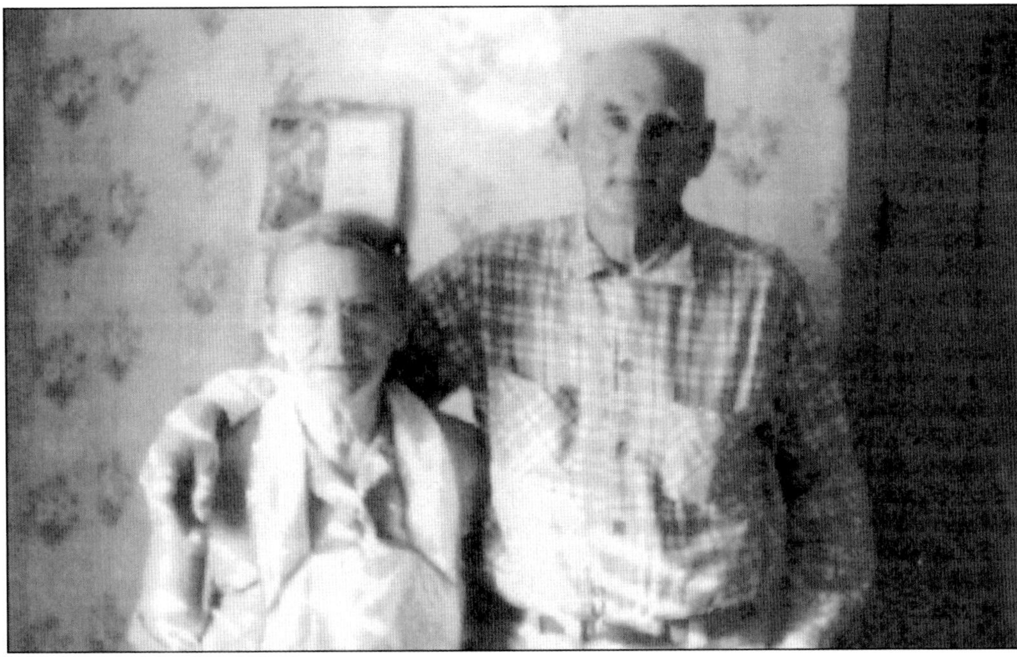

Neal and Ella Ida Meredith are shown here in their home. Ella was a wonderful cook, despite the lack of modern-day conveniences. Before electricity, they had an icebox. The iceman delivered ice to the house three times a week. They often made ice cream in the summer using their own cow's milk. Ice to freeze the ice cream was purchased at the Downs store. (Courtesy Lillie M. Moreland.)

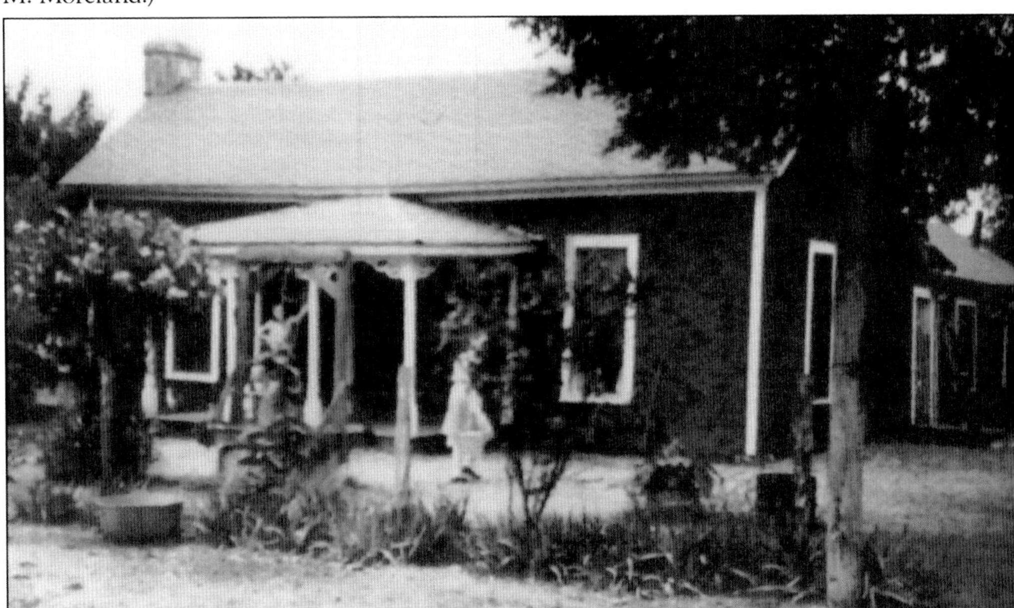

The home of the Meredith family stood at the intersection of Meredith Drive and Manchaca Road. Neal Meredith and his wife, Ella Ida Wirth Meredith, raised their three children, John Fred, Annie Mae, and Lillie Alice, here. When passing this home in the early 1900s, it emanated the mouthwatering aroma of homemade yeast rolls made by Ella. (Courtesy Lillie M. Moreland.)

The expanse of railroad tracks that cut through the heart of Manchaca provided a quiet and unique venue for Neal Mance Meredith and Ella Ida Wirth to take a stroll and get to know each other better. The young couple is shown here when they were dating, shortly before they married. (Courtesy Lillie M. Moreland.)

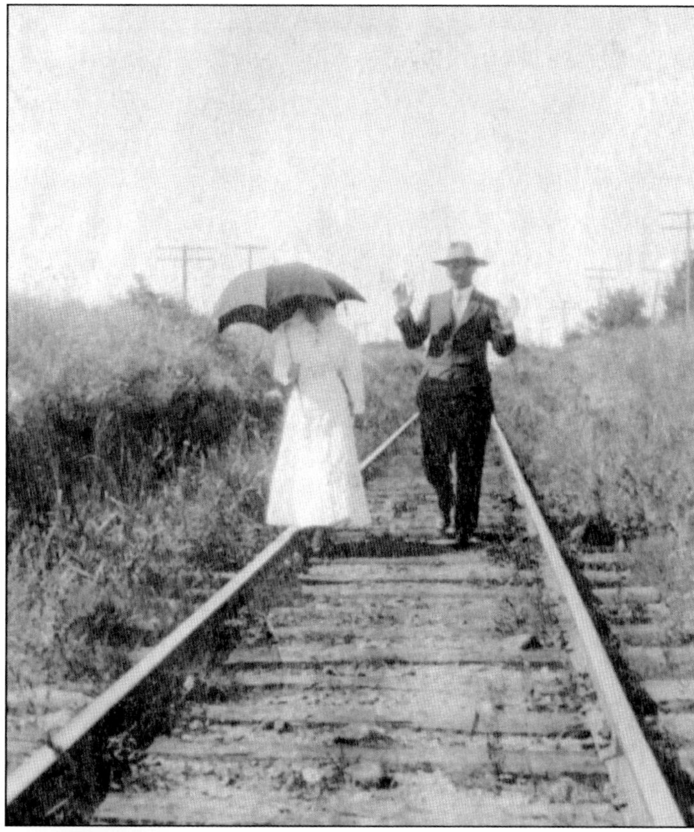

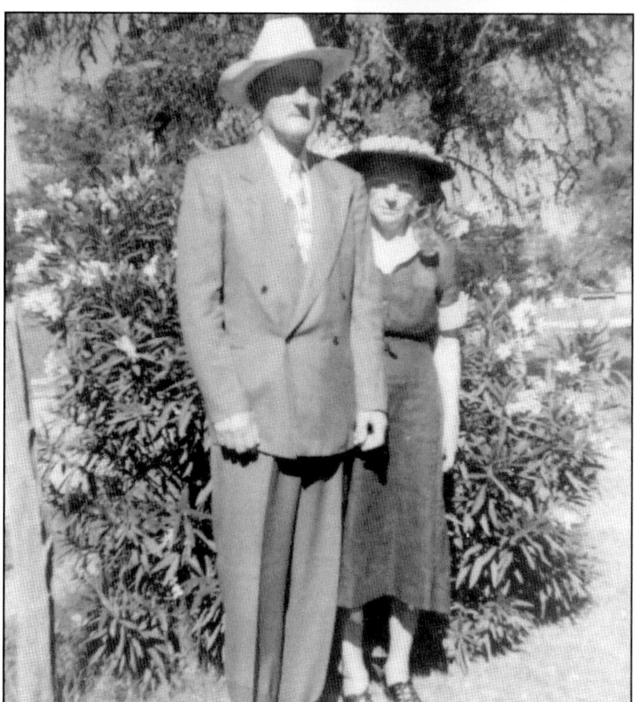

When Neal Mance Meredith and Ella Ida Wirth married, they joined two key families with rich histories in Manchaca. Neal was born in a log cabin on Bear Creek and Ella was born on property that is today part of San Leanna. (Courtesy Lillie M. Moreland.)

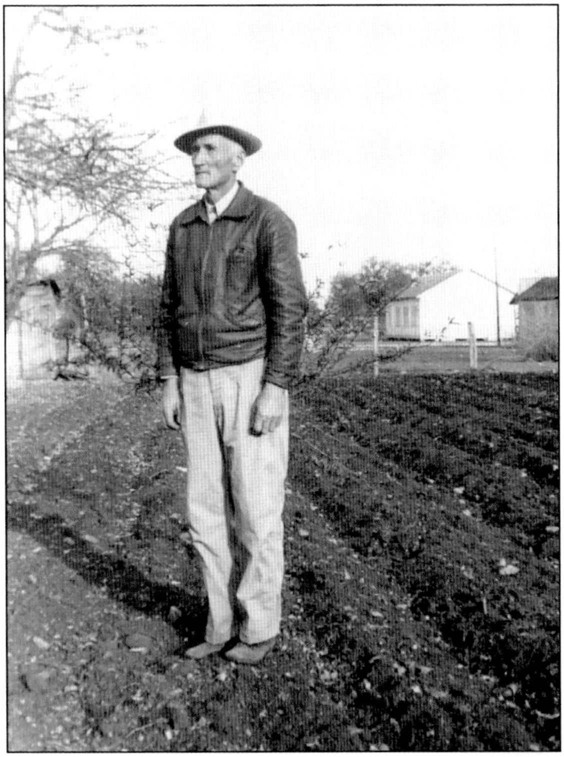

Neal Meredith is shown here in his newly plowed garden space near his home. For a time, Neal worked in the oil fields with his older brother. Later on in life, he inspected cattle for $100 a month. This photograph also records an early glimpse of the Baptist Church, which can be seen behind Neal on the right-hand side of the photograph. (Courtesy Lillie M. Moreland.)

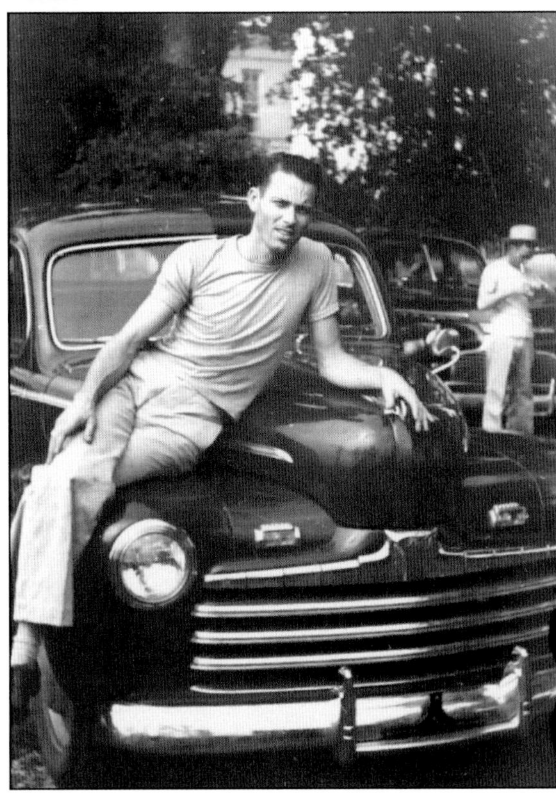

Young Odell Moreland is photographed here sitting atop this good-looking 1946 Ford. The 239 CID engine in this model gave it a lot of power under the hood. Automobiles played an important part in Odell's life later on. In 1954, he went into the damaged auto appraisal business. (Courtesy Lillie M. Moreland.)

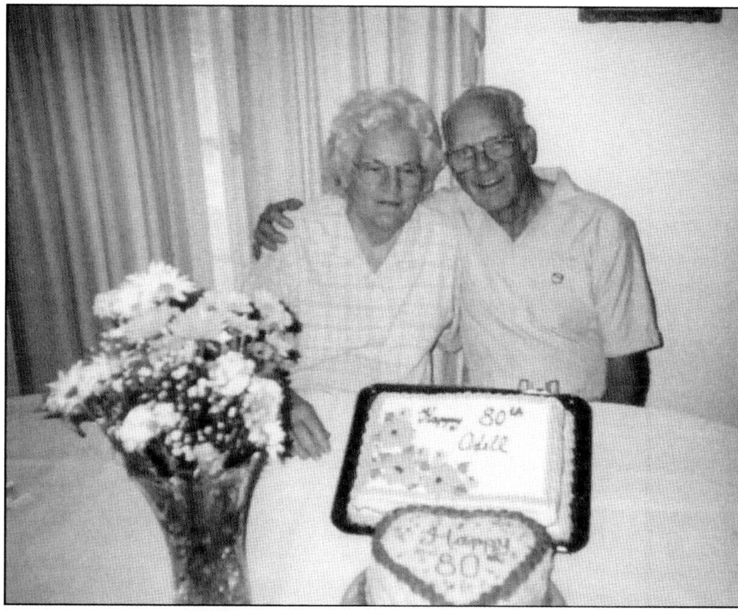

Longtime Manchaca resident Lillie Meredith met Odell Moreland on December 4, 1941, just three days before the bombing of Pearl Harbor. After he enlisted to fight in World War II, they married, but did not see each other again for three years, when they were reunited on Christmas 1945. They are shown here celebrating Odell's 80th birthday. (Courtesy Lillie M. Moreland.)

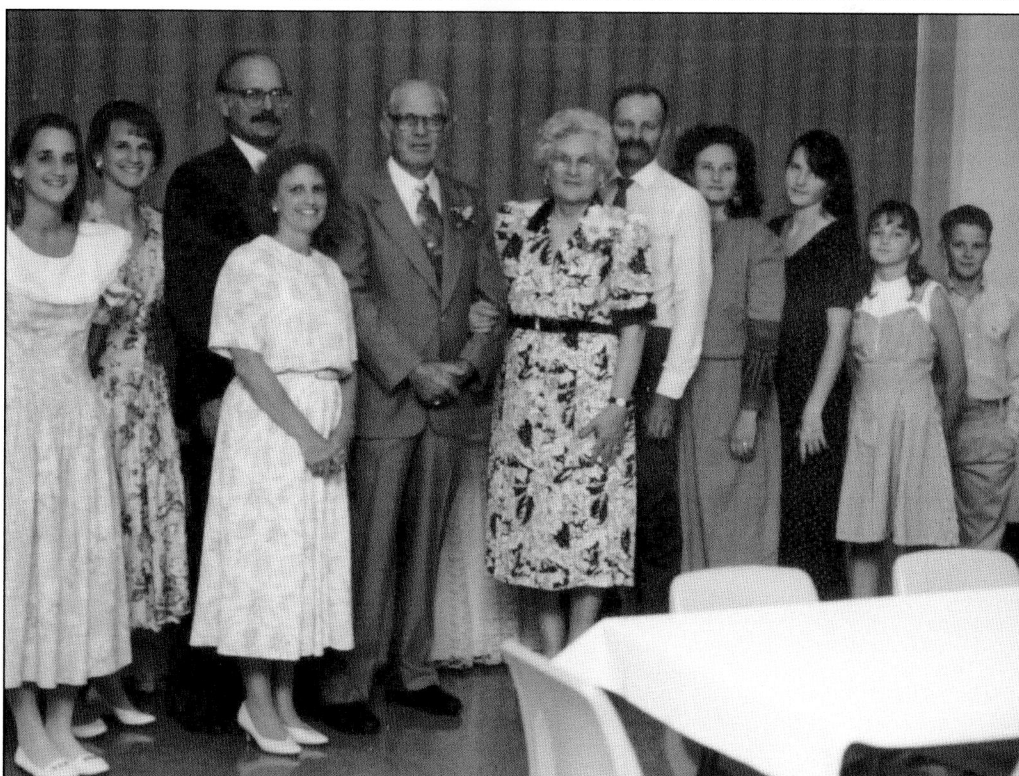

The Moreland family gathered in Fellowship Hall at Manchaca Methodist Church in September 1992 to celebrate the wedding anniversary of Lillie and Odell. Shown from left to right are Shana, Stacy, Nealan, Janice, Odell, Lillie, Glenn, Patty, Kenna, Aimee, and Ty Moreland. (Courtesy Lillie M. Moreland.)

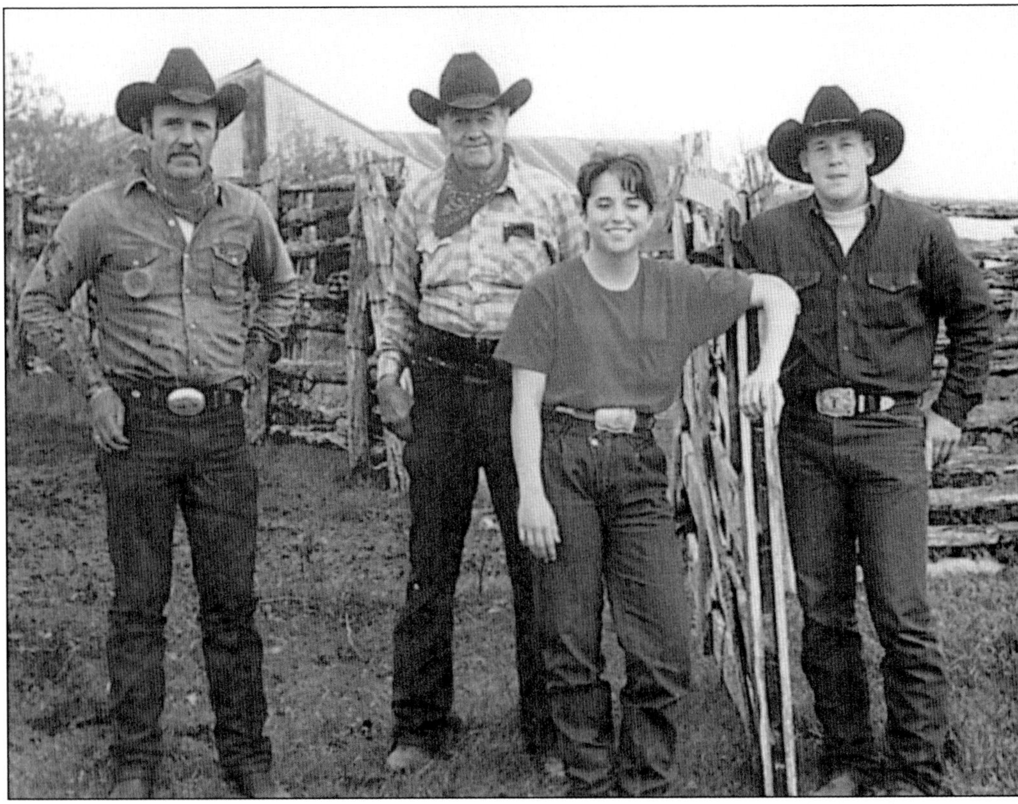

Having just finished working and branding some calves, these cowhands paused to get their photograph taken. Shown from left to right are Robert Puryear, Emory Puryear, Robin Puryear Luttrull, and Jeff Luttrull. Emory was foreman of the Heep Ranch. He leased this property, known as the Pope Place and located on the Heep Ranch, so he and Robert could run cattle on it. (Courtesy Jean and Robert Puryear.)

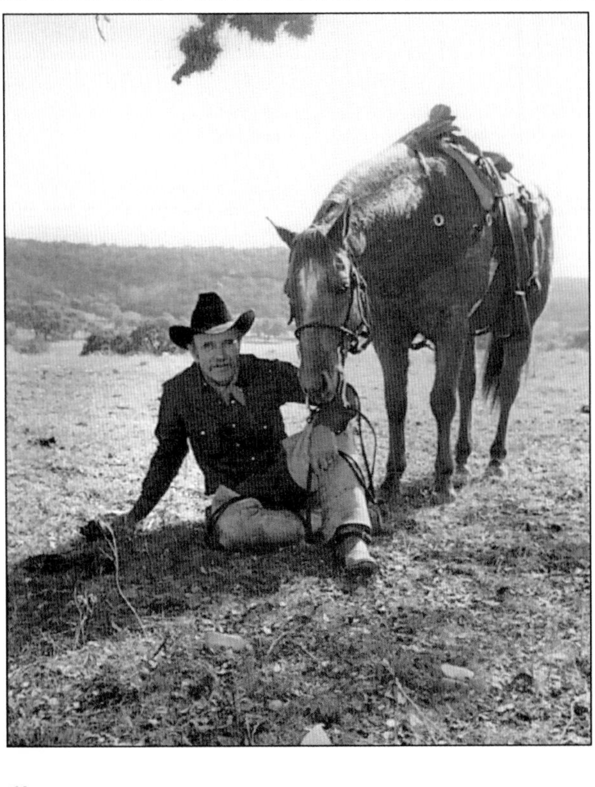

Having grown up at the Heep Ranch around horses and cattle all of his life, Robert Puryear easily fit the profile George Strait's agents were looking for when they hired cowboys for an upcoming video Strait was making. Robert is shown here, with his horse Snook, on location for the filming. (Courtesy Jean and Robert Puryear.)

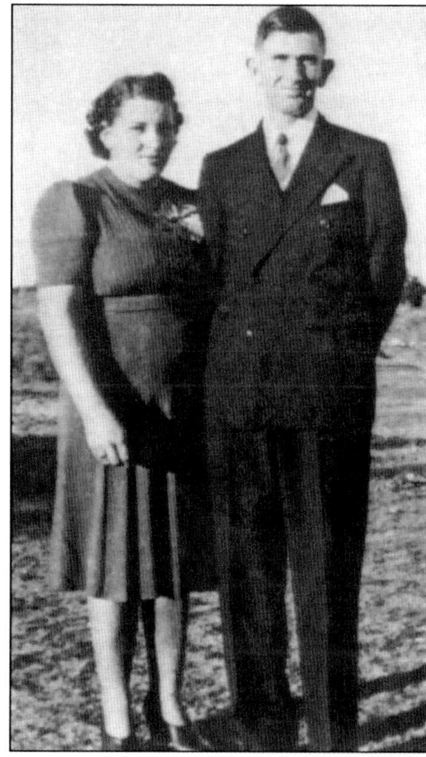

Doris Allen and Fred Siebert were married October 19, 1940, and are shown here on one of their special wedding anniversaries to commemorate the day. Doris was very interested in the history of Manchaca and compiled a written history of some of the main families and businesses. (Courtesy Joanne Deane.)

When the Frank and Hannah Blackwell estate was offered for sale in 1945, Joe and Ara Siebert, the parents of Fred Siebert, purchased the old 19th-century home Frank Blackwell had built. The Sieberts had a great appreciation for the history of the area and thoroughly enjoyed living in the old home. (Courtesy Joanne Deane.)

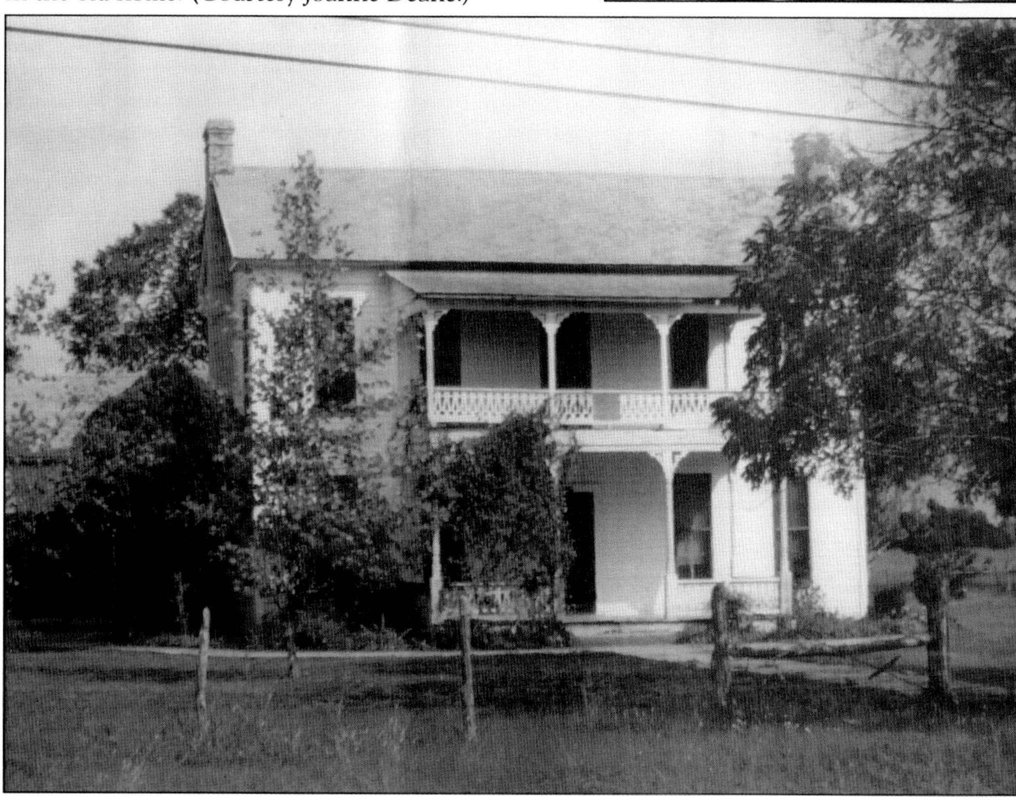

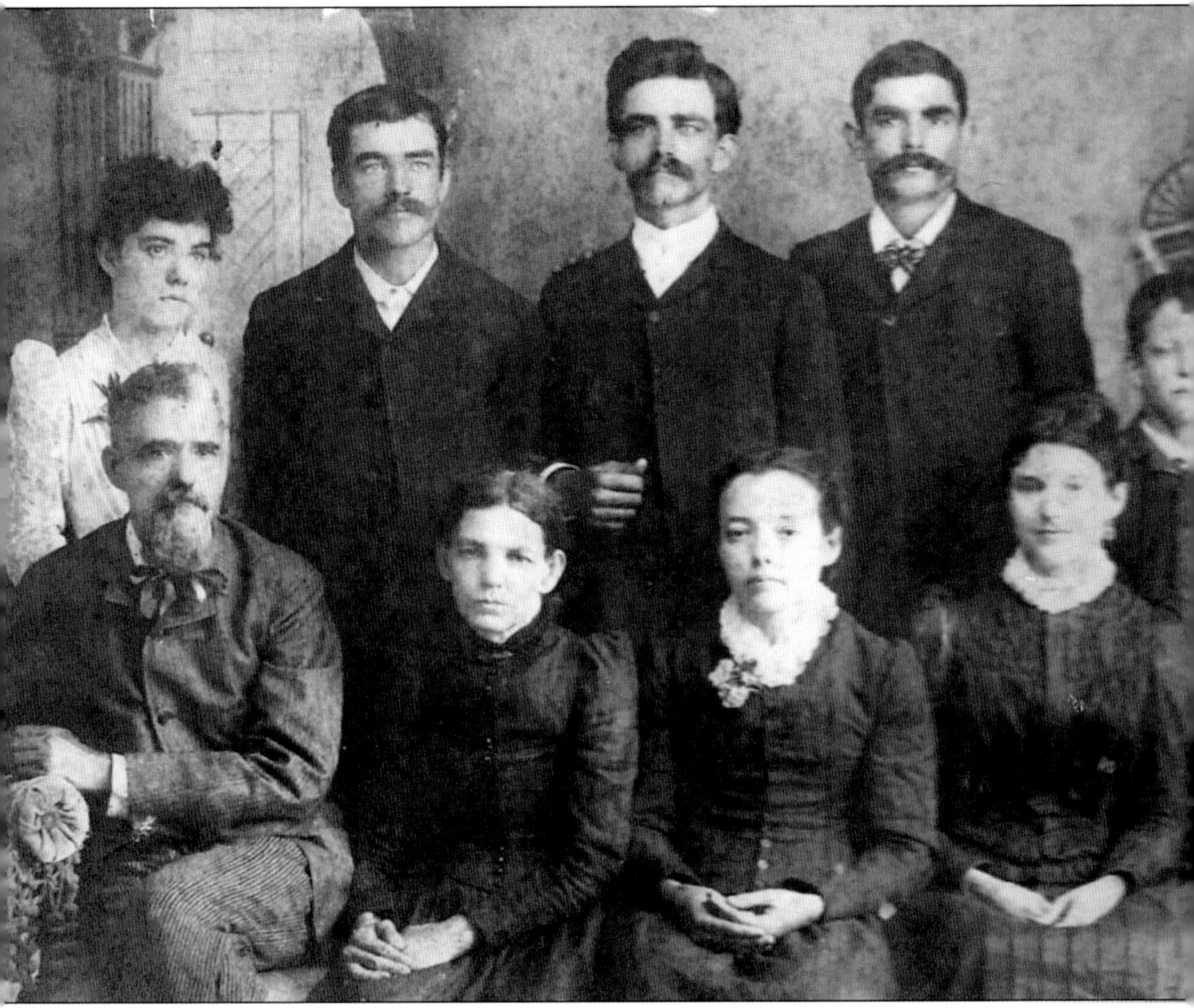

Standing in the far left corner of this image is Sarah Brooxie Parker Shepperd, who was born April 16, 1864, in DeWitt, Texas, to Alexander Hamilton Parker and Maryann Elizabeth Caddell. At the young age of 18, she fell in love with John Preston Shepperd. They were married on October 31, 1882, in Gillespie County, Texas. During her youth, her family moved from DeWitt to Goliad, Texas, and then on to Llano by 1880. She and her husband, John Shepperd, are shown on the 1900 census as residents of Manchaca. She died at the young age of 39 on October 14, 1903, and is buried along with her husband in the McQuistian Cemetery located off of Twin Creeks Road in Manchaca, Texas. (Courtesy Jewell H. Albright.)

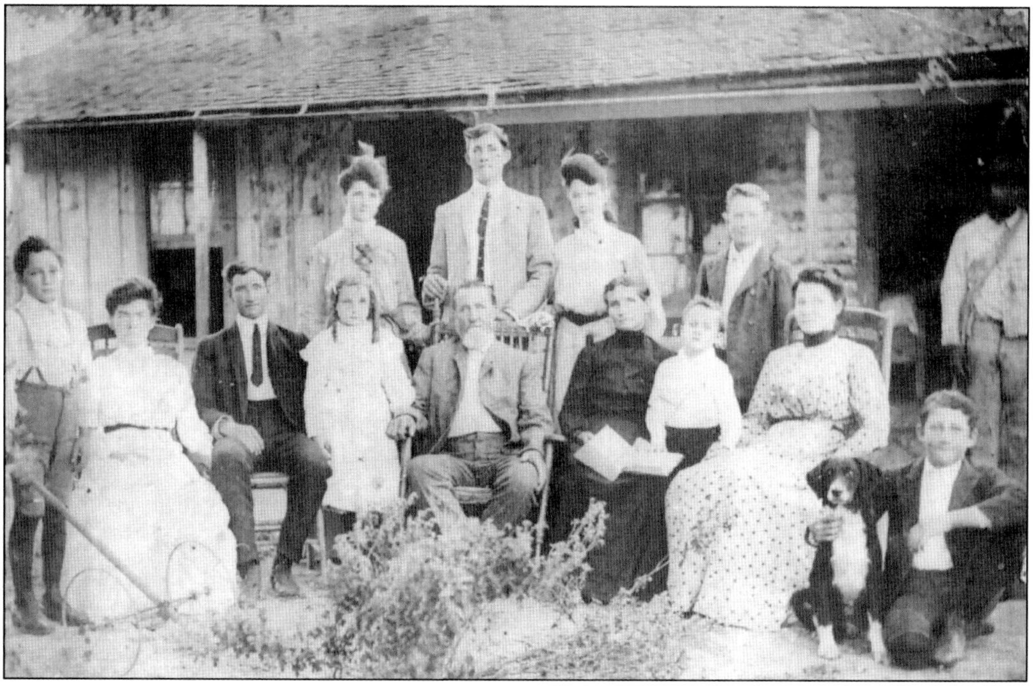

Seated in the middle of this family portrait are George Washington Strickland, who was born in 1844, and his wife, Nancy Jane Stockton Strickland, who was born in 1854. Their home in Manchaca can be seen behind them. It was located off of what is today Bliss Spillar Road. George and Nancy are surrounded by their children, grandchildren, extended family, and a trusted farmhand. Their youngest son, Marvin, is kneeling in the first row with his arm around his best pal, Old Rip. Marvin worked for the Austin-Travis County Health Department for 30 years, retiring in 1957, and was the first city sanitarian. Below are the tombstones of George Washington Strickland and his wife, Nancy, who are buried at Live Oak Cemetery. (Courtesy Wanda Stewart.)

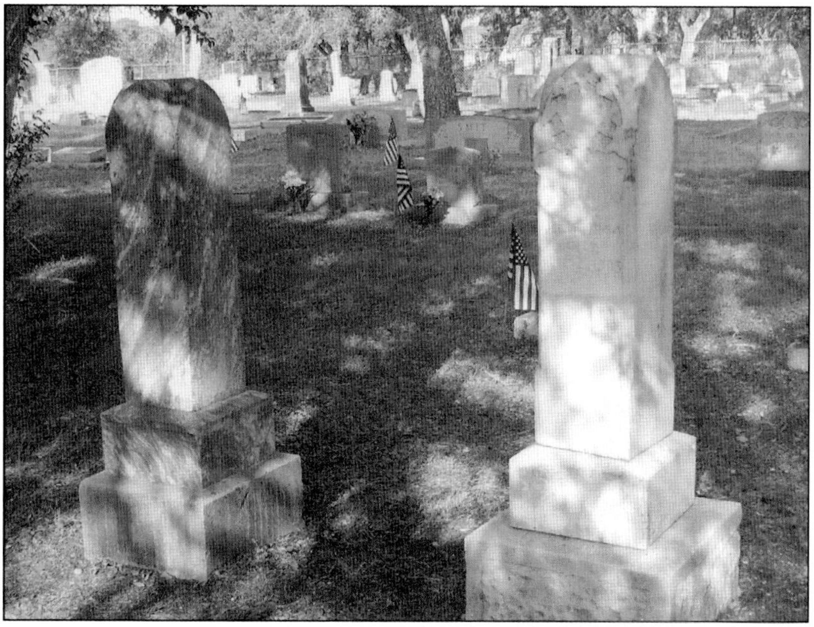

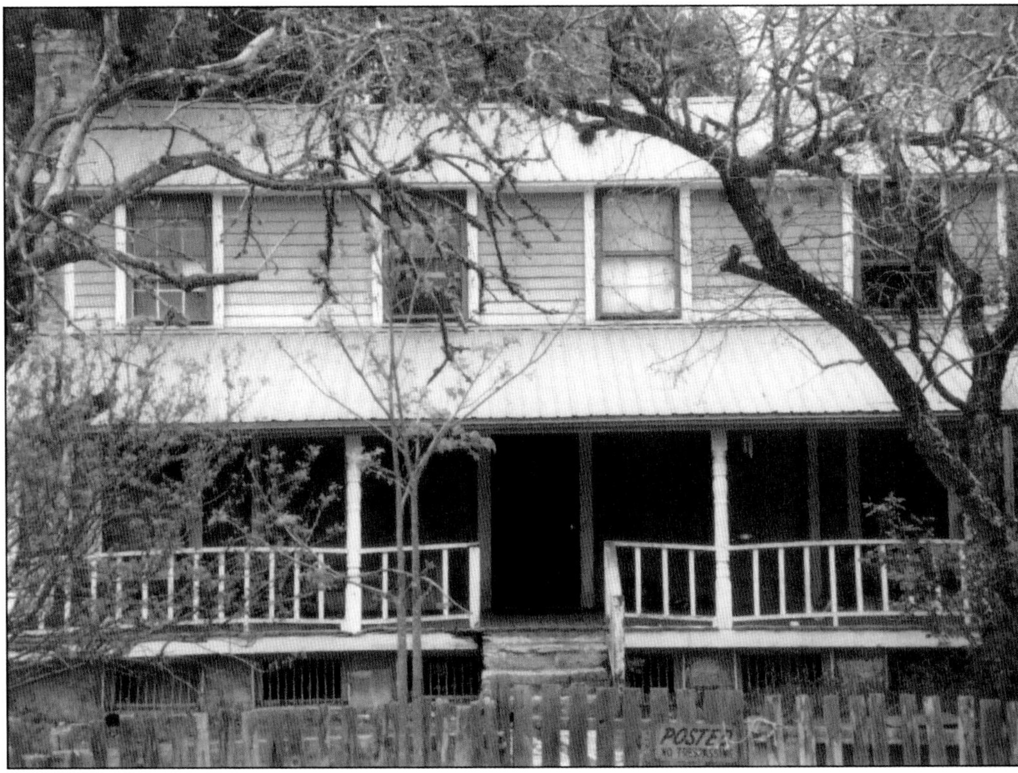


Three homes in Manchaca have been attributed to the Turleys. The chimney on this Turley home had the date of 1878 engraved into the stones. Of special interest in this home is the large basement where provisions could be kept cool. Unfortunately, the home was destroyed by a fire. (Courtesy Debra Tompkins.)

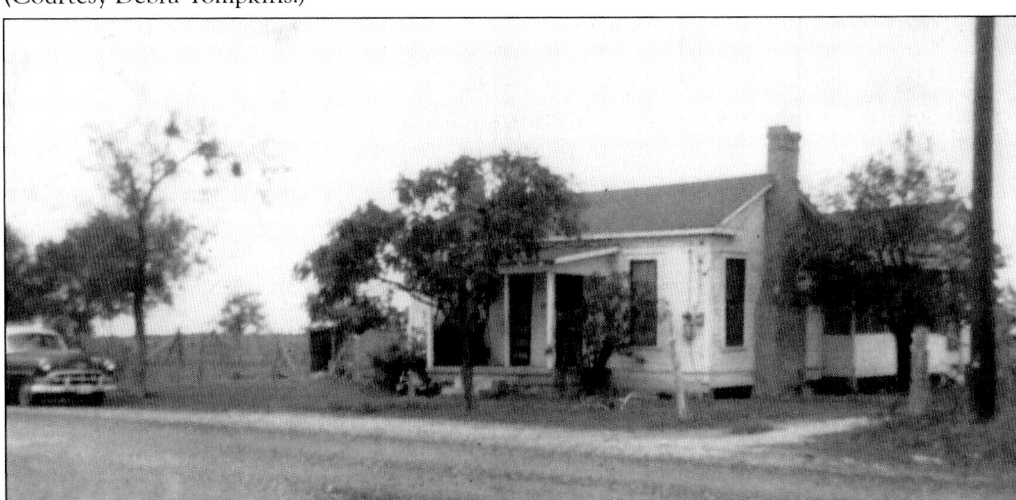

James Monroe Turley and Jane Soules, who married in Webberville in 1851, later settled in Manchaca in this country home. The Turleys were the parents of Edna Turley Carpenter. The home saw several owners after the Turleys. At one time, it was occupied by Nova and Luther Kessee and their three children, Maxine, June, and Everett. (Courtesy of Joanne Deane and the PICH 03029, Austin History Center, Austin Public Library.)

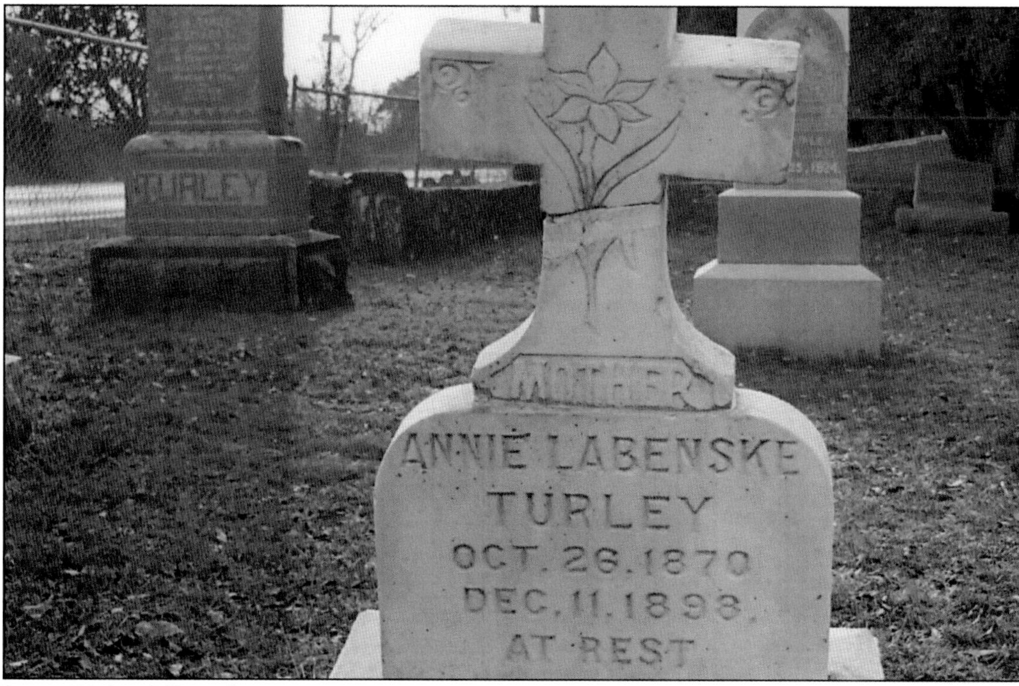


James Turley fell madly in love with Annie Labenske. Knowing full well she had the deadly disease tuberculosis, they married in February in 1890. Three years later, a son they christened Vernie was born to them. Tuberculosis ended up taking Annie's life in December 1898, at the young age of 28, leaving James a heartsick widower. (Courtesy Ann and Barry Trask.)

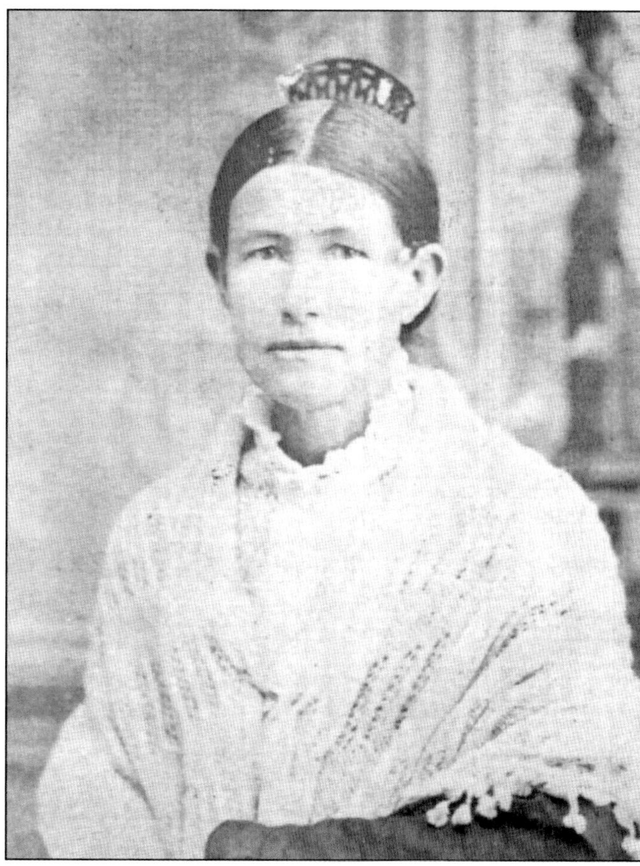

Jane Soules Turley, born in 1832, is shown here in 1880. At just under five feet tall and never weighing more than 90 pounds, she nonetheless carried the pet name of "Business," given to her by her husband, James Turley. Jane gave birth to 12 children, including Edna Turley Carpenter, and raised 3 stepdaughters. (Courtesy *Tales from the Manchaca Hills an Unvarnished Memoir.*)

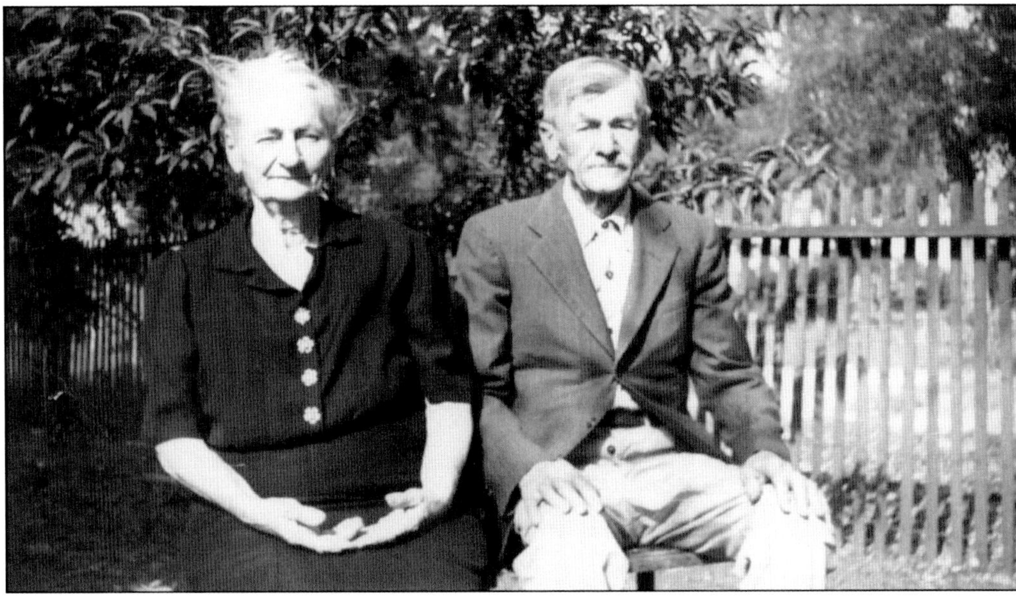

Freiderich Wilheim Wirth and his wife, Annie Meinecke of Carmine, lived on a 240-acre farm in Manchaca, where they raised eight children. Freiderich was known to all as Fritz. He was born in Danzig, West Prussia, Germany, in 1865, and he came to America in 1872 on the Barron Harbor steamship. His family first settled in New Braunfels and moved to Manchaca in 1879. (Courtesy Lillie M. Moreland.)

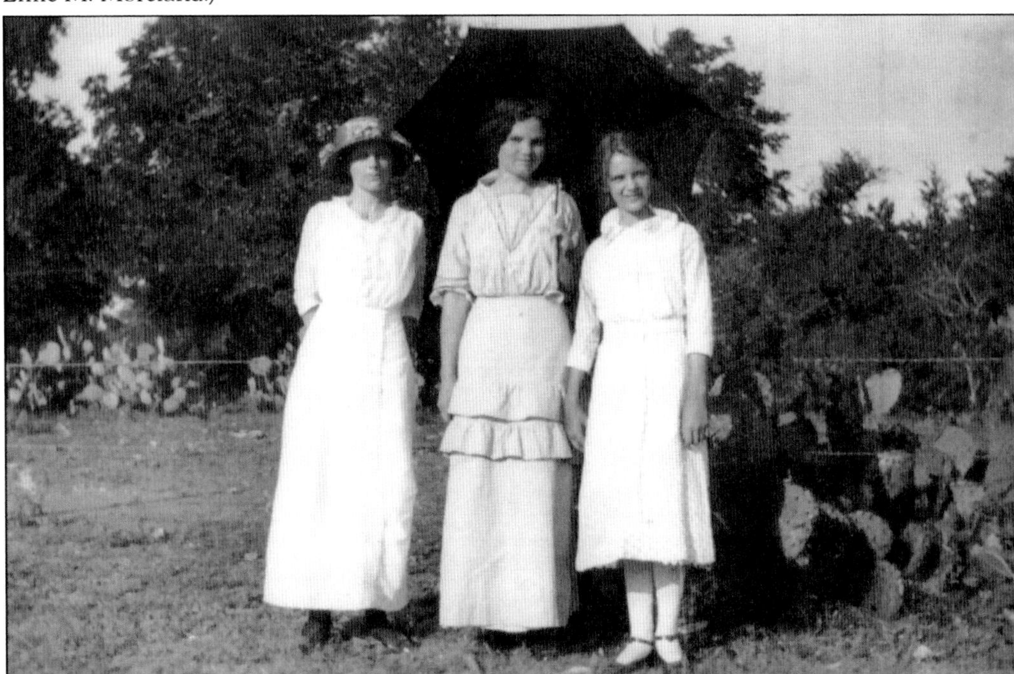

These lovely young ladies, shaded by their parasol, posed among the prickly pear cactus to show off their dress clothes. Standing from left to right are Nora Wirth, unidentified, and Lillie Wirth. Keeping those white stockings and dresses sparkling must have been a job considering the unpaved streets of Manchaca. (Courtesy Lillie M. Moreland.)

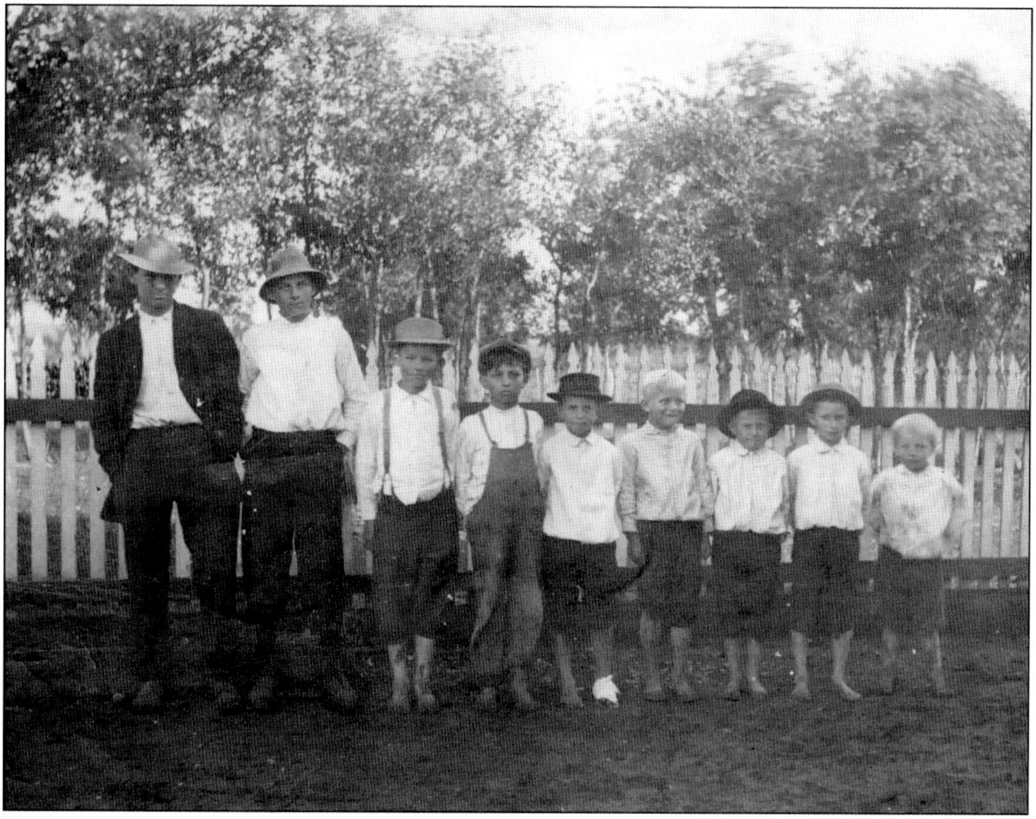

The neighborhood boys gathered for a stair-step photograph in the front yard of Annie and Fritz Wirth. It looks like the little ones of this "Manchaca Gang" preferred to go barefoot rather than submit to the confinement of any footwear. This may account for the bandage on the injured foot of one little fellow. (Courtesy Lilly M. Moreland.)

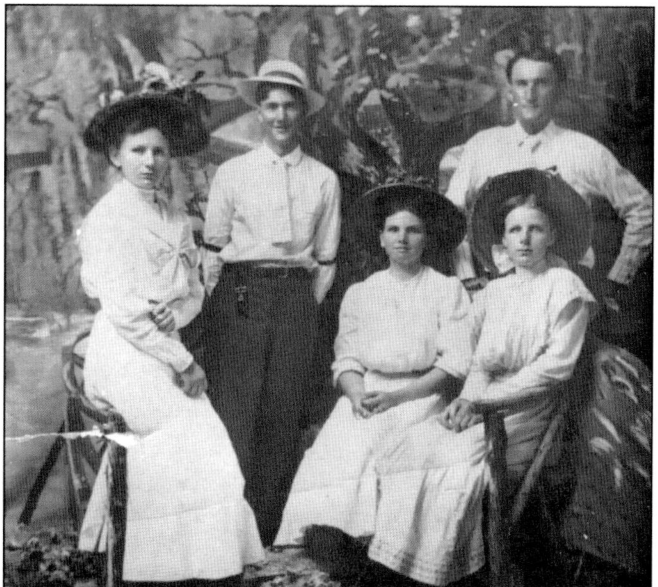

On a warm summer day in June 1909, these young people from Manchaca gathered for a photograph. Shown from left to right are Ella Wirth, Lewis Labenske, Mary Wilson, Nora Wirth, and Neal Meredith. Ella Wirth and Neal Meredith would go on to marry and raise their children in Manchaca. (Courtesy of Lillie M. Moreland)

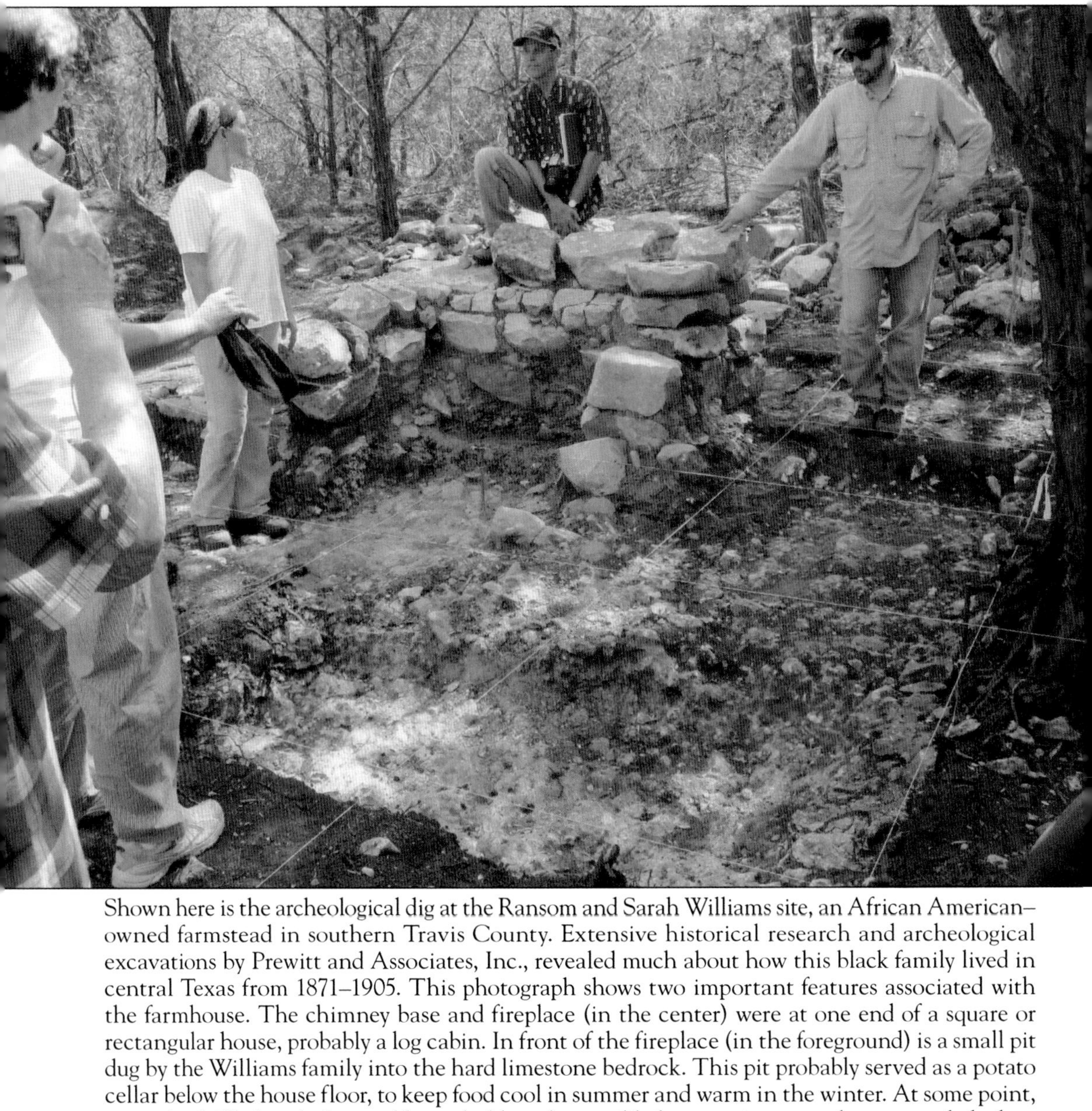

Shown here is the archeological dig at the Ransom and Sarah Williams site, an African American–owned farmstead in southern Travis County. Extensive historical research and archeological excavations by Prewitt and Associates, Inc., revealed much about how this black family lived in central Texas from 1871–1905. This photograph shows two important features associated with the farmhouse. The chimney base and fireplace (in the center) were at one end of a square or rectangular house, probably a log cabin. In front of the fireplace (in the foreground) is a small pit dug by the Williams family into the hard limestone bedrock. This pit probably served as a potato cellar below the house floor, to keep food cool in summer and warm in the winter. At some point, it was backfilled with dirt and household trash, possibly because it was no longer needed when the family acquired an icebox. Standing to the far left are MOCHA members visiting the site. In the center, from left to right, are archaeologists Jennifer McWilliams, Doug Boyd, and Aaron Norment. (Photograph by Barry Trask.)

Shown here are horse tack and harness artifacts found at the Ransom and Sarah Williams Farmstead. Shown counterclockwise from the upper left are a spur, a wiffletree center clip and hook, a plain bridle bit, a horseshoe and harness buckles, and part of a decorative snaffle bit. (Artifact photographs by Jennifer McWilliams and compiled by Sandy Hannum, used with permission of the Archeological Studies Program, Environmental Affairs Division, Texas Department of Transportation, Austin.)

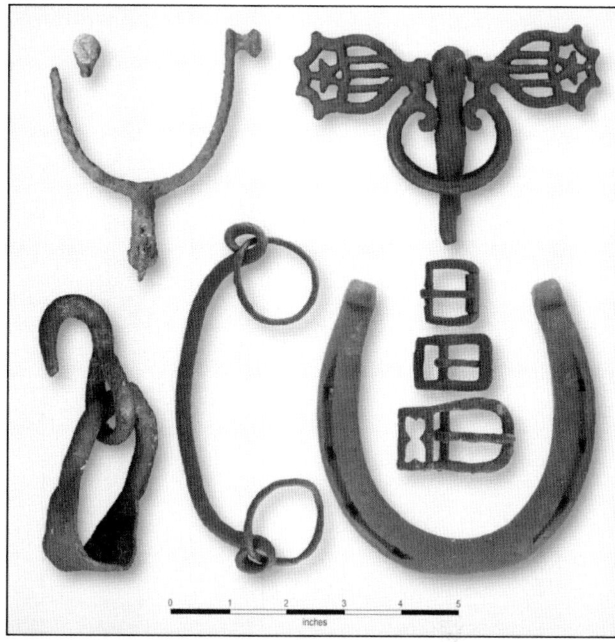


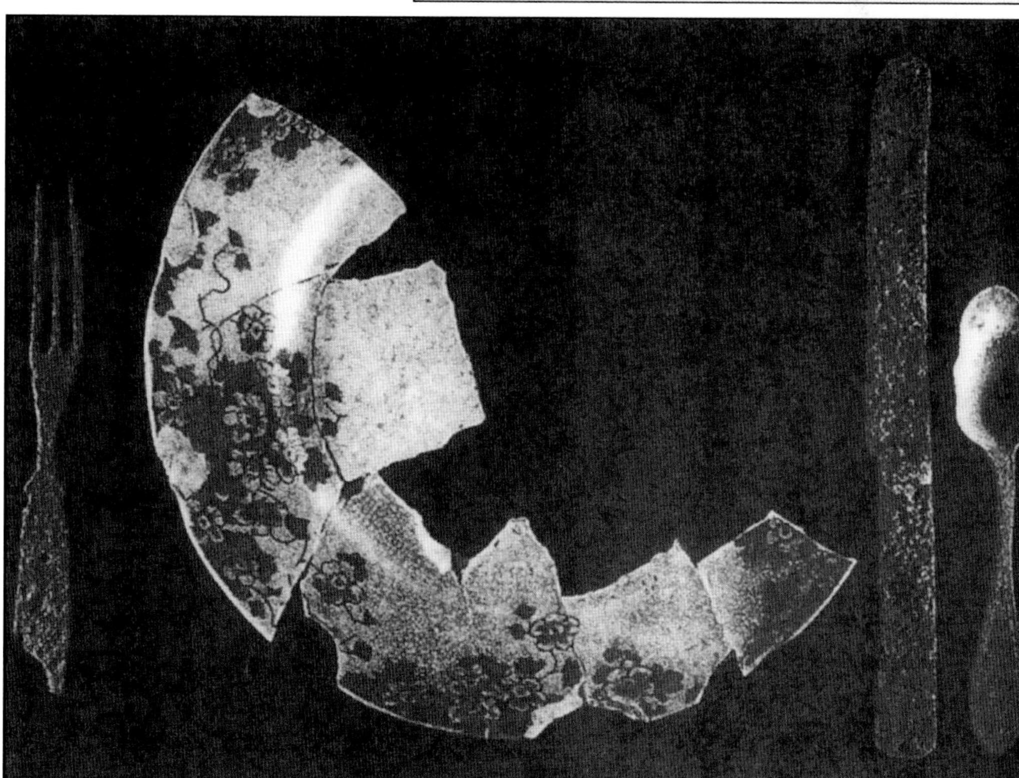

Shown above is a dinner place setting of kitchen artifacts recovered from the Ransom and Sarah Williams Farmstead. The transfer-printed plate was made by the English pottery firm Alfred Meakin, Ltd., between 1875 and 1897. (Photograph by Marsha Miller, College of Liberal Arts, University of Texas at Austin.)

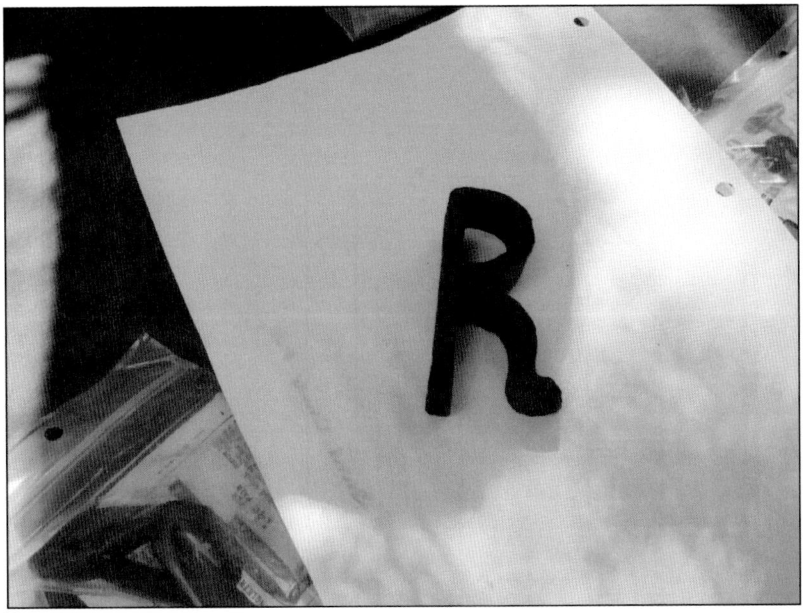

An iron letter "R," broken off of a branding iron that once belonged to Ransom Williams, is shown at left. According to the Travis County Brand Registry, Ransom Williams registered the letters "RA" as his horse brand on April 4, 1872. (Photograph by Barry Trask.)

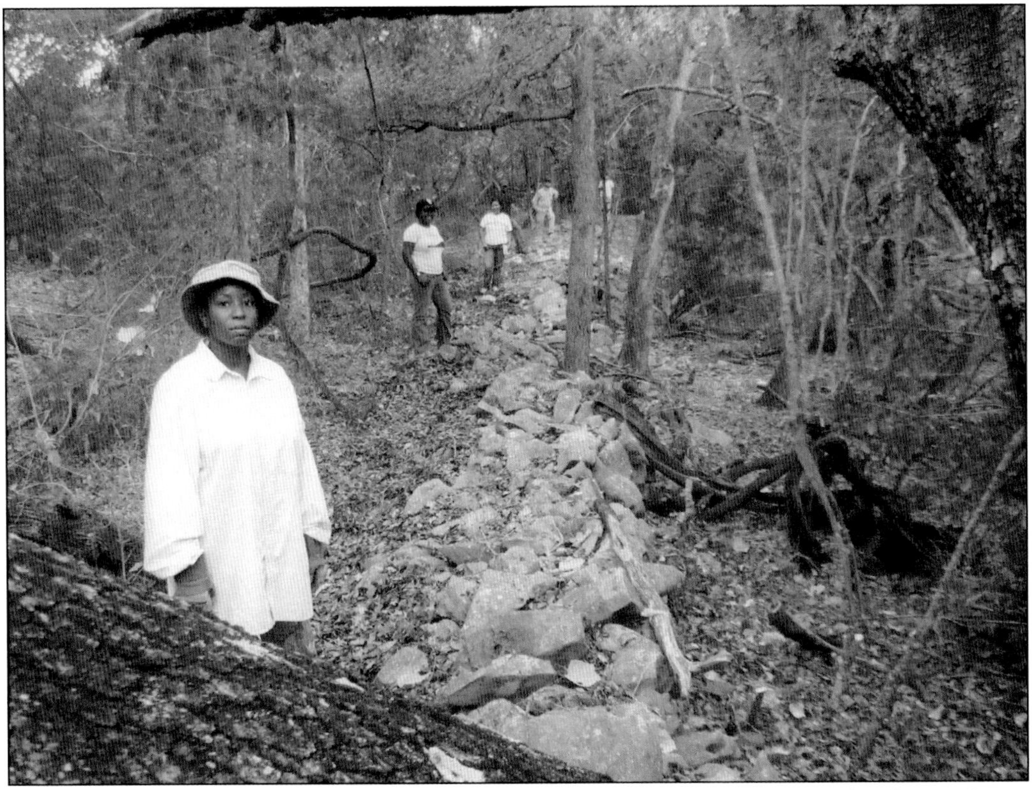

A massive rock wall that served as a livestock fence on the Williams Farmstead is shown above. Archeologists standing along the wall to provide scale are, from front to back, Jodi Skipper, Nedra Lee, Valerie Prado, Felton Pierre, Aaron Norment, and Jennifer McWilliams. (Photograph by Douglas K. Boyd, used with permission of the Archeological Studies Program, Environmental Affairs Division, Texas Department of Transportation, Austin.)

Taking photographs was a favorite activity to record holidays in 1926. The following Manchaca residents posed for the camera on Easter at a picnic at Manchaca Springs. Shown from left to right are (first row) young Ella Rae Cruze; (second row) Marie Stevenson, Nolen Cruze, Alice Cruze, John Fred Meredith and Leola Winberley. (Courtesy Joanne Deane.)

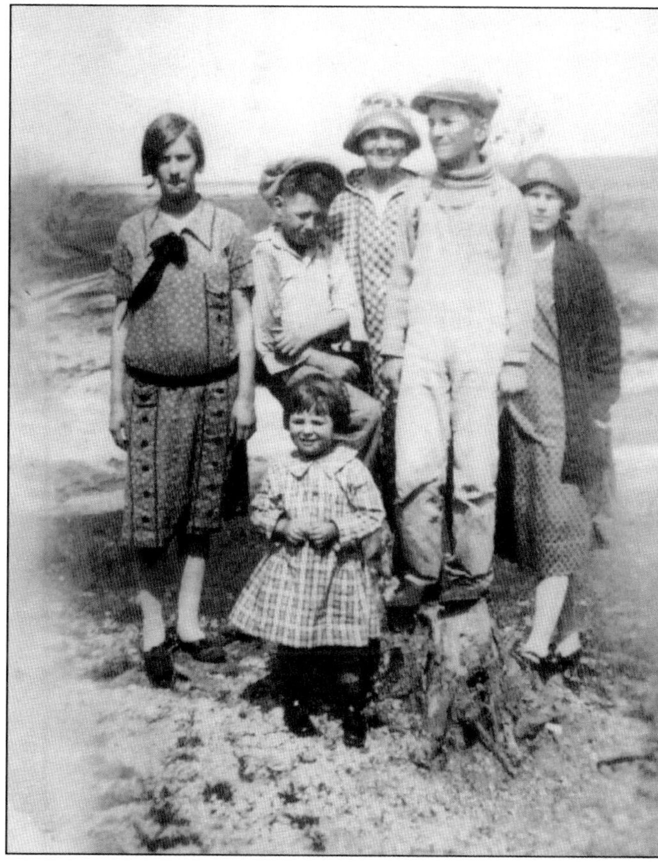

On Easter Sunday 1926, several families gathered at Manchaca Springs to celebrate the holiday. Shown here are members of the Stevenson, Bryant, Burton, Cruze, Wimberley and Meredith families. Young John Meredith, in the first row, appears to be shooting back at the camera with a homemade version of a cannon. (Courtesy Joanne Deane.)

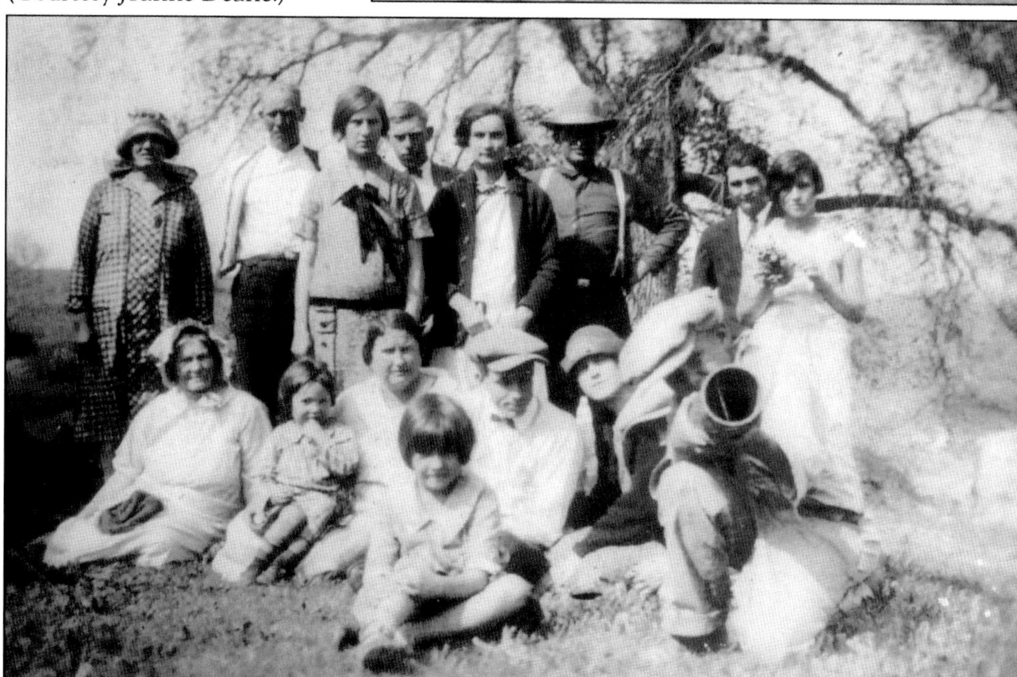

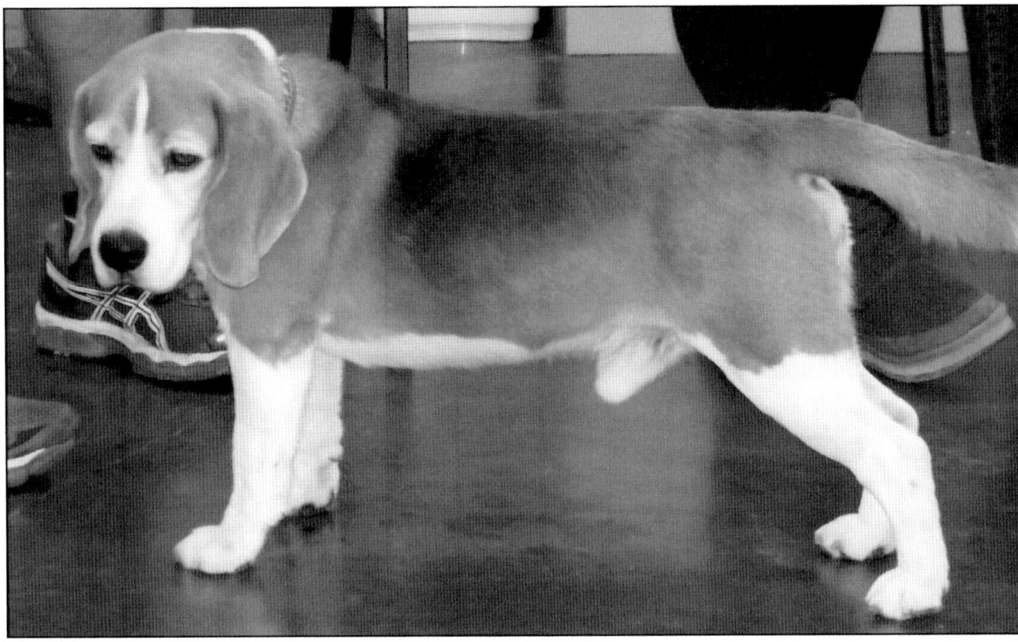

When Uno the beagle won Best in Show at the 2008 Westminster Dog Show, he went down in history as the first beagle to ever hold that title. Aaron Wilkerson from Manor, Texas, was Uno's handler for the Westminster show. When they were introduced to one another for the first time, an immediate and natural bond was formed. His owner, Caroline Dowell, says, "It was just a boy and his dog." Uno and Caroline reside in the village of San Leanna, just outside of Manchaca. His sweet and jaunty personality wins the hearts of all who meet him. Besides being extremely handsome, Uno is also a service dog who has brought many hours of fun and love to others. Uno is shown below serving as grand marshal of the village of San Leanna's 2011 Fourth of July Parade. He is escorted by Dan Huebner. (Both, courtesy Elizabeth Korts.)

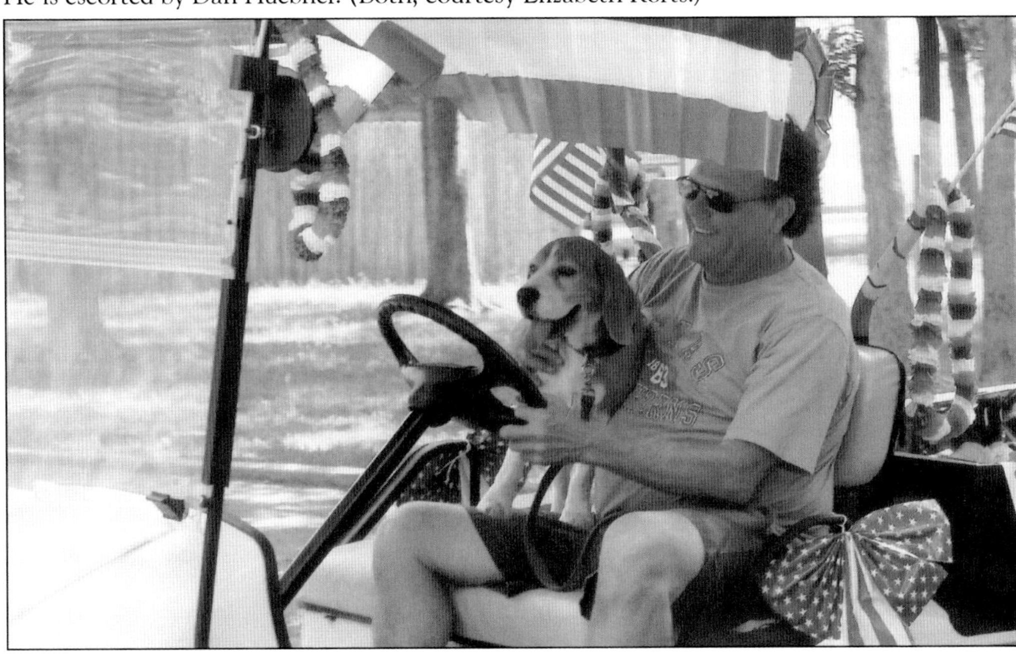

# *Three*

# Transportation and Commerce

The early stagecoach stop at Manchaca Springs brought many a traveler through the area, and they often returned to put down their roots. As the population increased around Manchaca, businessmen built several mercantile stores in the heart of town. One of the earliest establishments was the Ellison and Von Rosenberg General Merchandise store. Co-owner Dr. W.A. Ellison practiced medicine in town. The Summerrow family owned a general merchandise store and a cotton gin. Shawnee Thomas Carpenter owned a store and became a cotton gin owner. Pharmacist Frank Blackwell owned a general merchandise store that also dispensed medications. His store had the noted distinction of having the local post office situated within its walls. Advertisements placed in the Austin paper showed the competition and salesmanship of the Summerrows and Blackwells. Other well known establishments were the Labenske Store, the blacksmith shop owned by Joe Lamb, the J.B. Jones store, and later the Earl Jones Grocery. The International and Great Northern Railroad, which ran through town and touted the "Shortest and Best Route to and From Texas," brought merchandise to fill the local shops and gave the people of Manchaca an efficient way to get their goods to market.

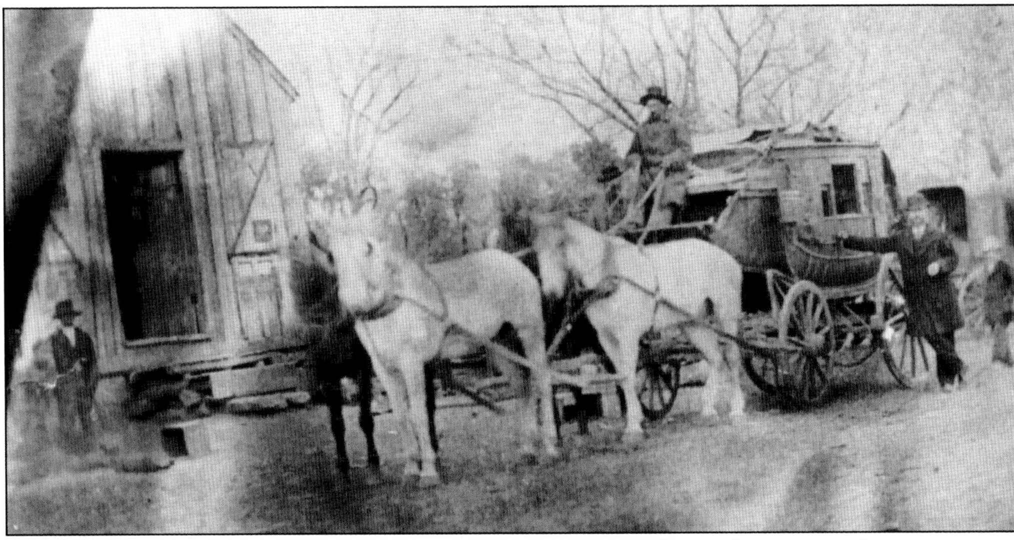

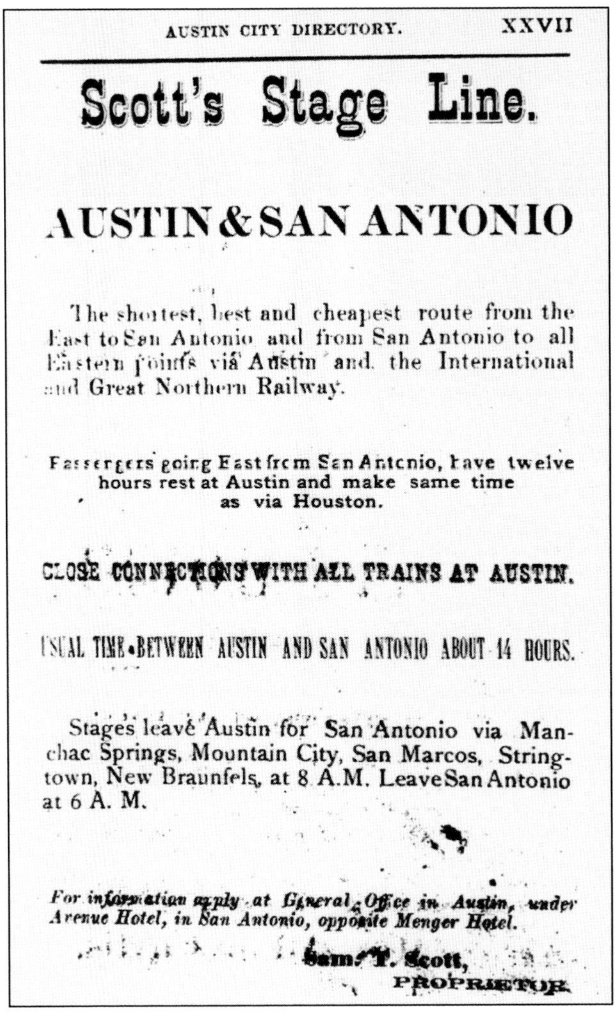

AUSTIN CITY DIRECTORY. XXVII

# Scott's Stage Line.

## AUSTIN & SAN ANTONIO

The shortest, best and cheapest route from the East to San Antonio and from San Antonio to all Eastern points via Austin and the International and Great Northern Railway.

Passengers going East from San Antonio, have twelve hours rest at Austin and make same time as via Houston.

CLOSE CONNECTIONS WITH ALL TRAINS AT AUSTIN.

USUAL TIME BETWEEN AUSTIN AND SAN ANTONIO ABOUT 14 HOURS.

Stages leave Austin for San Antonio via Manchac Springs, Mountain City, San Marcos, Stringtown, New Braunfels, at 8 A.M. Leave San Antonio at 6 A. M.

*For information apply at General Office in Austin, under Avenue Hotel, in San Antonio, opposite Menger Hotel.*

Sam. T. Scott,
PROPRIETOR.

This early stagecoach was photographed stopping at Manchaca Springs. An 1850 advertisement in the *Texas State Gazette* offered tri-weekly stage routes run by the Harrison and McCullough stage line. The route ran from Austin, through Manchaca Springs, then on to San Marcos, New Braunfels, and San Antonio. The 1877 city directory for Austin advertises Scott's Stage Line, which also stopped in Manchaca Springs. (PICA 19588, Austin History Center, Austin Public Library.)

*Mooney & Morrison's General Directory of the City of Austin for 1877–78* featured this advertisement for Scott's Stage Line that ran through Manchac [*sic*] Springs. Stage coach lines carried the mail. Bids to acquire routes were placed with the United States Postal Department. Each route carried a number. At least two routes ran through Manchaca Springs, 8564 and 6285. (Courtesy Austin History Center.)

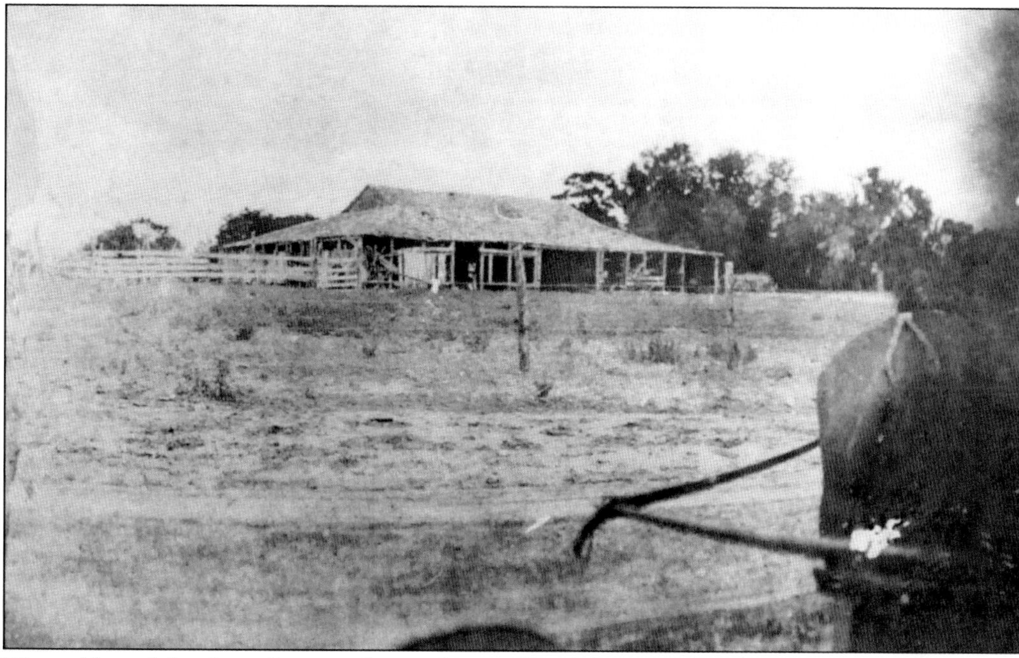

The stables at Manchaca Springs, shown above, offered the animals a place to rest and chow down. In 1850, the Harrison & McCulloch stage line left Austin at 3:00 a.m. and arrived in San Antonio 18 hours later at 9:00 p.m. They touted a four-horse stage, a nice upgrade from previous two-horse teams that ran the route. (PICA 19586, Austin History Center, Austin Public Library.)

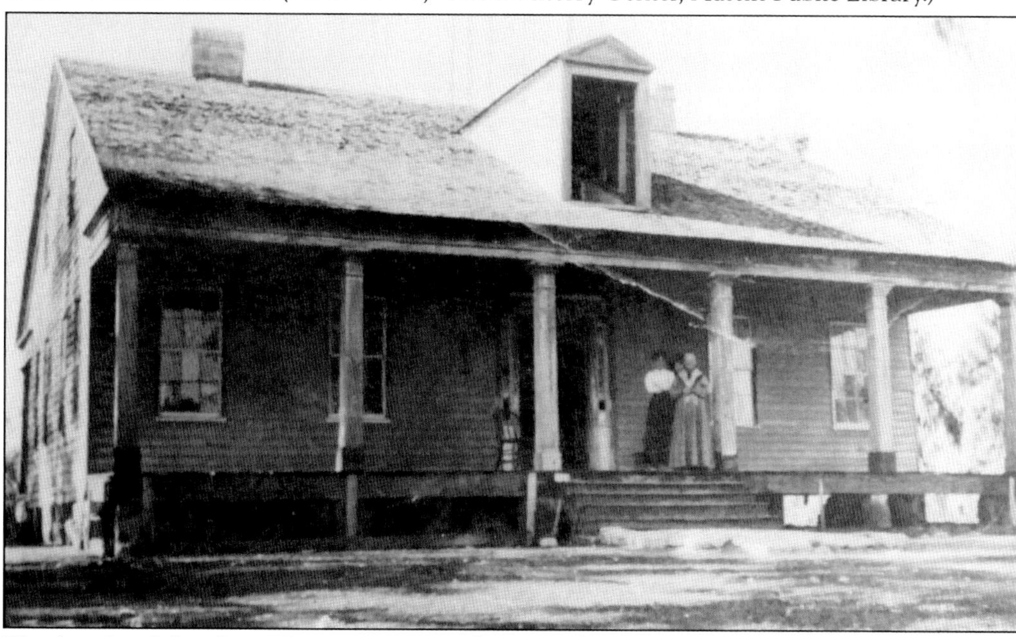

The hotel at Manchaca Springs was a welcome sight to stage travelers. Frederick Olmsted recorded his experience at the springs in the 1850s in his book *A Journey through Texas*. He noted a bountiful table set with preserved fruits, ham, fresh bread, and tea. They were waited on by neatly dressed girls who offered the travelers drinks in silver cups. (PICA 19585, Austin History Center, Austin Public Library.)

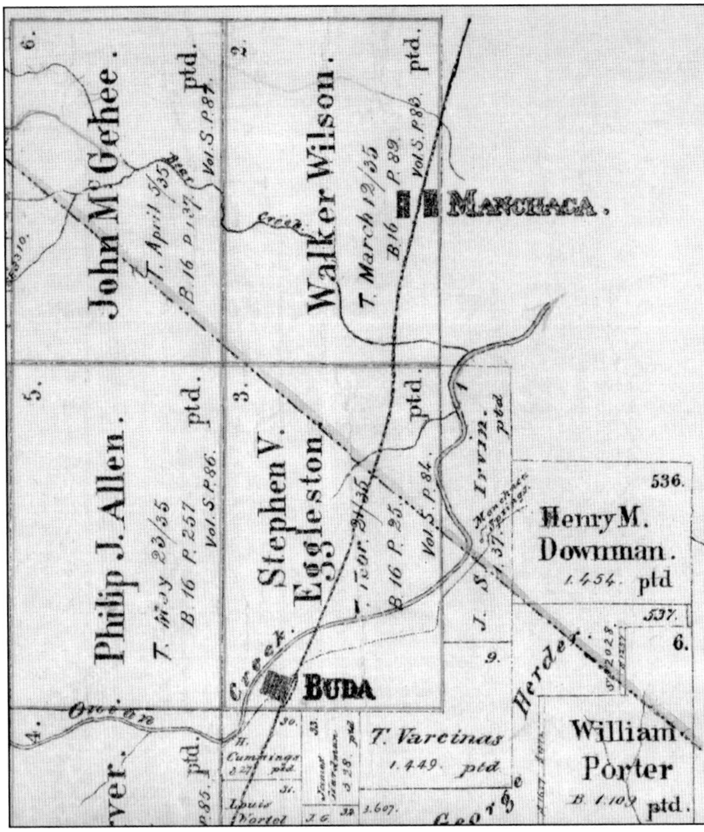


Manchaca is shown here in 1880 with the train tracks running through the middle of town. When the International and Great Northern Railroad came to Manchaca, growth for the little town followed close behind. The addition of dependable transportation to and from local markets attracted merchants and farmers to settle in the area. (Map of Hays County, 1880, No. 16848. Courtesy of the Texas General Land Office, Austin.)

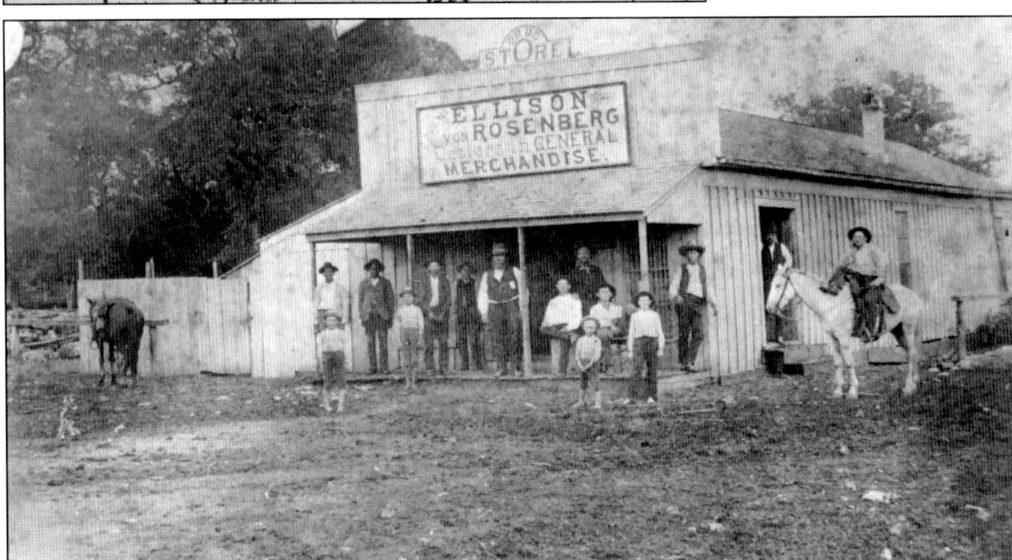


In 1889, Dr. W.A. Ellison and P. Von Rosenberg set up this general merchandise and drug store in Manchaca. Dr. Ellison was a much loved and highly revered physician, and he delivered many babies in Manchaca. *The Medical World, Volume 5*, published in 1887, carried two articles submitted by him. In one article, he states he "attended 176 different women in 243 confinements." (PICA 03596, Austin History Center, Austin Public Library.)

Mary Emily McCuistian Ellison was the daughter of Rebecca and John Jordan McCuistian. She is buried in the McCuistian Cemetery. Mary was the wife of Manchaca physician Dr. W.A. Ellison, and mother of Sudie, Lena, and Willie Ellison. Being a healer himself, it must have been terribly frustrating to lose his dear wife at the young age of 38. (Courtesy Ann and Barry Trask.)

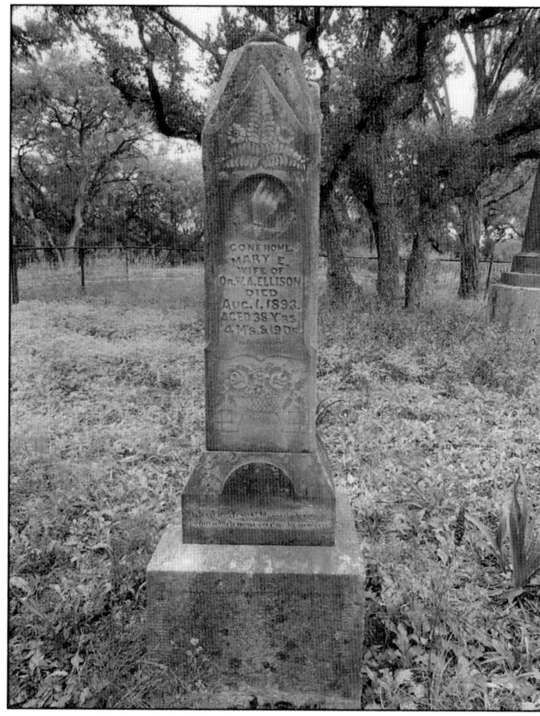


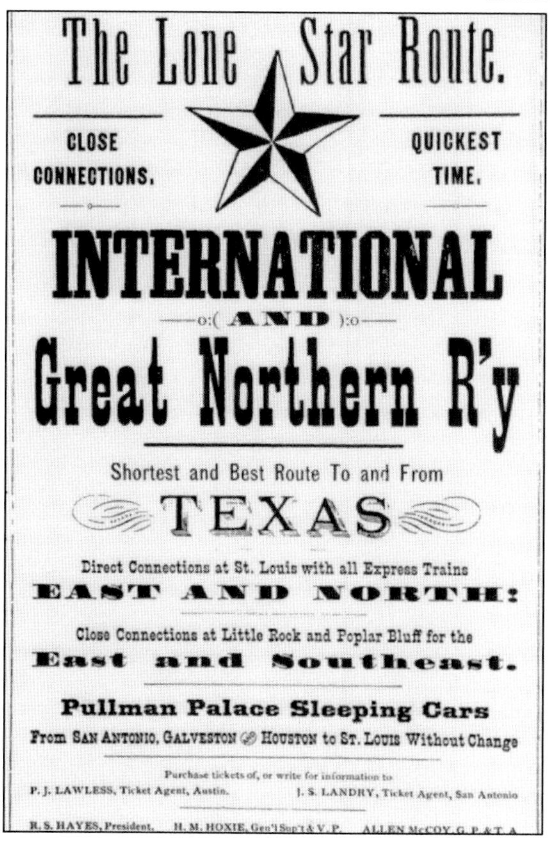


The International and Great Northern Railroad had reached the city of Austin by 1876, and by 1880 the line was completed through Manchaca. This advertisement for the railroad, touting the latest accommodations in sleeping cars, appeared in *Morrison & Fourmy's General Directory of the City of Austin for 1881–1882*. (Courtesy Austin History Center, Austin Public Library.)

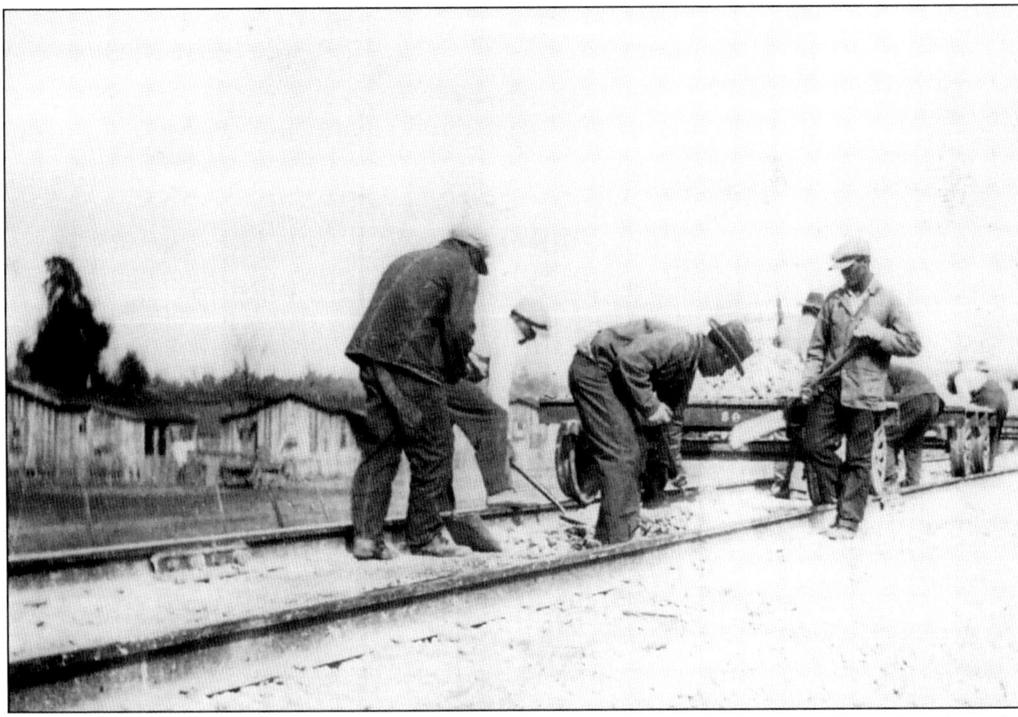

Taken in the late 1930s, this photograph shows workers making repairs to the railroad tracks. Throughout the years, changes and repairs were required to keep the tracks in good working order. Railway Section Houses, built by the International and Great Northern Railroad to house its workers and provide storage, can be seen in the background. (Courtesy of Joanne Deane.)

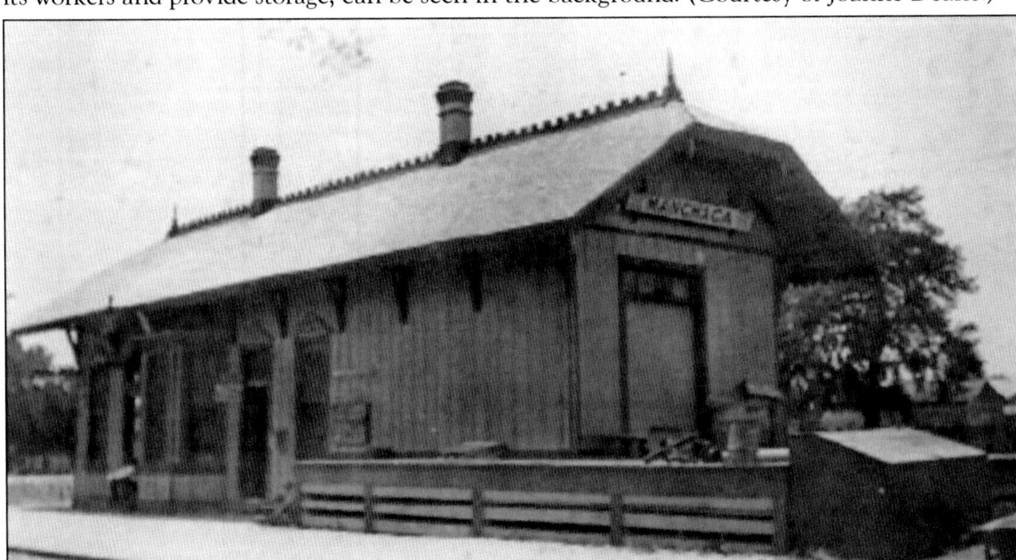


The train depot in downtown Manchaca was the heart of the town for decades until it disappeared in the 1940s. In times gone by, old men would sit out front and whittle or pitch washers or horseshoes. Children played under the shade of the spreading oaks and the telegraph operator located in the depot announced advance weather information to all interested parties. (Courtesy Lillie M. Moreland.)

The International and Great Northern Railroad handled incoming and outgoing mail as it passed through town. Lillie Meredith Moreland is standing next to the mail hook, where the mailbag was placed for the train to pick up. Railroad operators left the incoming mailbag here as well, allowing residents to retrieve their mail. (Courtesy Lillie M. Moreland.)

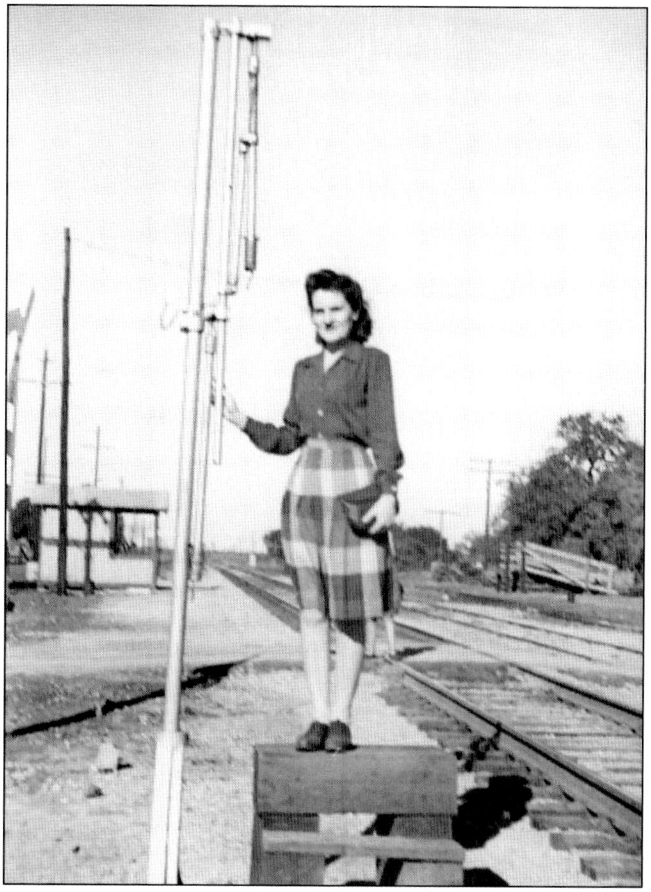

Neal Meredith worked on the roads for the county. He is shown here in 1910 holding the reins of his team of mules. The town of Manchaca had no paved streets or street signs at this time. (Courtesy Lillie M. Moreland.)

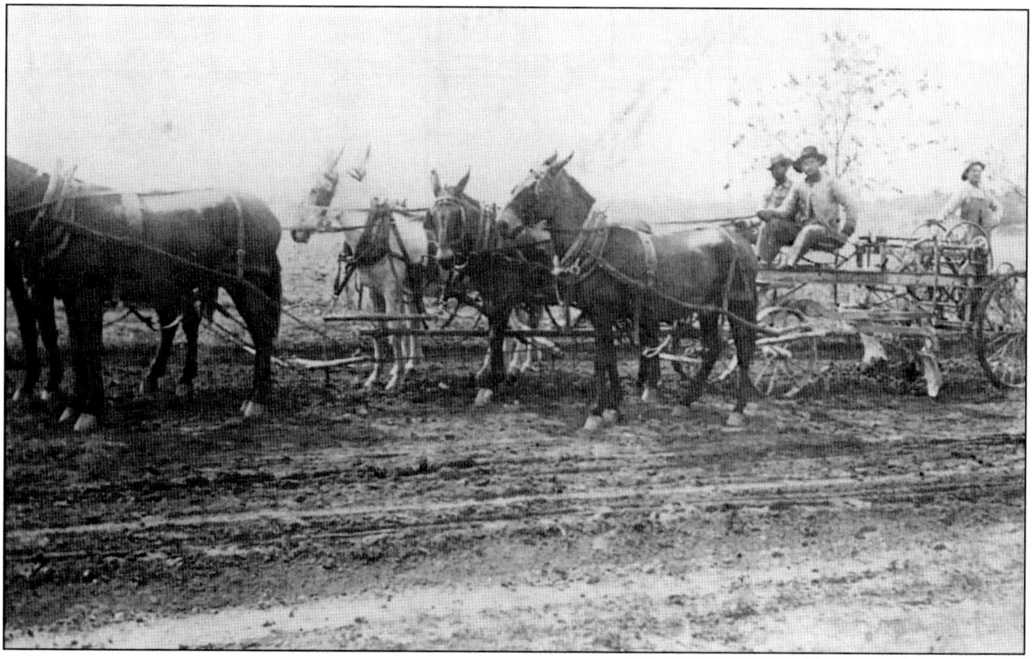

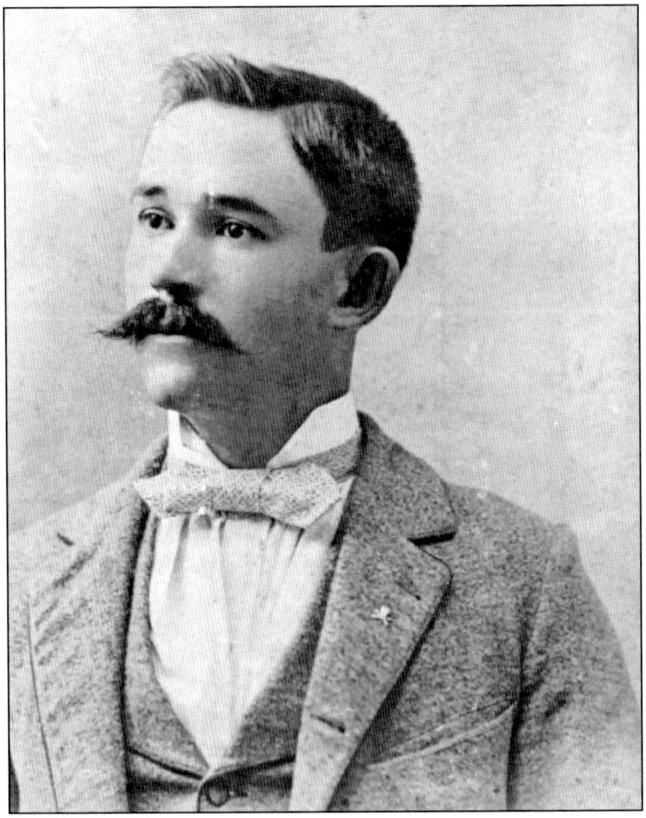

When Shawnee Thomas Carpenter asked Edna Turley to marry him, he wrote, "If I get you for $1.50 (for the cost of a marriage license) it will be the best buy I ever made." Shawnee Thomas is shown here in 1895 at the age of 21. In 1897, Shawnee married Edna at the Manchaca Methodist Church. He became a successful businessman in town. (Courtesy *Tales from the Manchaca Hills an Unvarnished Memoir.*)

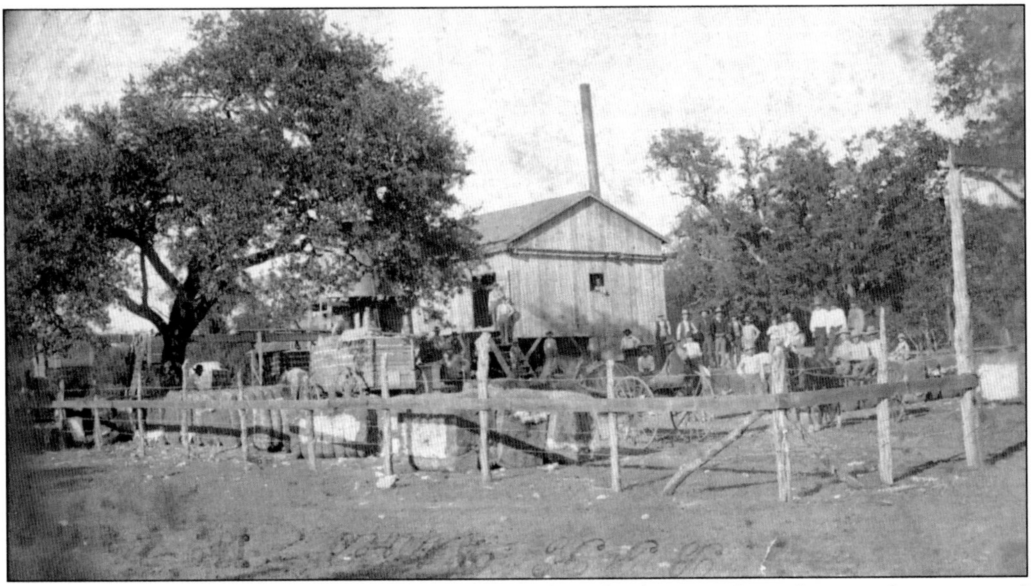

This Manchaca cotton gin stood along the railroad tracks that ran through town. It was owned and operated first by W.P. Summerrow, and later by Shawnee Thomas Carpenter. The cotton ginned here was grown within five miles of the facility. Longtime Manchaca residents remember that in its heyday, it would gin 5,000–6,000 bales of cotton each fall. (Courtesy PICA 03597 Austin History Center, Austin Public Library.)

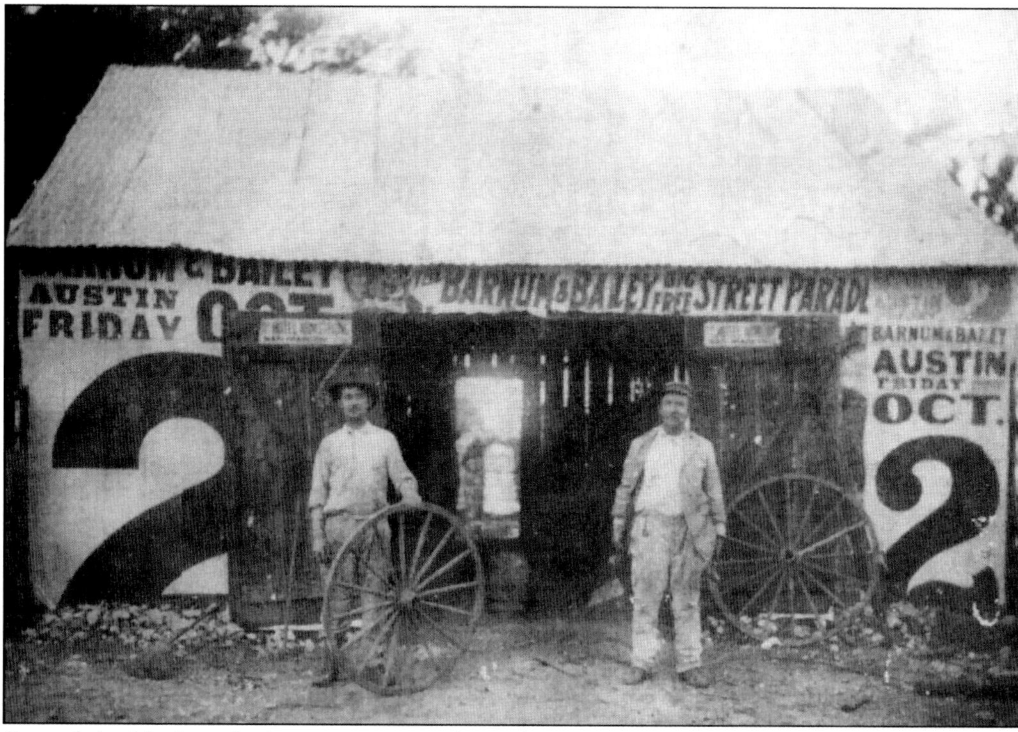


One of the blacksmith shops in town is shown here in 1908. The circus advertisement on the front may have been creative use of an old billboard. According to the federal census of 1910, there were several blacksmith shops in the bustling community of Manchaca. Shown here are Calvin Swank, left, and Joseph T. Lamb, owner. (Courtesy Caroline O'Brien.)

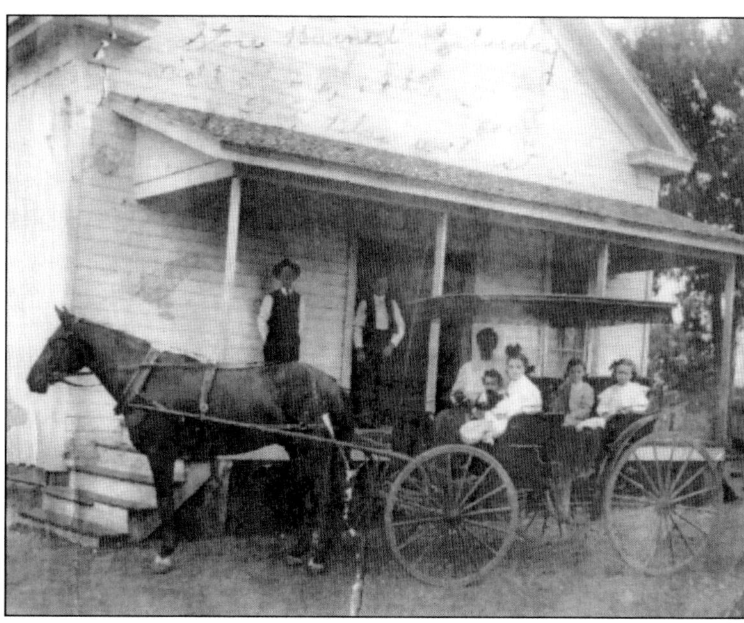

The Blackwell Store was a pivotal business in early Manchaca. Posed here on the front porch of the store are owner Frank Blackwell, left, and his employee Pat Cunningham in the doorway. Shown in the front seat of the buggy, from left to right, are Frank's wife, Hannah, with daughters Blanch and Bruce. Sitting in the rear are Bernice, on the left, and Beatrice Blackwell. (Courtesy Joanne Deane.)

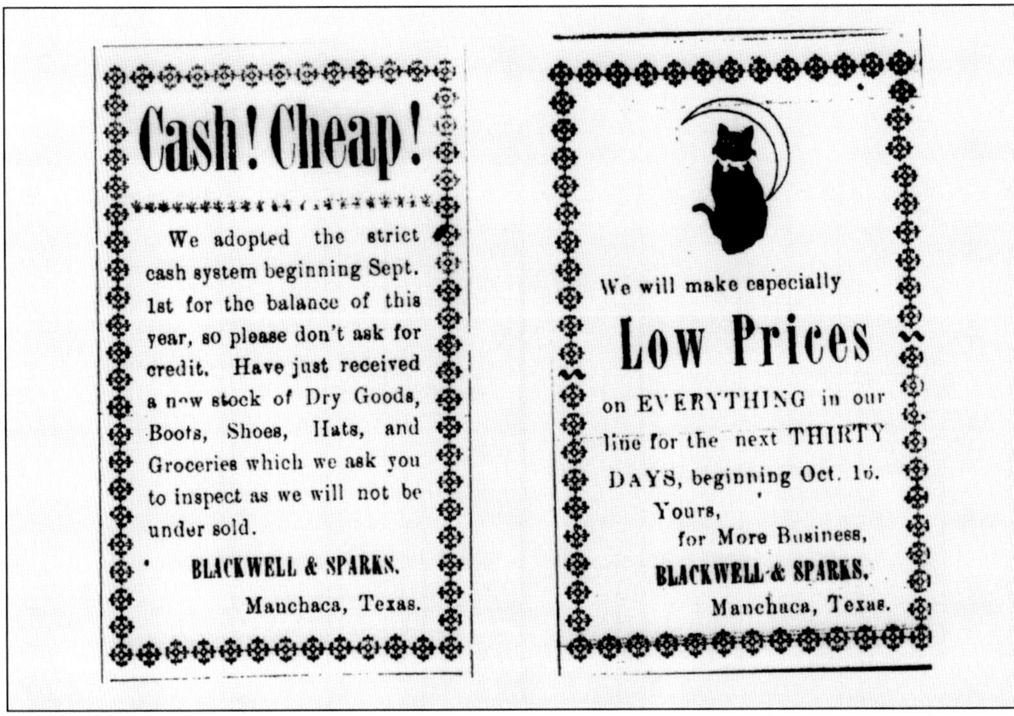


Manchaca merchants Blackwell & Sparks knew the importance of good advertising. These 1901 advertisements that ran in the *Texas State Democrat Farm and Home* paper show their competitive spirit in pricing and the knowledge that cash is king. Besides offering general merchandise and groceries, their establishment also provided prescriptions, filled by pharmacist Frank Blackwell. The addition of the town post office in the front of the store was a welcome service to Manchaca residents. (Courtesy Austin History Center, Austin Public Library.)

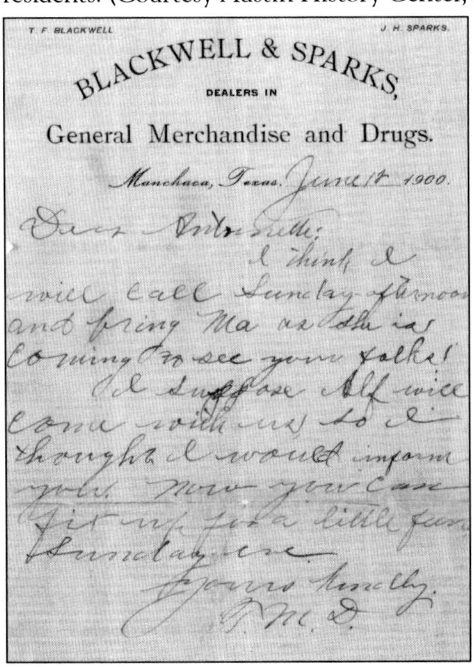

T. F. BLACKWELL J. H. SPARKS

BLACKWELL & SPARKS,

DEALERS IN

General Merchandise and Drugs.

Manchaca, Texas, June 1st 1900.

Dear Antoinette:

I think I will call Sunday afternoon and bring Ma as she is coming to see your folks. I suppose Alf will come with us so I thought I would inform you. Now you can fix up for a little fun Sunday eve.

Yours kindly,

T. M. D.

Thomas Dunnahoo (pen name Scarlet) and Cordie Labenske (pen name Antoinette) wrote informative columns about Manchaca for the *Texas State Democrat Farm and Home Newspaper* during the turn of the century. Their acquaintance blossomed into love in 1900, when Thomas began courting Cordie. Here, he used notepaper from the local store to set up a date. (Courtesy Marilyn Dunnahoo McLeod.)

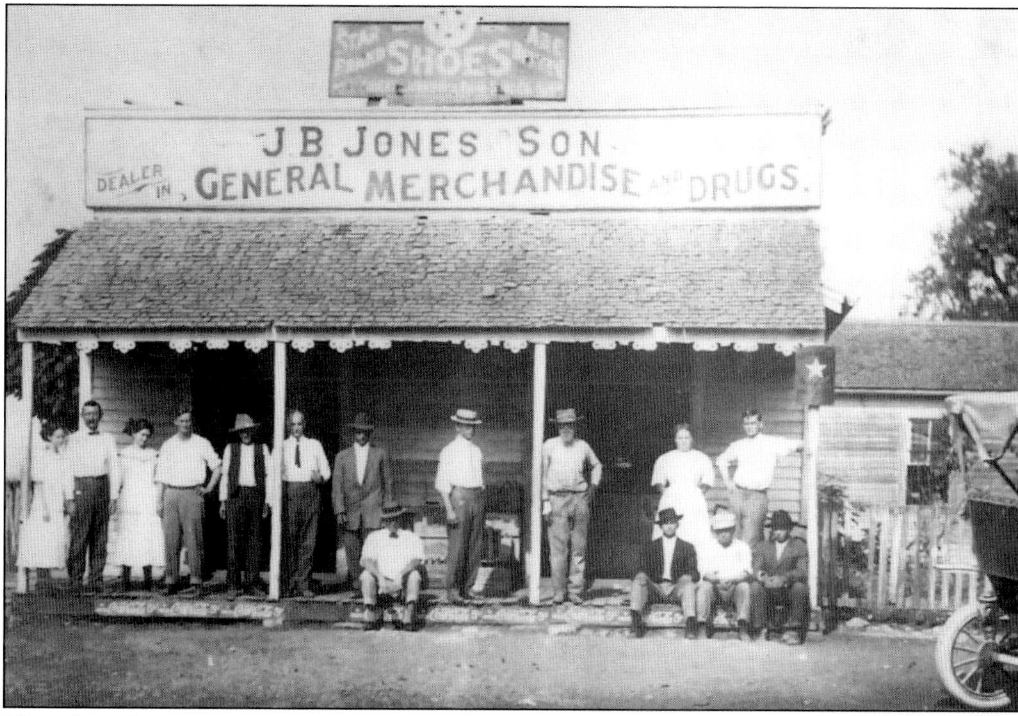


There have been two stores carrying the Jones name in the town's past. This is a photograph of the J.B. Jones & Son store around the year 1918. Of those standing on the porch, the only person identified is Daniel Labenske, who is sixth from the left. Labenske also owned a shop in town. (Courtesy Anne Jones.)

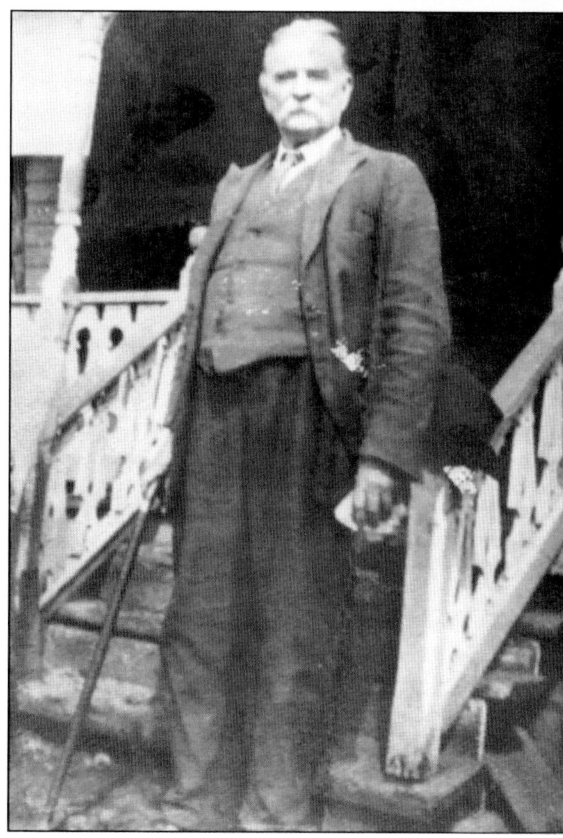

Daniel Labenske moved into town from his farm on Bear Creek and opened a general merchandise store. He would sit outside under the shade of a large oak tree and usher people inside. As they left, he would record their purchases in his credit ledger or collect their payment in cash. He had great trust in his customers, whom he had known for decades. (Courtesy Virginia Dunnahoo.)

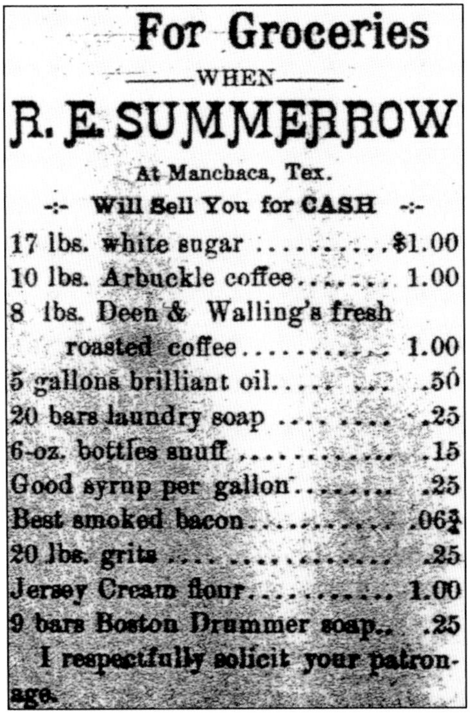


The growing town of Manchaca supported several mercantile stores around 1900. Mr. R.E. Summerrow ran a nice establishment and submitted this advertisement to the *Texas State Democrat Farm & Home* newspaper. Compared to today's prices, he certainly had some great bargains! (Courtesy Austin History Center, Austin Public Library.)

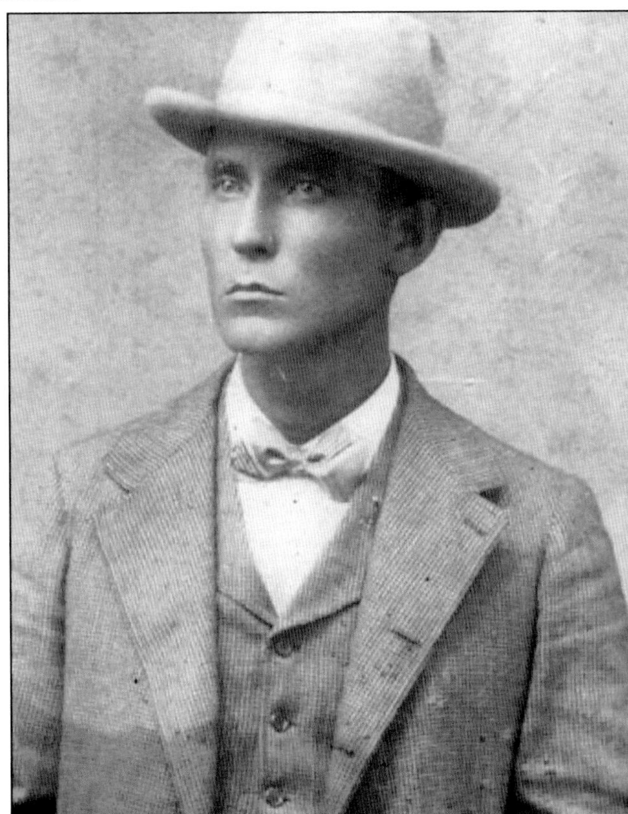

The Summerrow family made many contributions to early Manchaca. Ed Summerrow, shown at right, was a geologist. His father, M. Edward Summerrow, was elected postmaster of Manchaca in 1883. Robert E. Summerrow filled that position in 1896 and owned a mercantile store in town. In 1899, the *Texas State Democrat Farm and Home* paper reported that W.P. Summerrow owned the Manchaca cotton gin, and that Robert Summerrow had imported fish from Washington that he planned to release into the local creeks. (Courtesy Earlayne Chance.)

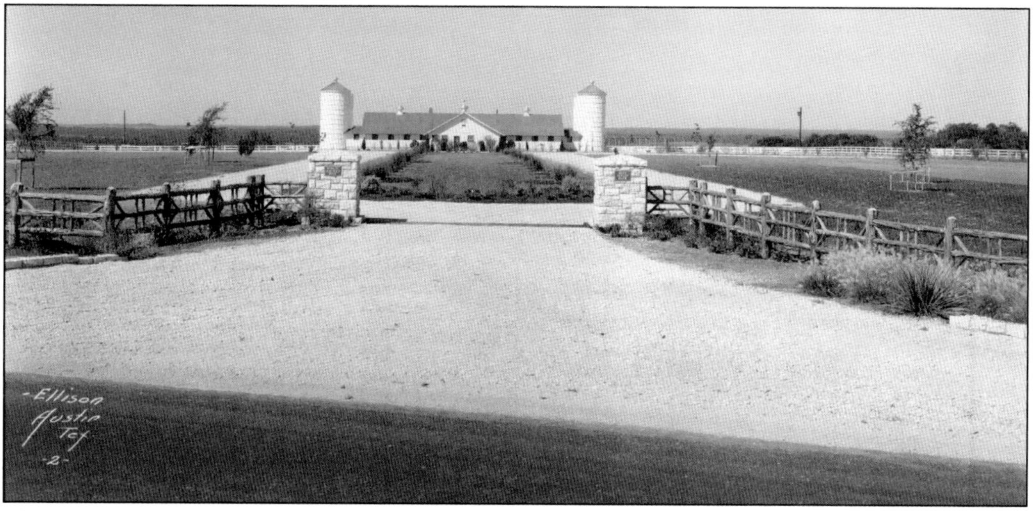

Shown here is the barn for Heep Dairy, located off Puryear Road and owned by successful oilman Herman Heep. Milking was done at 4:00 a.m. and 4:00 p.m. in a room with a glass wall that allowed up to 20 visitors to watch the entire milking process. Herman was president of the American Jersey Association. When they experienced financial problems, he used his keen business sense to turn things around. (CO9468, Austin History Center, Austin Public Library.)

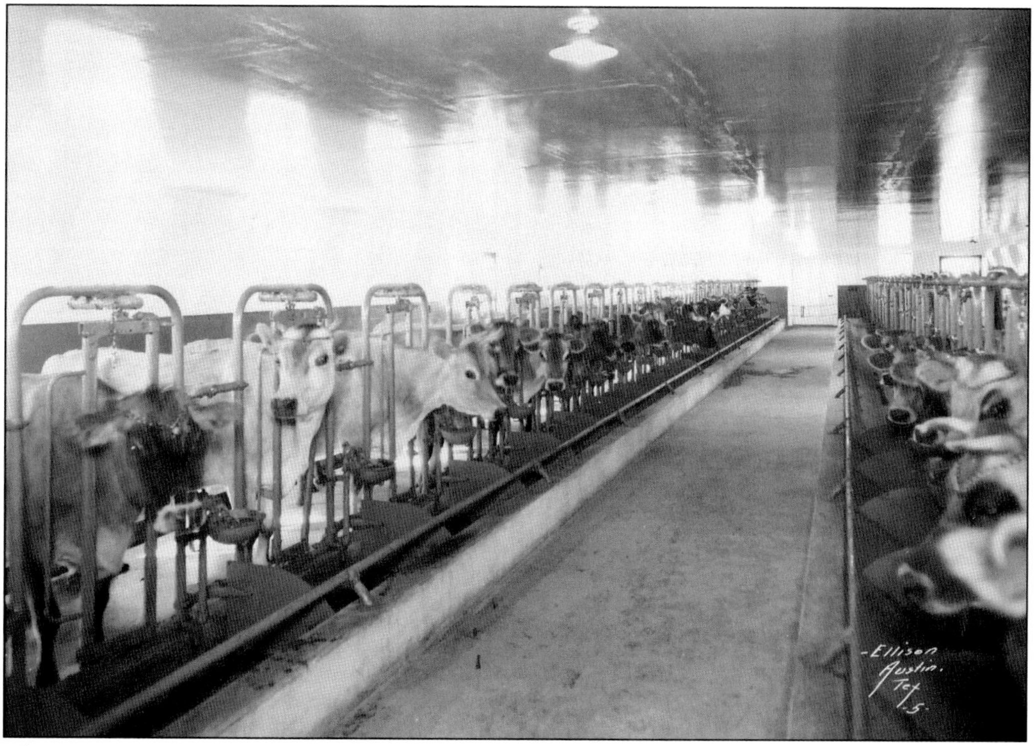

These prize-winning Jerseys were a familiar sight to Joe Armstrong, who was employed at Heep Dairy. Joe remembers earning $3 a day, plus room and board. Lyndon Baines Johnson and Sam Rayburn often visited the dairy. During the Texas drought of the 1950s, Herman Heep bought land in Oregon and shipped his prize herd there, where water and grass was plentiful. (CO9473, Austin History Center, Austin Public Library.)

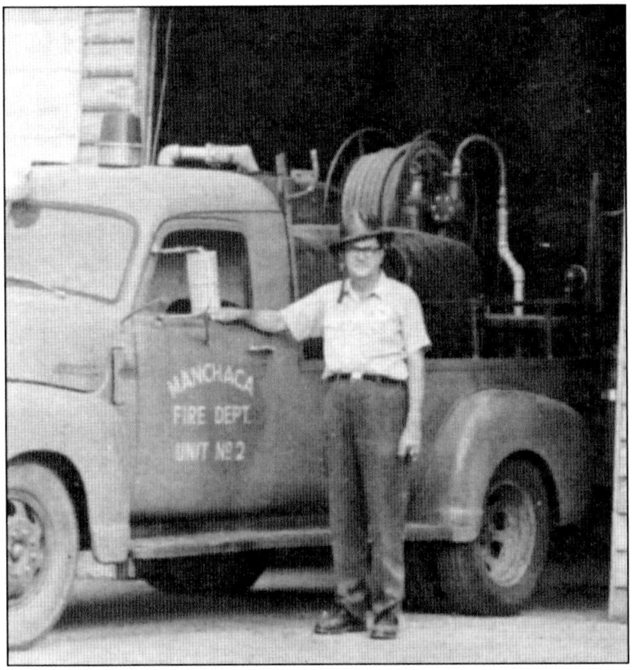


The Manchaca Volunteer Fire Department was established in 1967, with contributions collected in a box placed on the counter at the Country Corner Store owned by Ray and Ethel Turner. Ray is shown at left standing next to old Unit No. 2. The creation of the fire department was a community effort, with Manchaca resident Jack Garner leasing land to the department for $1 a year (which he never collected). (Courtesy Carolyn and Curtis Turner.)

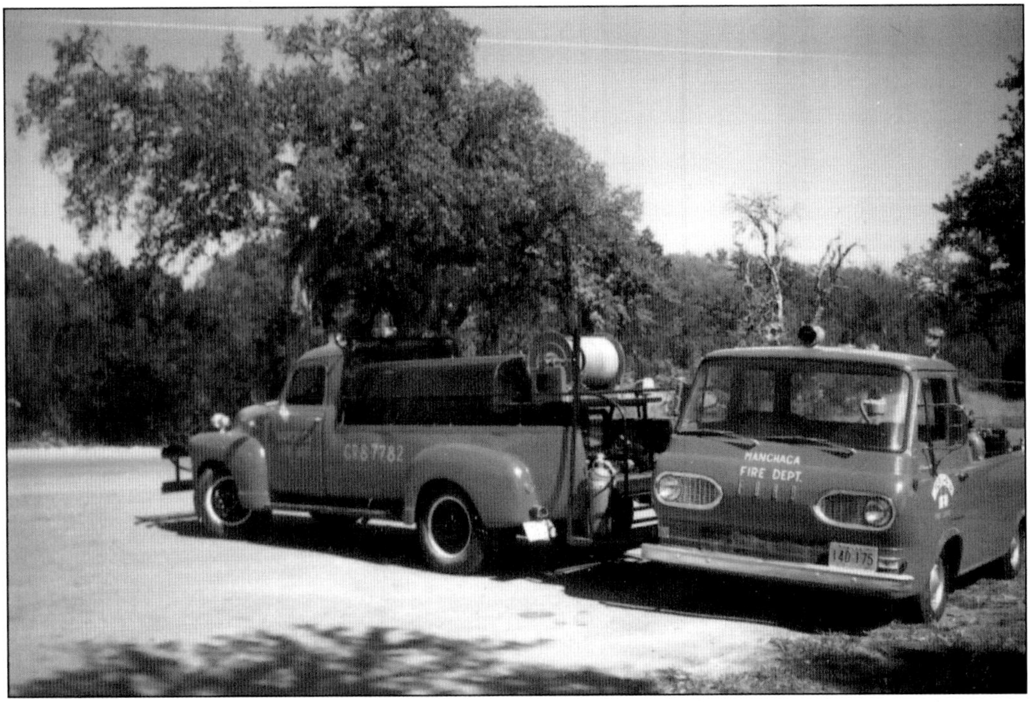


The fire department's first truck was obtained at an auction for $1,137, which was all there was in the box collected at the Country Corner Store. It was a 1961 Ford Econoline, at right in this photograph. It originally belonged to the King Ranch. On July 15, 1967, they were first called into action, when their help was requested to extinguish a grass fire at Brown School Ranch. The original board for the department consisted of Ray Turner, Gene Williams, Randolph Walker, W.P. Nance, and Mr. Moser. (Courtesy Carolyn and Curtis Turner.)

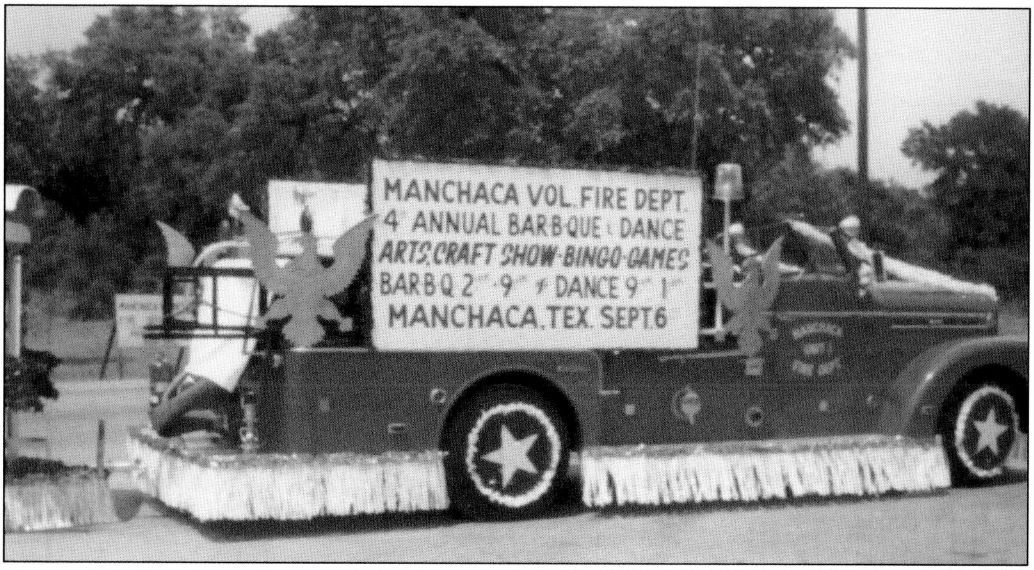


Engine No. 1 is shown here in 1976. It was refurbished for parade duty by Randolph Walker and his son-in-law Gene Robison. The parade often took over an hour to reach its destination at the fire hall on FM 1626. Star Flight would sometimes do a flyover if they were in the area and not busy. Parade marshals included Jake Pickle and Ann Richards. (Courtesy Carolyn and Curtis Turner.)

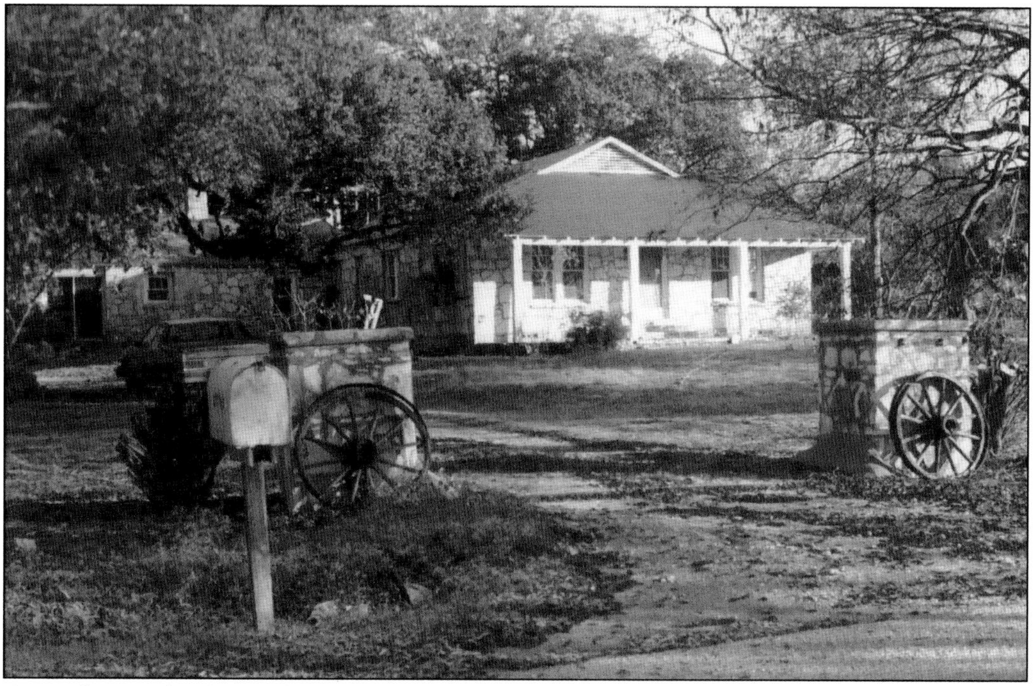

Around 1940, developer Lloyd Arnold moved to this home, on land that would one day become San Leanna. He also owned a dairy in the area. Eventually, he began purchasing acreage to develop a subdivision. This would become a place where Austin residents could retreat to a second home away from the fast paced city. Cattle and peacocks were a common sight in the subdivision and added to the country feel. (Courtesy Jim Payne.)

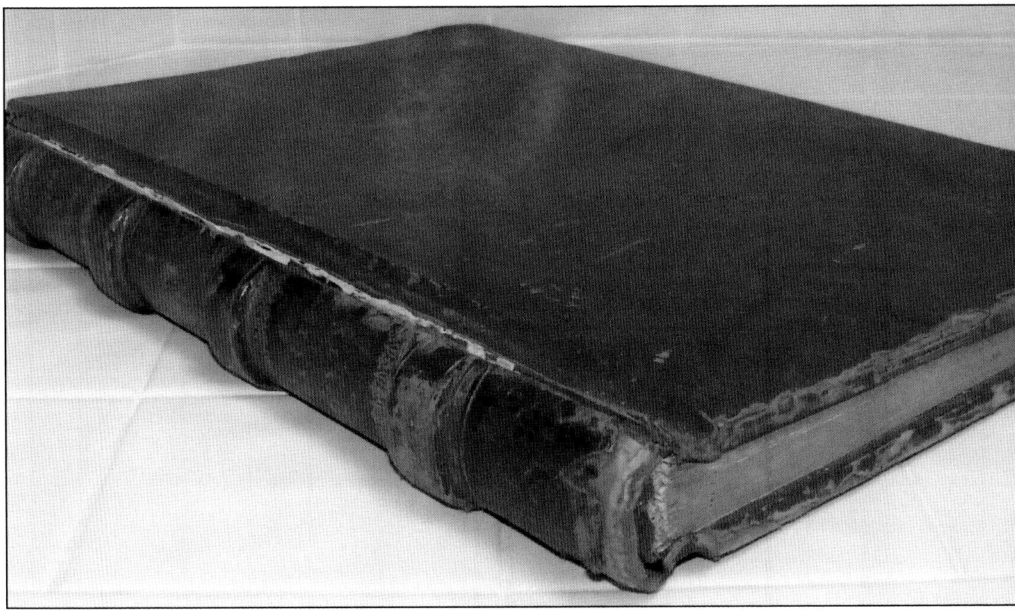

Tom Dunnahoo was the constable of Manchaca for years, but it was not a paying, full-time job by any means. Tom recorded his income and expenditures in this old ledger book. His constable position entitled him to police work at the local auto races that paid $3 for the night. He collected $9.60 from impounding stock for the Radams in 1928, and he often sat on the grand jury, which paid $4 a day. Other means of bringing in some cash included selling hay, cotton, corn, turkeys, and his house painting services. In 1928, he sold a bale of cotton weighing 532 pounds for $82.96. (Both, courtesy Marilyn Dunnahoo McLeod.)

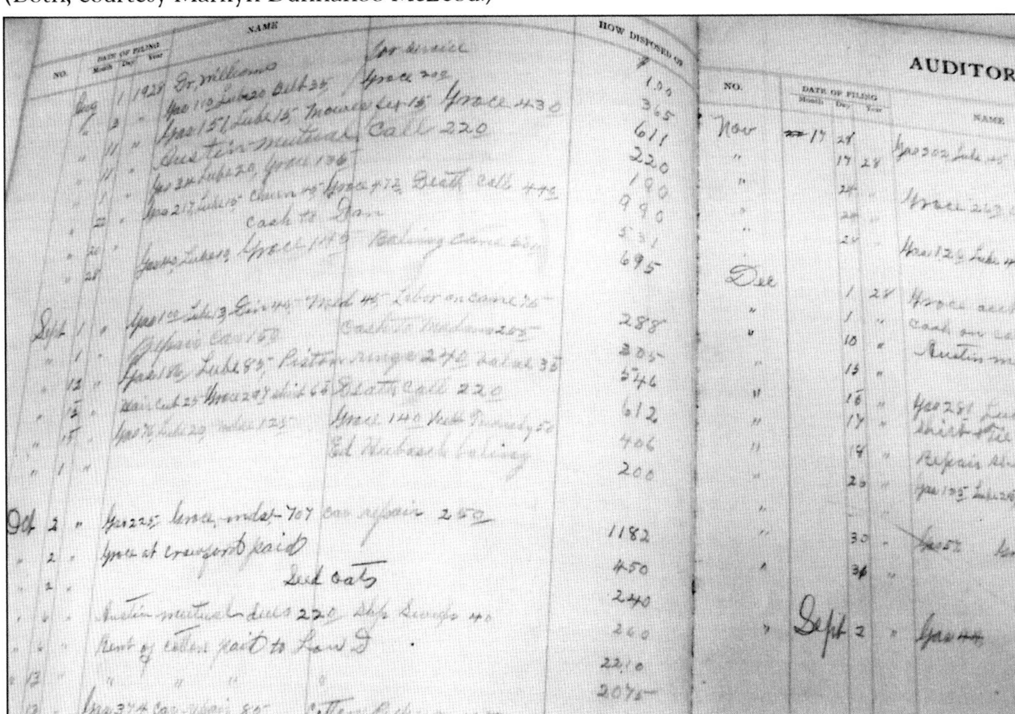

# *Four*

# SCHOOL DAYS

Growth in the bustling community of Manchaca sparked the need to educate the increasing number of children of the area. The first school was set up in 1877 in the Old Rock Church that was located on Twin Creeks Road. This was a tuition school. The first public school was built in 1883 and was located on the northeast corner of FM 1626 and Manchaca Road. In 1905, a new brick school with a bell tower was built. Growth came at a rapid pace for the small town, and by 1910 the brick school was expanded by adding a second story.

Also documented in Manchaca was an African American school. The school building no longer exists, but the address for its old location is 753 FM 1626. In addition to these two schools, there was a Hispanic school situated on Polk Road on the north side of FM 1626. Around 1956, the three schools were consolidated.

The current public school was built in 1976. It is located across the street from the location of the old two-story school. The bottom floor of that old two-story building is still standing and is used as a private school today.

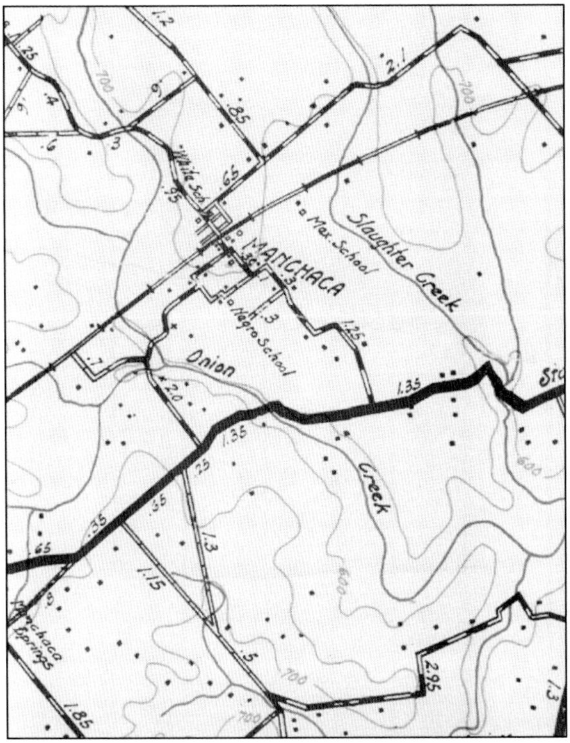


In 1932, the Travis County Engineering Department prepared a wonderfully detailed road map of the county. This section shows Manchaca. Manchaca had three schools at that time, and each one is noted on the map. (Courtesy Perry-Castaneda Library, University of Texas.)

The first school building constructed in Manchaca can be seen in the background of this 1902 Manchaca School group photograph. It was a board-and-batten structure of the old box type. In 1905, the community built a new brick school to accommodate their growing population. (Courtesy Lillie M. Moreland.)

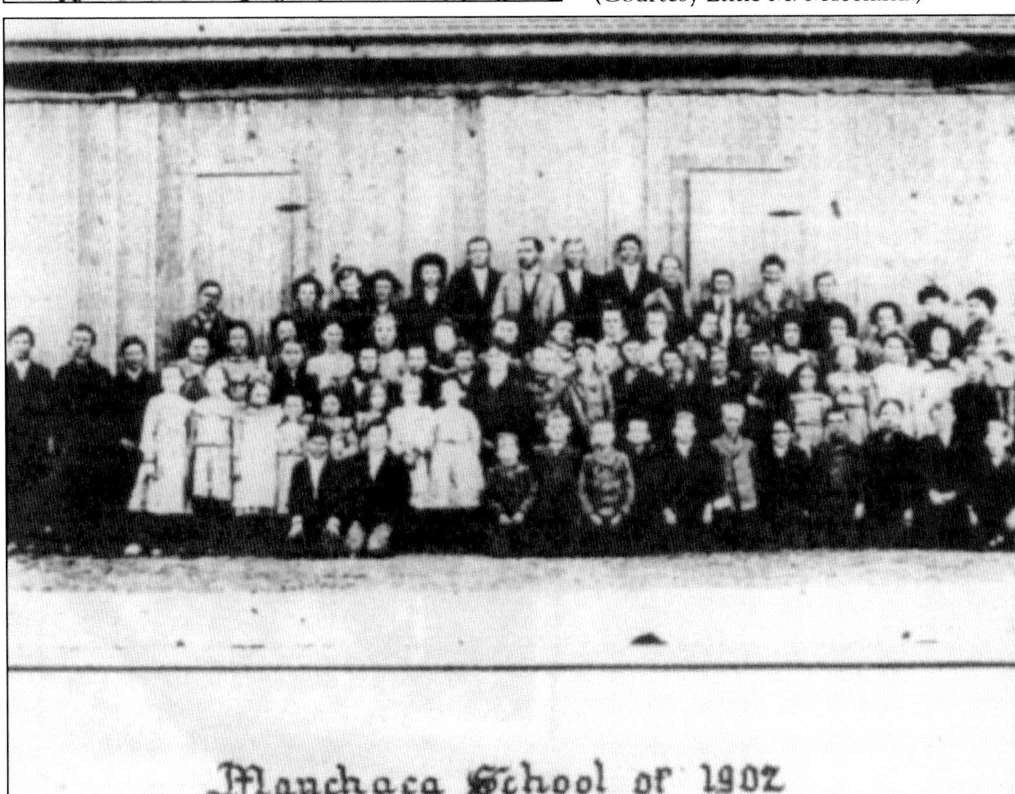

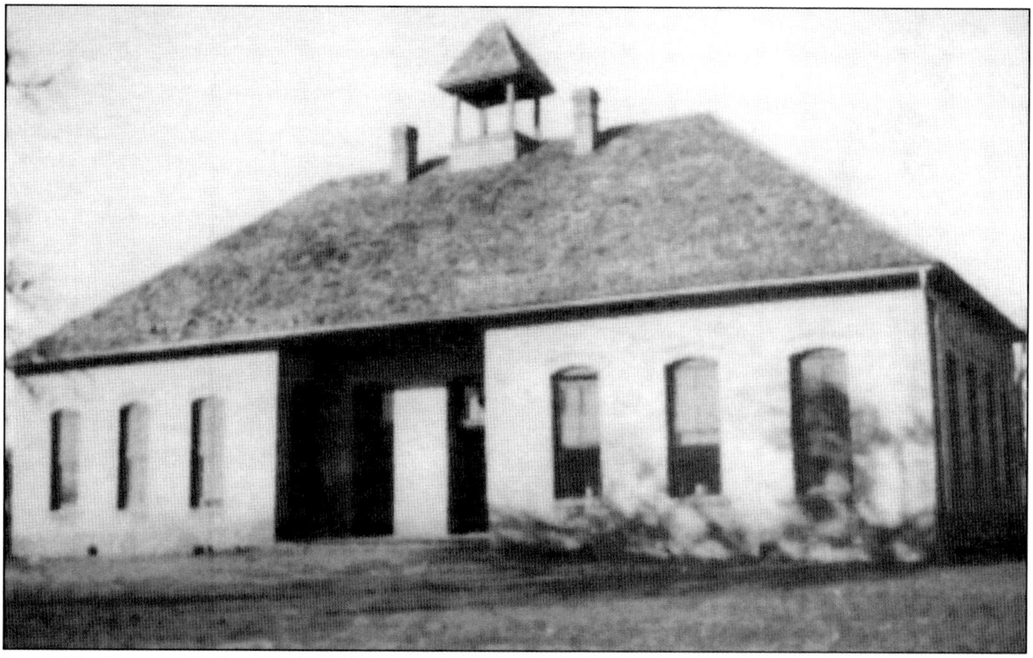

In 1905, this sturdy brick schoolhouse with a bell tower was built to accommodate the growing number of students in the area. This population growth spurt has been attributed to the fact that the International and great Northern Railroad ran through town, making commerce much more convenient for the residents. (Courtesy Lillie M. Moreland.)

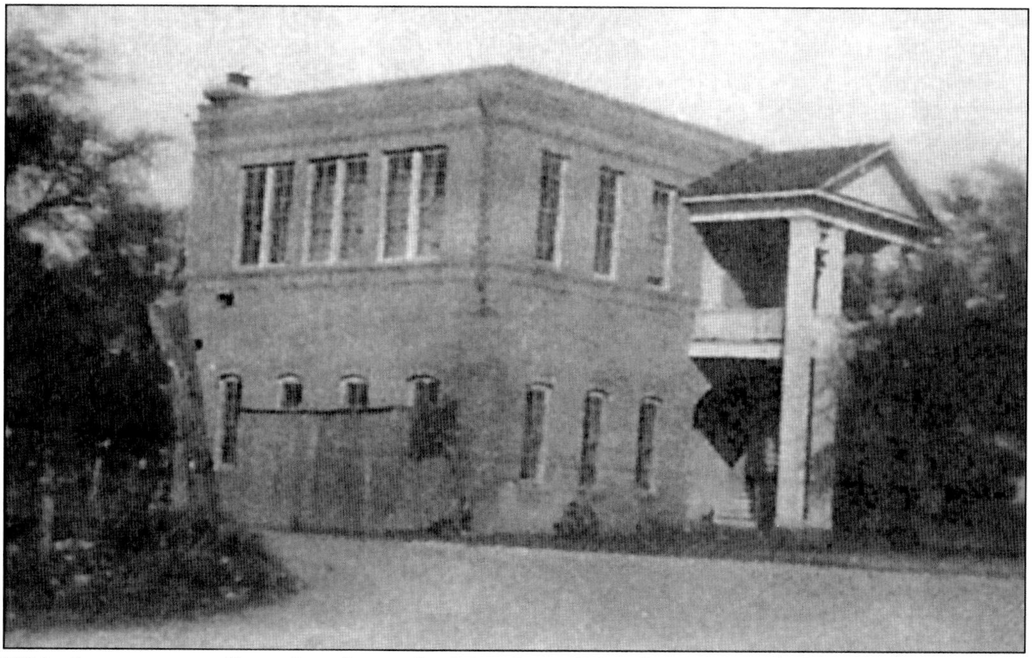

With the growing influx of students, the Manchaca School was expanded with a second story. Local brick layer William Birkner helped with this project. The additional space held a cafeteria and an auditorium. After the addition, the school was able to offer seven grades to its students. (Courtesy Lillie M. Moreland.)

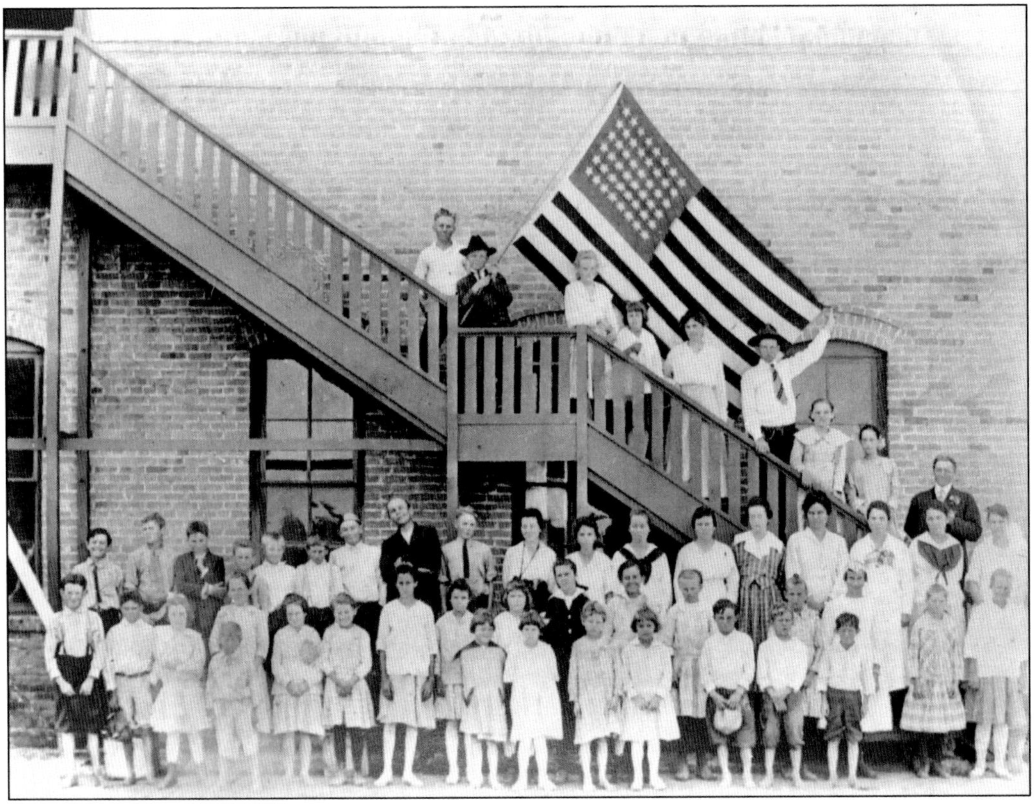

The entire student body of Manchaca School gathered for a group photograph in 1917. From left to right are (first row) three unidentified, Bertha Ellis, Mable Birkner, Joe Sanders, unidentified, and Jewel Sanders; (second row) Red Deane, five unidentified, Tommy Deane, Lillian Dunnahoo, four unidentified, Jewel Lovett, unidentified, Alice Fritts, and Audrey Swank.; (third row) six unidentified, Buck Carpenter, Claude Martin, Fred Turner, two unidentified, Bertha Cook, Alma Bradley, Bernice Blackwell, unidentified, Jodie Hewitt, Lillian Martin, and Lillie Wirth; (fourth row, on stairs) Jim Fritts, Harry Wirth, unidentified, Dolly Birkner, unidentified Zapalac, Bill Bradley, two unidentified, and Professor Humble. A few years after this large class photograph was taken, Harry Wirth graduated from the eighth grade and received the certificate, shown below, guaranteeing his eligibility for admission into the ninth grade. At this time, J.W. Peeler was teacher and principal of the school. He also taught there during World War II. (Both, courtesy Lillie M. Moreland.)

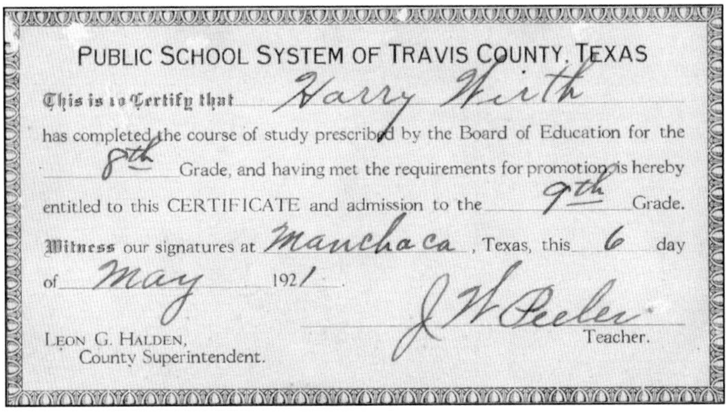

PUBLIC SCHOOL SYSTEM OF TRAVIS COUNTY, TEXAS

This is to Certify that Harry Wirth has completed the course of study prescribed by the Board of Education for the 8th Grade, and having met the requirements for promotion, is hereby entitled to this CERTIFICATE and admission to the 9th Grade.

Witness our signatures at Manchaca, Texas, this 6 day of May 1921.

LEON G. HALDEN,
County Superintendent.

J W Peeler
Teacher.

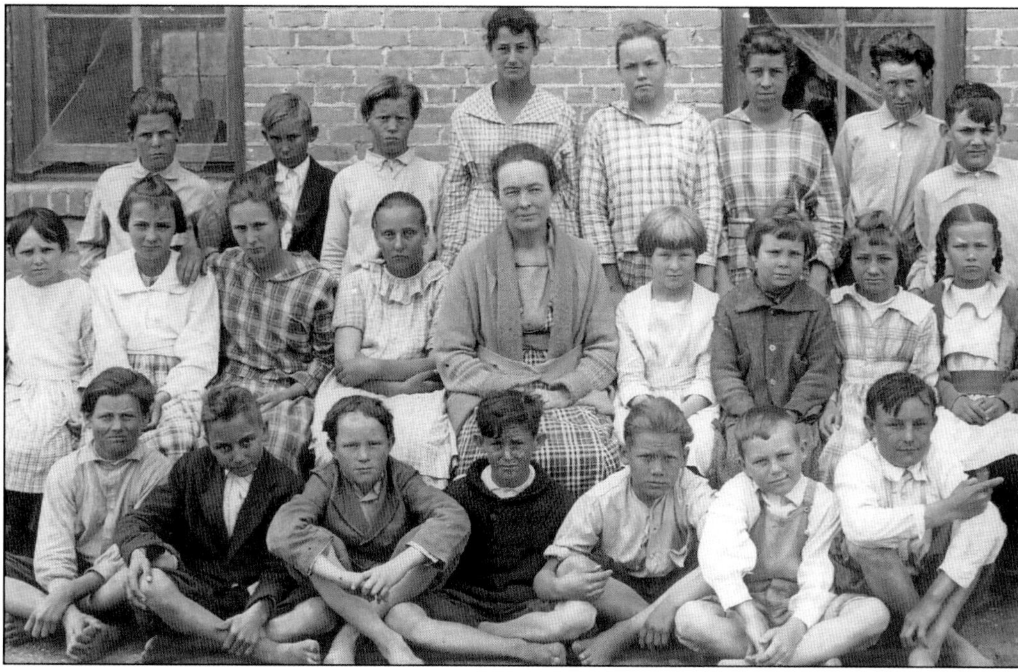

Teacher Edna Turley Carpenter is shown here in 1920, surrounded by her students. In this photograph, the only child identified in the first row is John Blanton Deane, who is fourth from the left. Shown from left to right in the second row are three unidentified students, Mattie Lee Ward, teacher Edna Carpenter, Genevieve Dunnahoo, Cordelia Dunnahoo, and two unidentified girls. The third row, from left to right, shows three unidentified, Tommie Deane, two unidentified, Joe Forrest Deane, and an unidentified boy. (Courtesy Joanne Deane.)

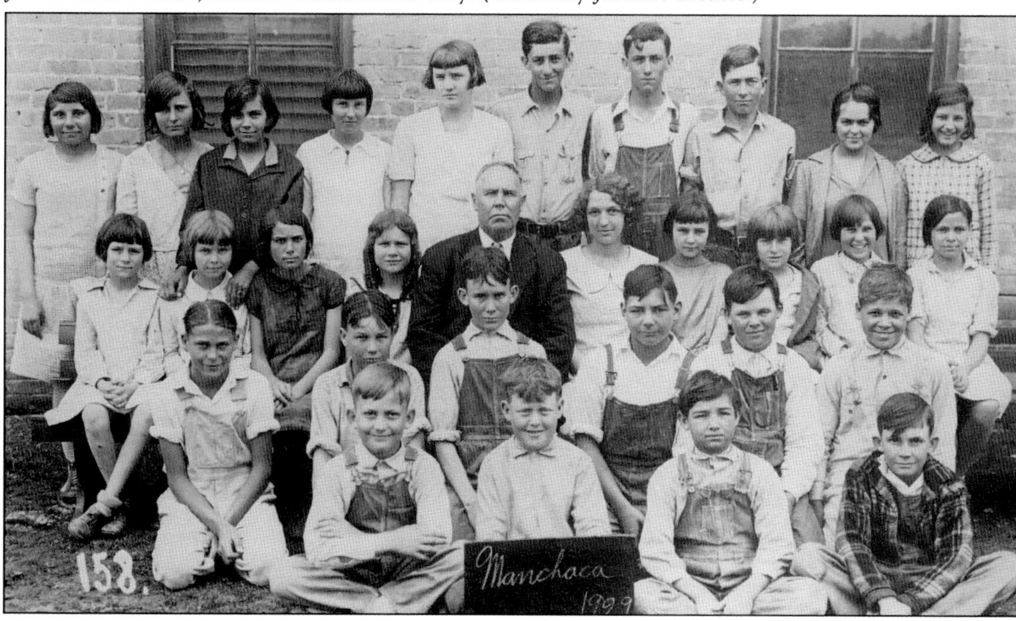


A few smiling faces among the more serious peer into the camera in this 1929 Manchaca School photograph. The overalls worn by the boys easily transitioned from school to farm work. (Courtesy Joanne Deane.)

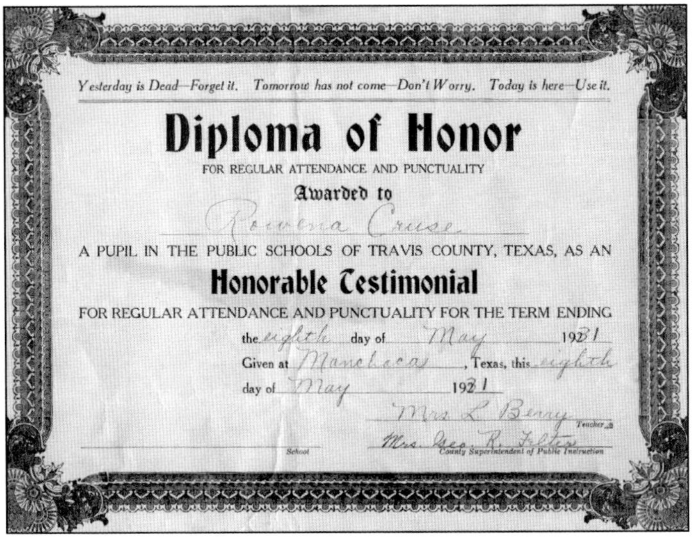
Yesterday is Dead—Forget it. Tomorrow has not come—Don't Worry. Today is here—Use it.

**Diploma of Honor**

FOR REGULAR ATTENDANCE AND PUNCTUALITY

Awarded to

Rowena Cruse

A PUPIL IN THE PUBLIC SCHOOLS OF TRAVIS COUNTY, TEXAS, AS AN

**Honorable Testimonial**

FOR REGULAR ATTENDANCE AND PUNCTUALITY FOR THE TERM ENDING

the eighth day of May 1931

Given at Manchaca, Texas, this eighth

day of May 1931

Mrs L. Berry, Teacher

School

Mrs. Geo. R. Felter, County Superintendent of Public Instruction

Rowena Cruze was on time to school every day and had perfect attendance in 1931. She was honored with a "Diploma of Honor" declaring her accomplishments. Note the saying at the top; "Yesterday is Dead—Forget it. Tomorrow has not come—Don't Worry. Today is here—Use it." Despite the misspelling of her last name, Rowena kept this certificate all of her life, so we know she felt the past was not to be forgotten. (Courtesy Joanne Deane.)

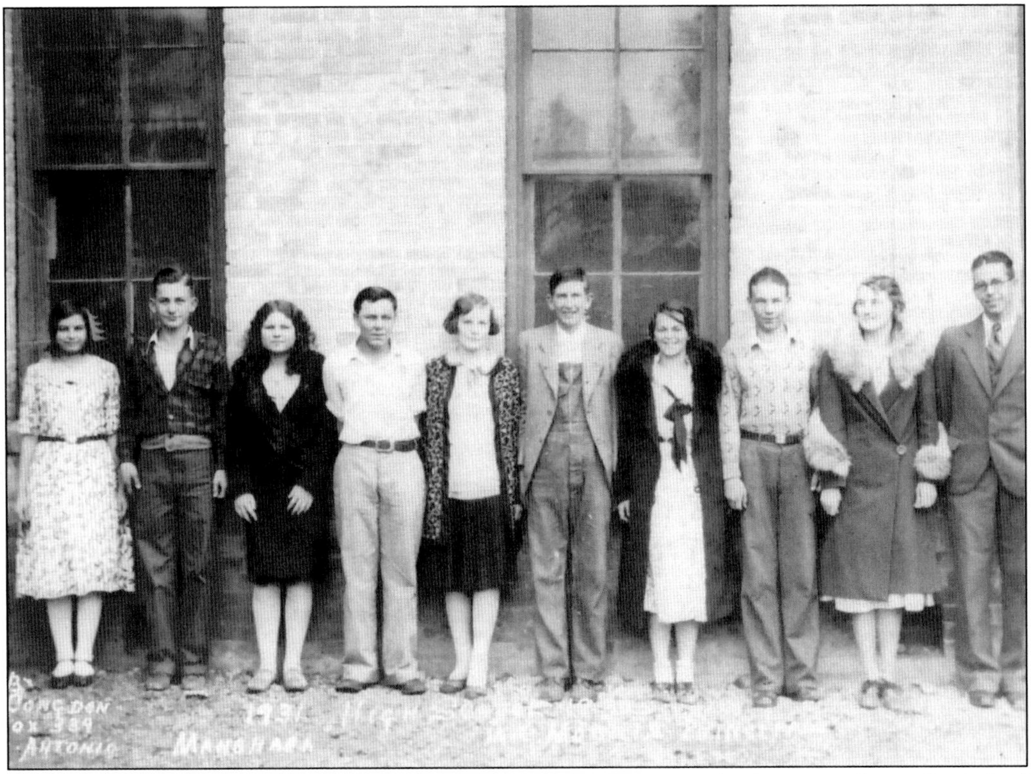

In 1931, the graduating class of Manchaca High School consisted of nine students. Each had high expectations for what the future would bring. Shown from left to right are Alma Grace, Ben Swank, Winifred Dunnahoo, unidentified, Eula Mae McMahan, Fred Siebert, Pauline Peeler, Senter Downs, Doris Thigpen, and teacher Bill Morris. (Courtesy Lillie M. Moreland.)

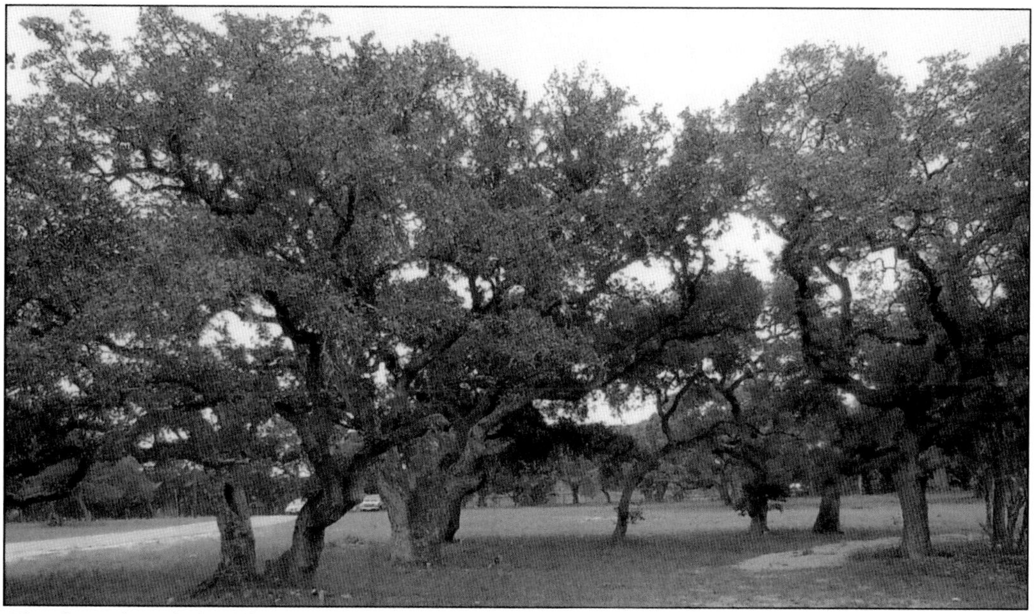

The first church building in the community was built on this property, donated by John J. McCuistian in 1872. Located just west of Live Oak Cemetery, it was known as the Old Rock Church and acted as the building for the first school, which was organized in 1877. Professor A. H. Decherd was hired to teach 70 pupils during the week. He was assisted by his daughter Annie. The Old Rock Church was torn down in 1941. (Courtesy Ann and Barry Trask.)

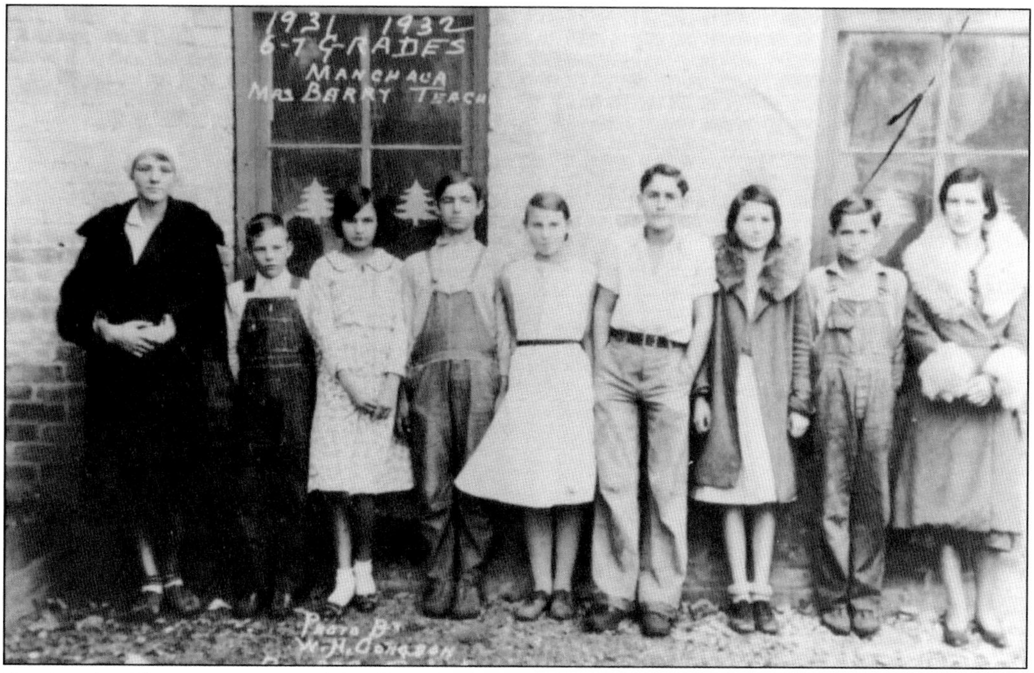


During the Christmas season, Mrs. Berry's sixth and seventh grade class at the Manchaca School gathered outside for their class photograph. Shown from left to right are unidentified, Brythal B. Thigpen, Rowena Cruze, Ben Grace, Fannie Behrens, Robert Sanders, Annie Mae Meredith, Joe Sanders, and Mrs. Berry. (Courtesy Lillie M. Moreland.)

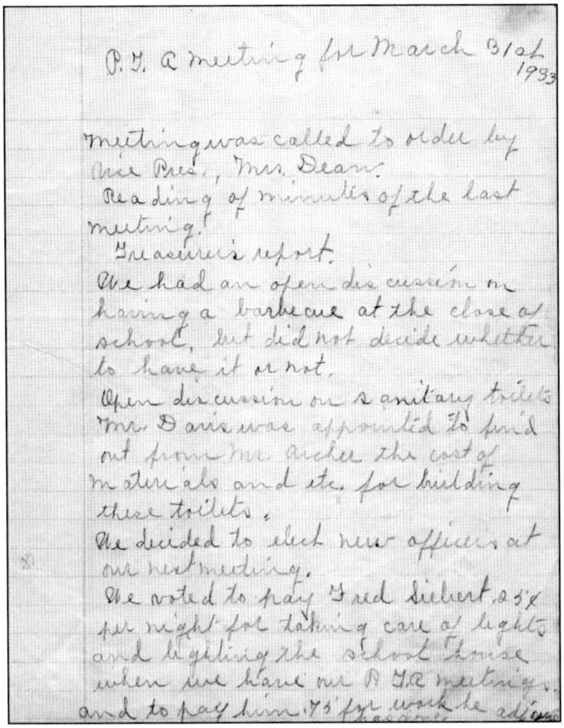

P.T.A. meeting for March 31st 1933

Meeting was called to order by Vice Pres., Mrs. Dean.
Reading of minutes of the last meeting.
Treasurer's report.
We had an open discussion on having a barbecue at the close of school, but did not decide whether to have it or not.
Open discussion on sanitary toilets. Mr. Davis was appointed to find out from Mr. Archer the cost of materials and etc. for building these toilets.
We decided to elect new officers at our next meeting.
We voted to pay Fred Siebert 25¢ per night for taking care of lights and lighting the school house when we have our P.T.A. meeting, and to pay him 75¢ for work he ad…

The Manchaca PTA has always been an active group of interested parents. Notes from a 1933 meeting indicate they wanted to update the restrooms at the school with "sanitary toilets." They also voted to pay Fred Siebert twenty-five cents a night for taking care of the lights at the school. At the height of the Great Depression, this had to be welcome news to Fred. (Courtesy Lillie M. Moreland.)

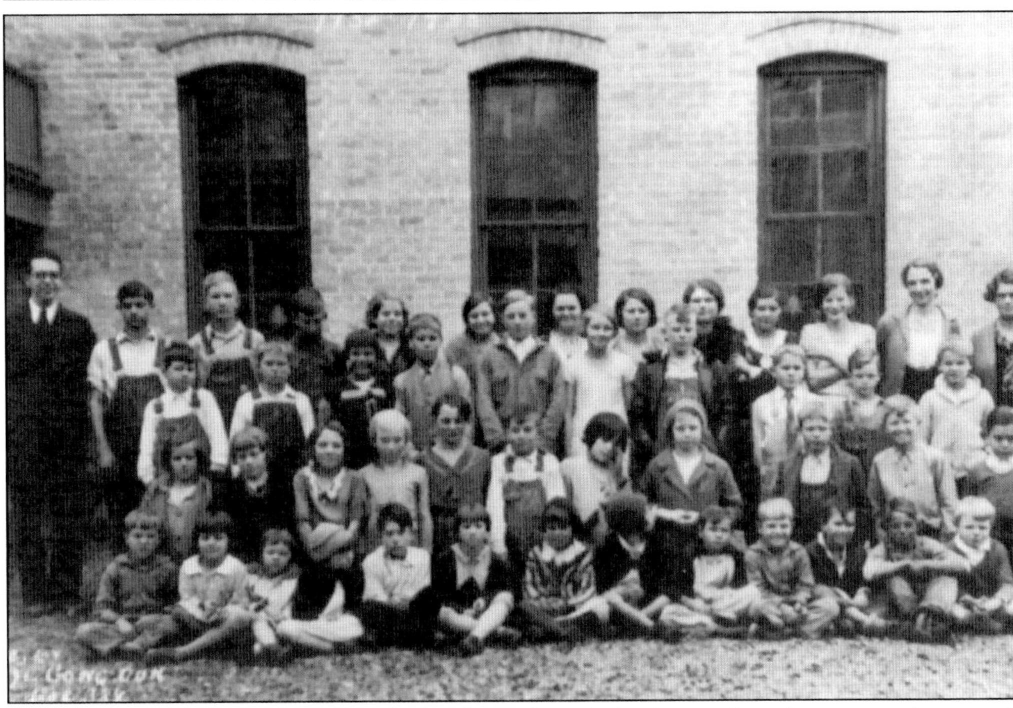

In the early 1930s, the entire student body of Manchaca School turned out for a group photograph. Everyone was well dressed. From the looks of them, you would never know the economic trauma that America was going through. Principal Bill Morris is on the far left with teachers Mary Armbruster and Audrey Swank, left to right, on the end of the last row. (Courtesy Lillie M. Moreland.)

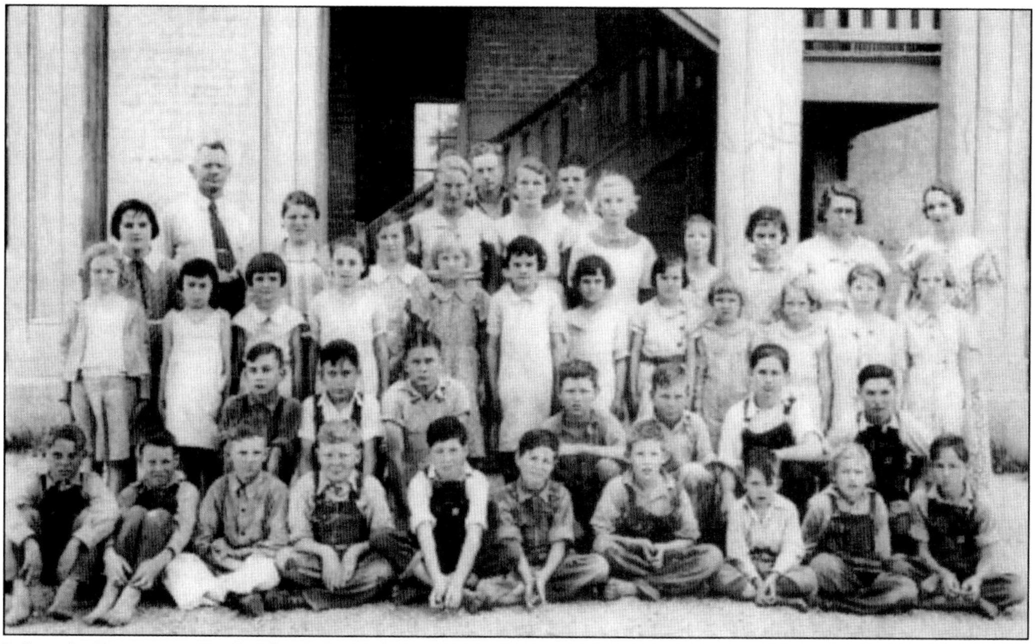

John A. Ramsey, on the far left in this 1935 image, was the seventh grade teacher and principal. To his right and just below him is student Lillie Meredith. The two female teachers standing on the far right in the fourth row are, Audrey Swank Dawson, on the left, and Mary Armbruster, on the end. In the second row on the far right are Jim Dunnahoo, on the end, and his brother Seth, next to him. (Courtesy Lillie M. Moreland.)

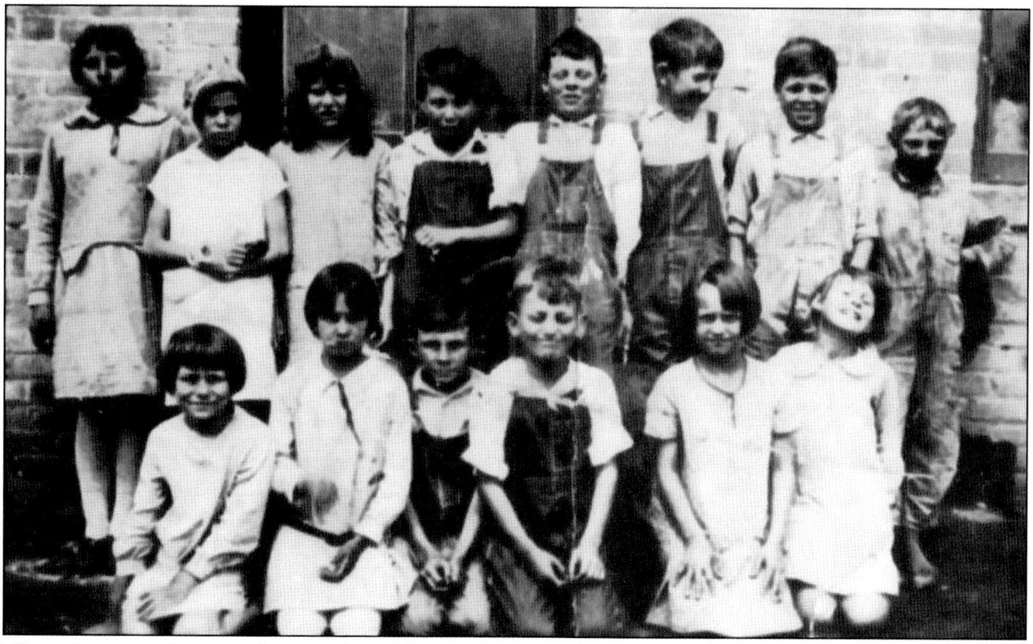

This photograph was taken in the 1930s at the Manchaca School. Shown from left to right are (first row) Annie Mae Meredith, Rowena Cruze, unidentified, Ben Swank, Charlotte Rylander, and Fannie Behrens; (second row) two unidentified, Winnie Dunnahoo, and five unidentified. (Courtesy Lillie M. Moreland.)

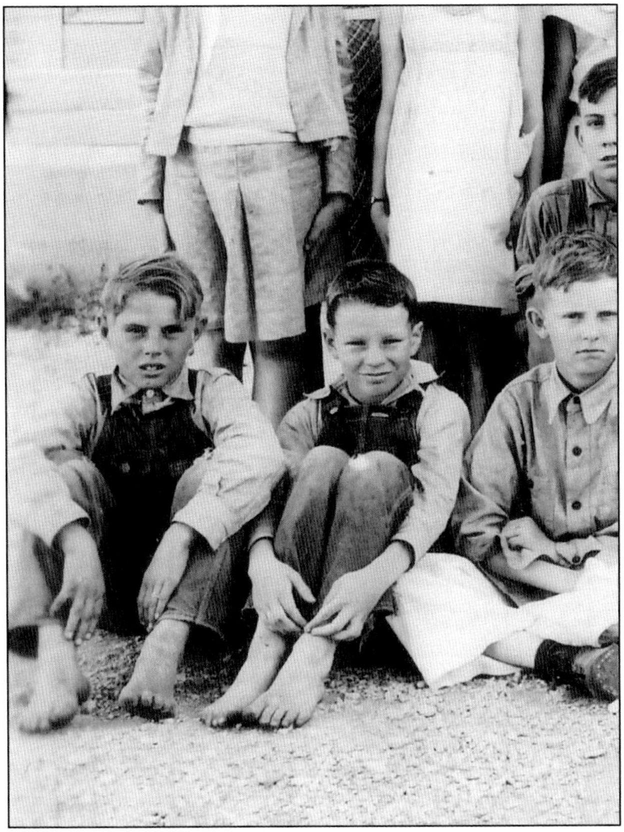

From left to right in this 1935 photograph are school boys Walter Hector, R.B. Edmiston, and Alfred Birkner. Behind Alfred is Tom Waggoner. (Courtesy Lillie M. Moreland.)

Shown here is the Manchaca School student body posed in front of the old school in 1916, before the second story was added on to the building. (Courtesy Lillie M. Moreland.)

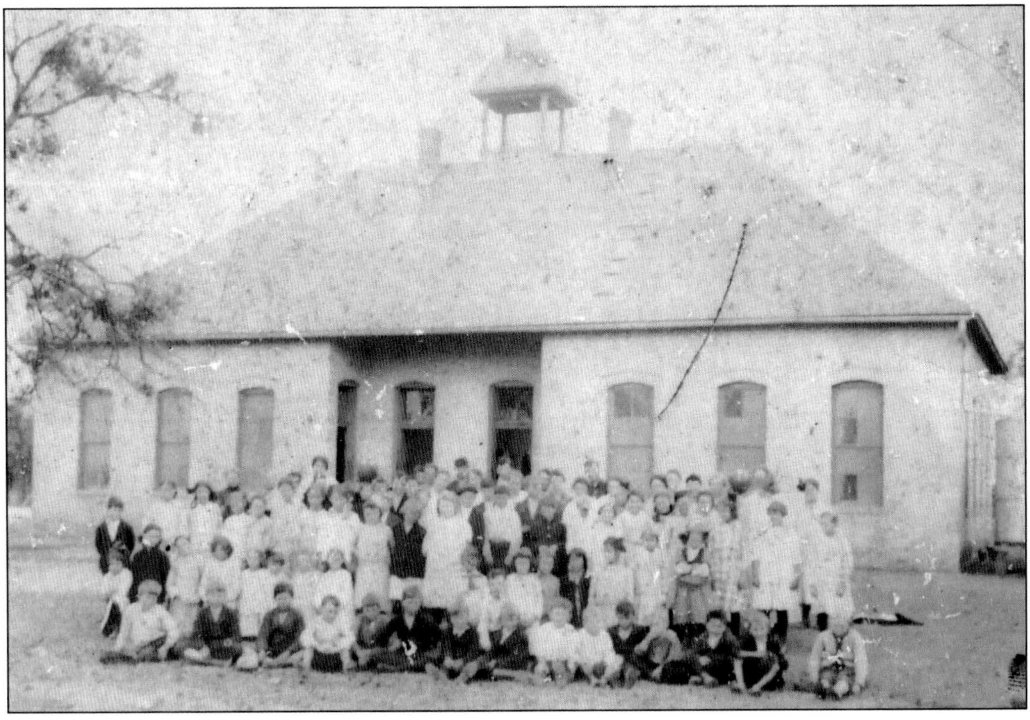

# *Five*

# SPIRITUAL GROWTH

The first place of worship erected in the Manchaca area was the Old Rock Church, owned by the Cumberland Presbyterian Congregation. This one-room building was constructed by the men of the community in the 1870s. Spiritual camp meetings took place regularly outside under a brush arbor, located close to the Old Rock Church on Onion Creek. By 1879, a permanent shed-type structure was built to replace the arbor. The camp grounds adjoined the property that makes up Live Oak Cemetery.

In 1873, the Methodist community included 80 people, headed up by Rev. Sam A. Whipple. Manchaca Methodist Church was formally organized by 1874. In their earliest days, they worshiped in the Old Rock Church, borrowed from the Presbyterian congregation. A wooden church was built in town to house the congregation in 1892. In 1957, the wooden sanctuary was replaced with a new brick sanctuary.

By 1918, Manchaca Baptist Church was established by Pastor Webb Townsley and 10 charter members. They held their first services in Woodmen's Hall. Later, they built a wooden sanctuary, which was modified and added to as the congregation grew. Several new sanctuaries have served the congregation throughout the years.

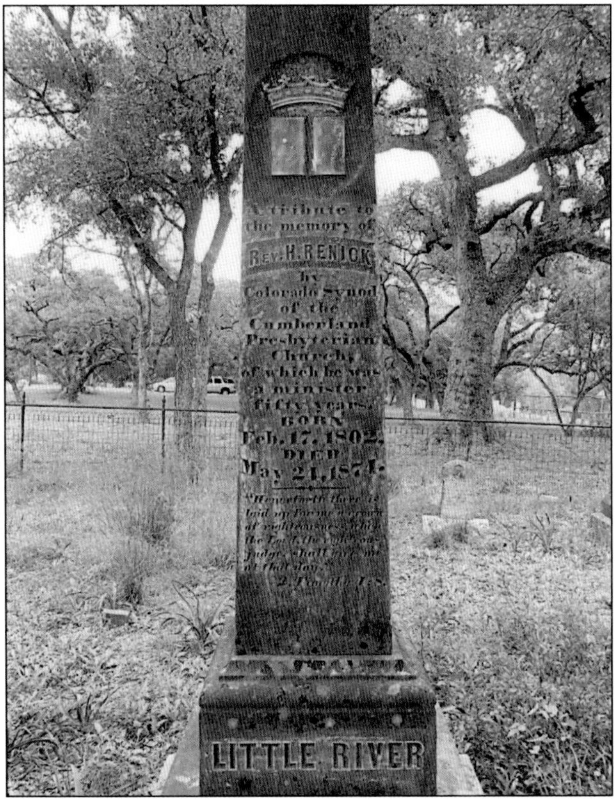


The Reverend Henry Renick was born in Kentucky and was first received as a candidate for the Presbyterian ministry at the age of 20. He moved to Onion Creek by 1872. "Little River" at the base of his tombstone refers to Little River Synod, which became part of the Colorado Synod in 1849. The reverend is buried at the McCuistian Cemetery in Manchaca. (Courtesy Ann and Barry Trask.)

The image below shows the old Manchaca Baptist Church, located north of FM1626 and Deane Road. This building has been updated and modified but still stands today. To acommodate the growing congregation, new sanctuaries were built in 1961 and 2004. (Courtesy Joanne Deane.)

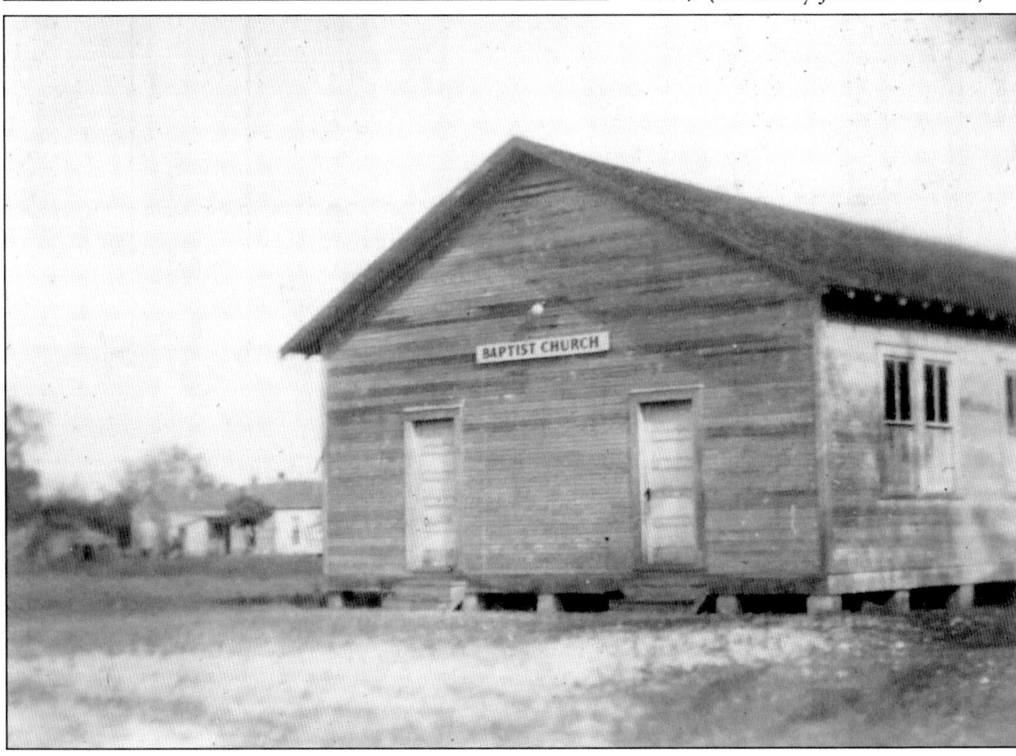

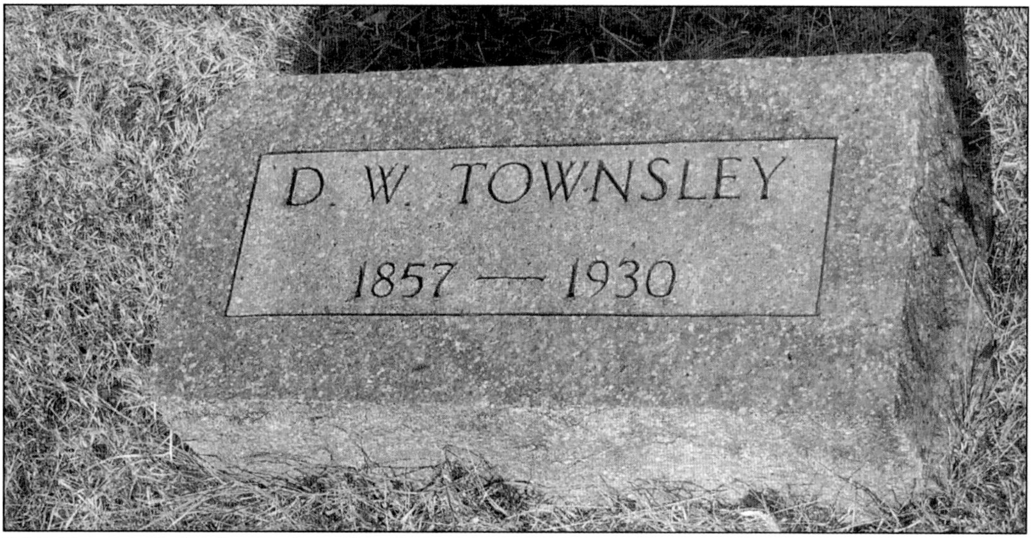


D.W. Townsley's death certificate lists him as Rev. D.W. Townsley and notes that he was a "Minister of the Gospel." He is buried in Live Oak Cemetery by the side of his loving wife, Addie Ruby Townsley, who passed away 10 years after him. They were married in Hays County on October 3, 1877. According to census information, the "D.W." stood for Daniel Webster, and he is sometimes listed as Webster. He is most likely the man who established the Manchaca Baptist Church in 1918 and is listed in their records as Webb Townsley. Mr. and Mrs. Townsley's son Webb died at the age of 18, and his burial is recorded in an Austin newspaper on March 15, 1908. (Courtesy Ann and Barry Trask.)

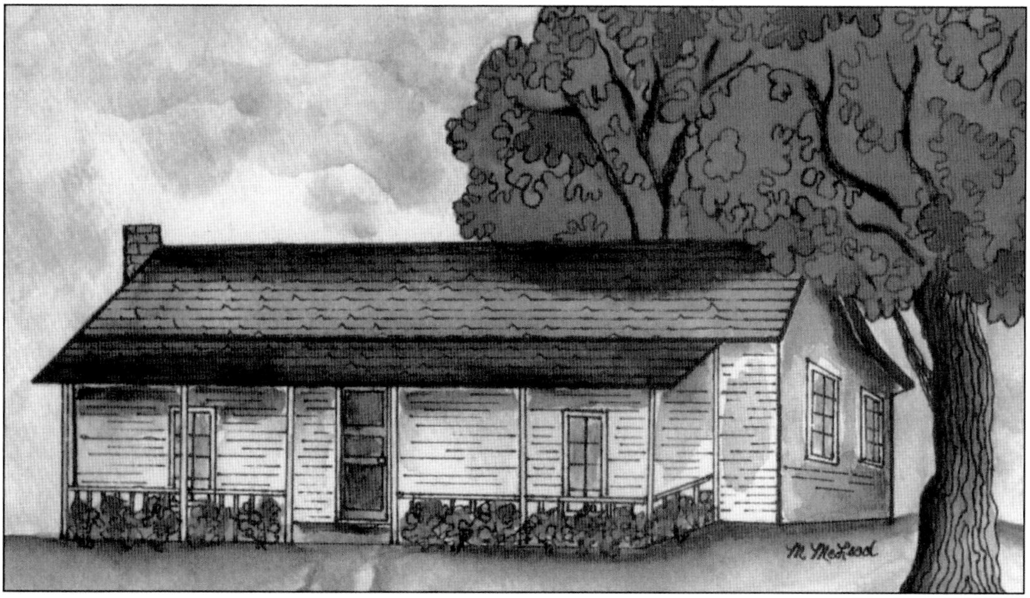


The Manchaca Methodist Church parsonage is shown in the sketch above. The parsonage played an important part in the lives of many Manchaca families, because the church made it available to them if it was unoccupied. When Lil and Odell Moreland married, their first home was in the parsonage. During the Depression, the Tom Dunnahoo family lived here. In 1923, Virginia Ann Dunnahoo, Tom's mother, passed away here. (Courtesy Lilly M. Moreland and Marilyn Dunnahoo McLeod.)

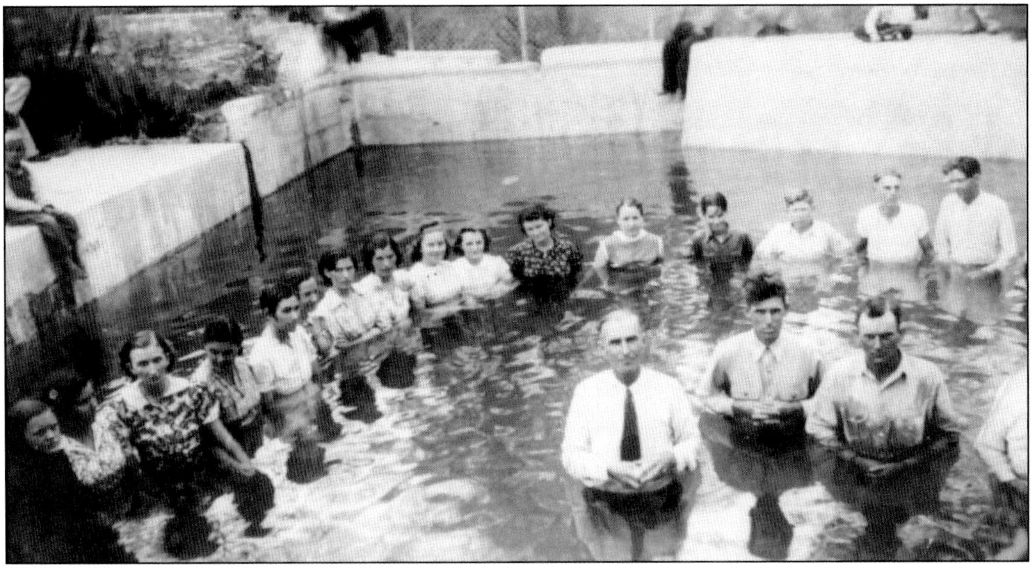

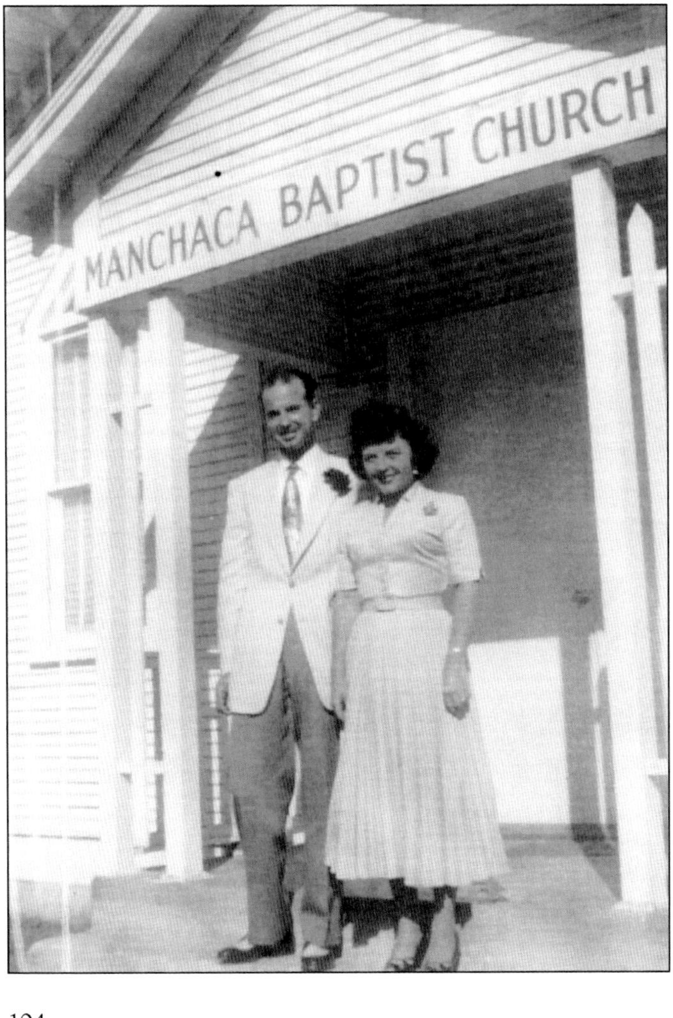


A group of adults from Manchaca Baptist Church traveled to Bluff Springs on a clear spring day to be baptized by Brother Cole. To commemorate the occasion, they all joined hands and faced the camera prior to the baptism for this group photograph. (Courtesy Joy Simmons.)

Jo and Leo Holden met at the Manchaca Baptist Church, and soon knew they were meant to be together for a lifetime. Determining to wait for marriage until after Leo returned from World War II, the couple exchanged their vows shortly after the war's end. They stayed very active in church, and Jo taught many a Sunday school class. (Courtesy Joy Simmons.)

Vera Holden Felps had been an active member of Manchaca Baptist Church since 1939. In 1947, she married Alton Polk, who was a watchmaker as well as a small-appliance repairman at his shop located at Fourth Street and Congress. Vera was a clerk at the Travis County Tax Collector's office. (Courtesy Joy Simmons.)

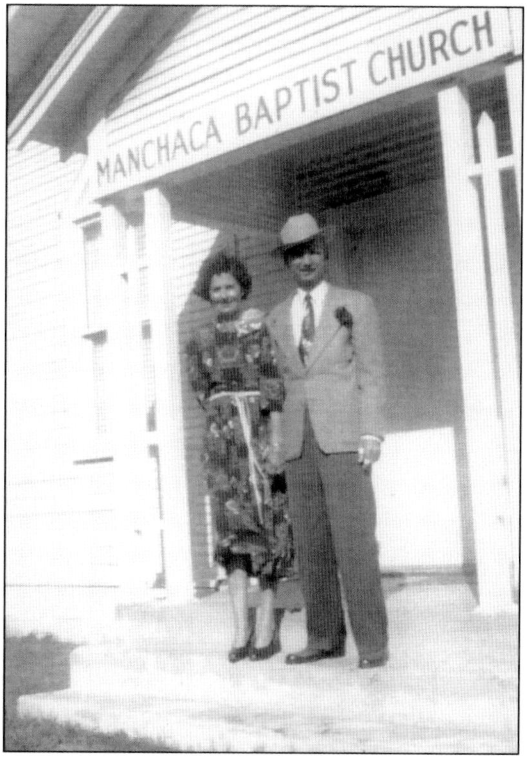


Manchaca United Methodist Church was declared a historical church by the Texas Historical Commission in 1984, when this marker was placed at the church. The church was formally organized by 1874. The first building was a wooden structure, erected in 1892 on an acre of land purchased for $75 on November 8, 1891, by church trustees William Chappell, Daniel W. Labenske, and Alfred Gatlin Matthews. It was used until 1957, when it was replaced with a new, brick sanctuary. (Courtesy Lillie M. Moreland.)

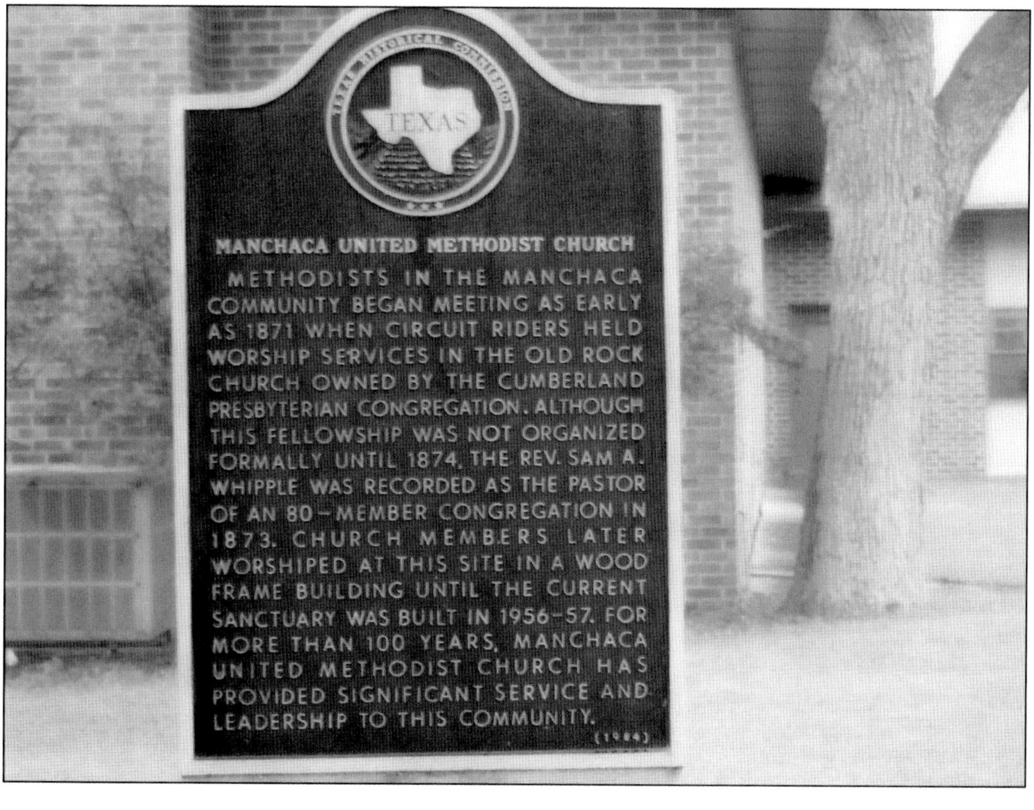

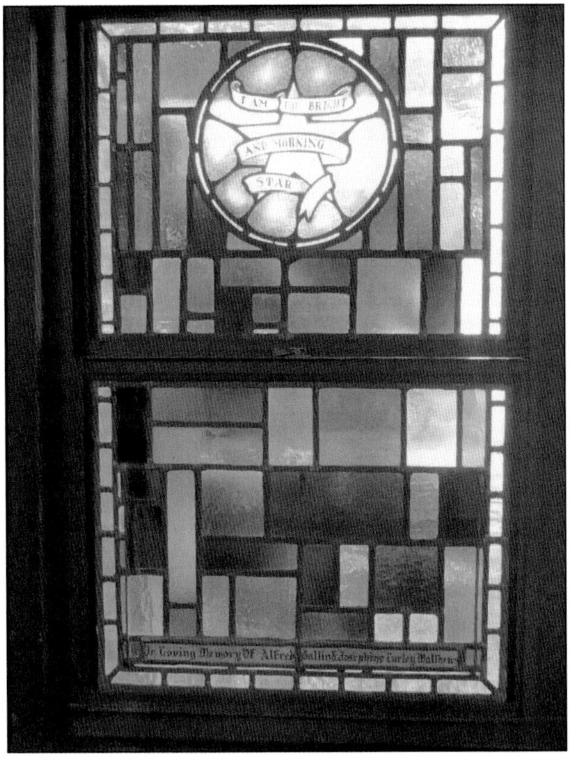


This window at Manchaca Methodist Church is dedicated to Alfred Gatlin Matthews and his wife, Josephine Turley Matthews. He was affectionately referred to as Captain Matthews for his Civil War service. Alfred said they were never mustered out, and when they realized it was all over, they just got on their horses and came home. He became a Mason in 1871, and belonged to Onion Creek Lodge. (Courtesy Ann and Barry Trask.)

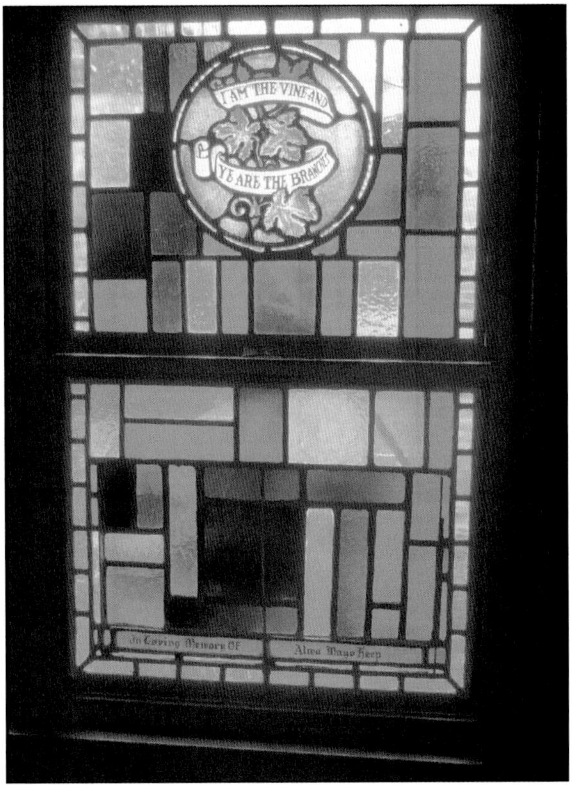


Alma Heep was a very active member of Manchaca Methodist Church. A descendant of the Burditt and Eanes families, she married Frederick Heep in 1894. Her son Herman was a generous and successful businessman. When the old 19th-century church building needed refurbishing and new carpet, her son offered to match the total contributions made by all of the other donors. (Courtesy Ann and Barry Trask.)

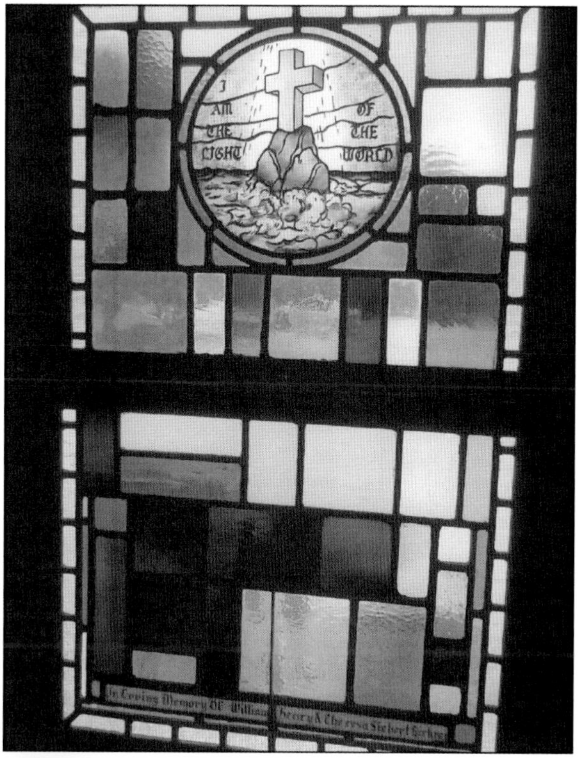


William Henry and Theresa Siebert Birkner were well known residents of Manchaca. Both were born in the 1870s and are buried in Live Oak Cemetery. The Birkners were successful farmers whose motto was, "The harder I work, the luckier I get." This window at Manchaca Methodist Church is dedicated to them. (Courtesy Ann and Barry Trask.)

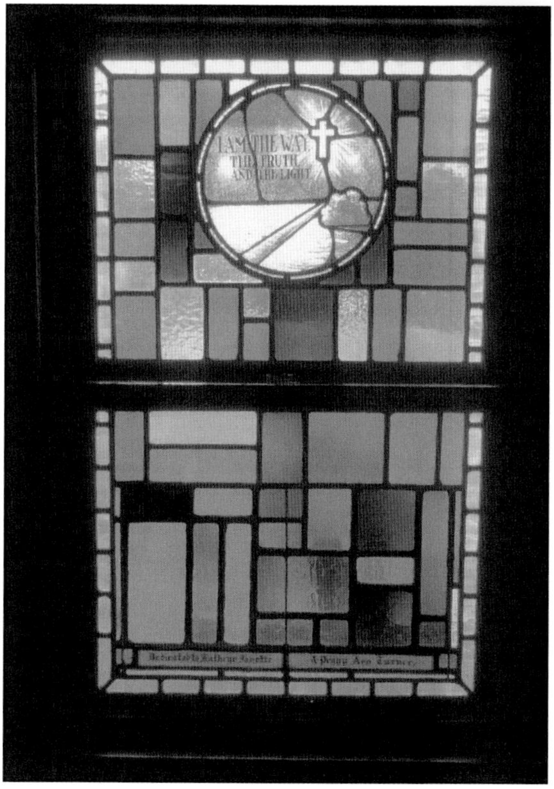


Rev. James Turner, pastor of Manchaca Methodist Church in the 1950s, dedicated this window to his daughters, Kathryn Janette and Peggy Ann. The church underwent major renovations under Reverend Turner. The story of escaped convict Russell Brooks volunteering to help lay the bricks for the church made the national news. (Courtesy Ann and Barry Trask.)

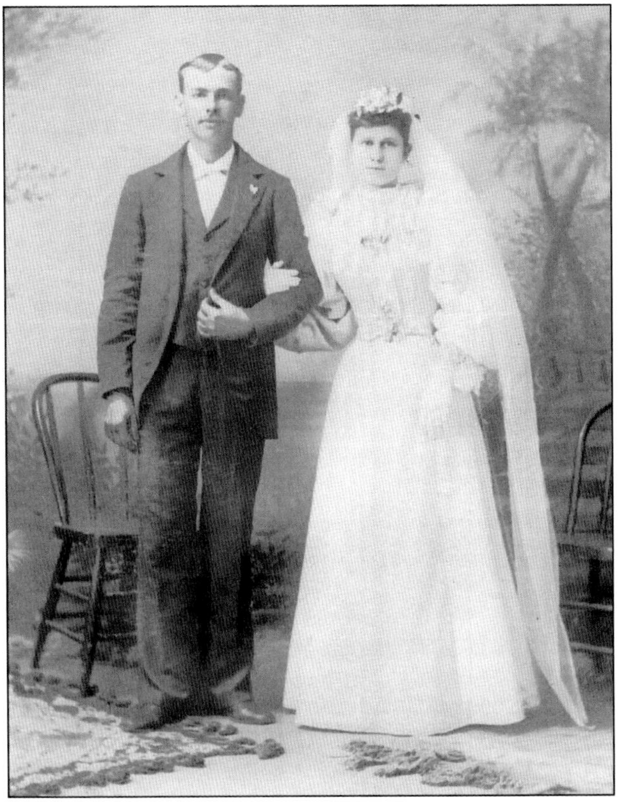

William Henry Birkner and Theresa "Tracy" Siebert posed for this beautiful wedding day photograph on February 3, 1897. The Birkners were very active members of Manchaca Methodist Church and the community as a whole. William helped build the schoolhouse in Manchaca as well as Manchaca Methodist Church. "Tracy" added to his success as a farmer, parents of eight, brick and stone masons. (Courtesy Jackie Patton.)

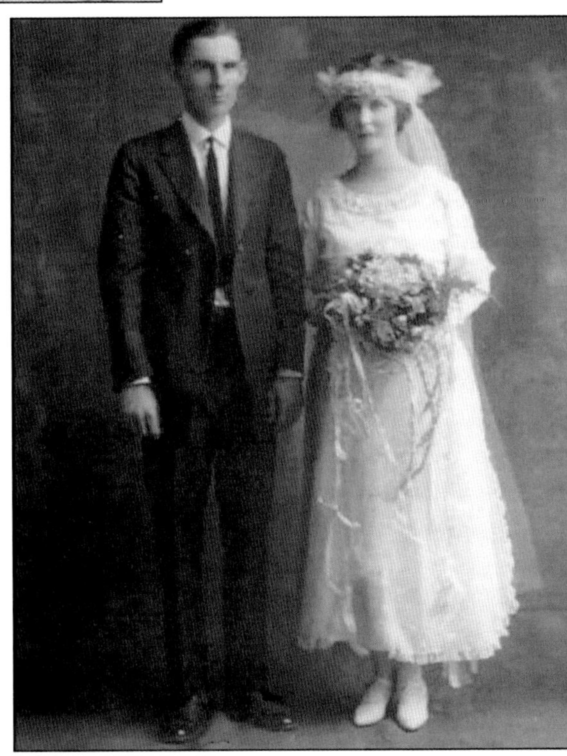

On July 25, 1923, a wedding united Minnie Helen Birkner, daughter of William and Theresa Birkner, and Frith Owens. Frith's father, Henry Bascom Owens, had been the minister of Manchaca Methodist Church from 1916–1918. Both Minnie and Frith graduated from college. Minnie taught school, and Frith became a geologist. Their loving marriage produced eight children. (Courtesy Betsy Wilkinson.)

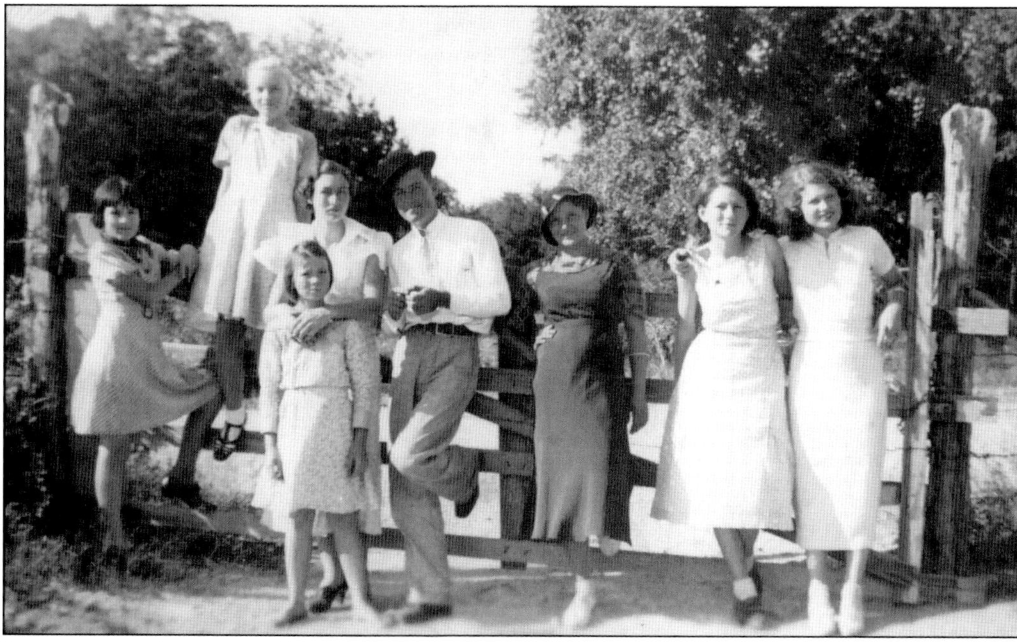

Pausing on a Sunday walk after church along FM 1626 in 1936 are, from left to right, Lillie Meredith, Alice Scott, Oleta Scott (in front), Itascia Scott (behind Oleta), Clay Sellers, Lillie Hector, Annie Mae Meredith, and Winnie Dunnahoo. This property is now owned by Caroline Dowell. (Courtesy Lillie M. Moreland.)

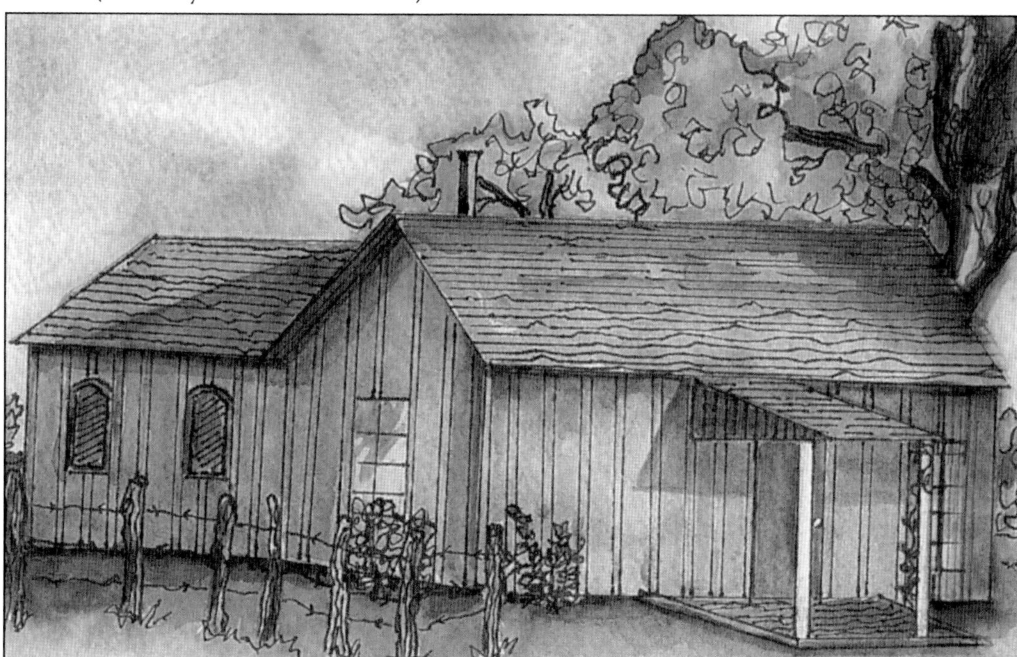

The Bethel African Methodist Episcopal Church parsonage in this sketch was built to house the pastor of the congregation. It served its purpose well for many years but was later destroyed by fire. The church was built on Bethel Church Road near the village of San Leanna. (Courtesy Lillie M. Moreland and Marilyn Dunnahoo McLeod.)

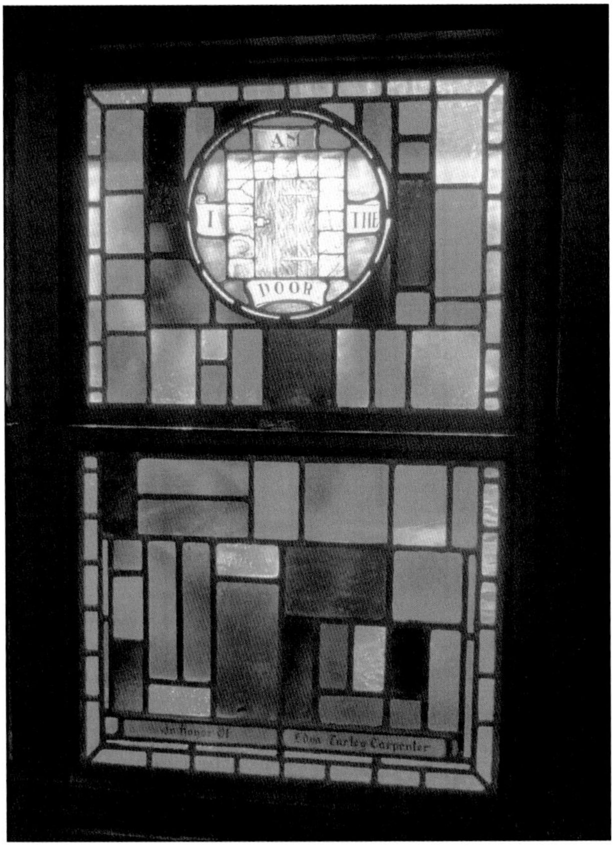


Edna Turley Carpenter was an active member of Manchaca Methodist Church and was well known in the community. Edna taught school in Manchaca for many years, encouraging children to continue their education. Born in 1872, Edna spent most of her life in Manchaca. She is buried in Live Oak Cemetery. (Courtesy Ann and Barry Trask.)

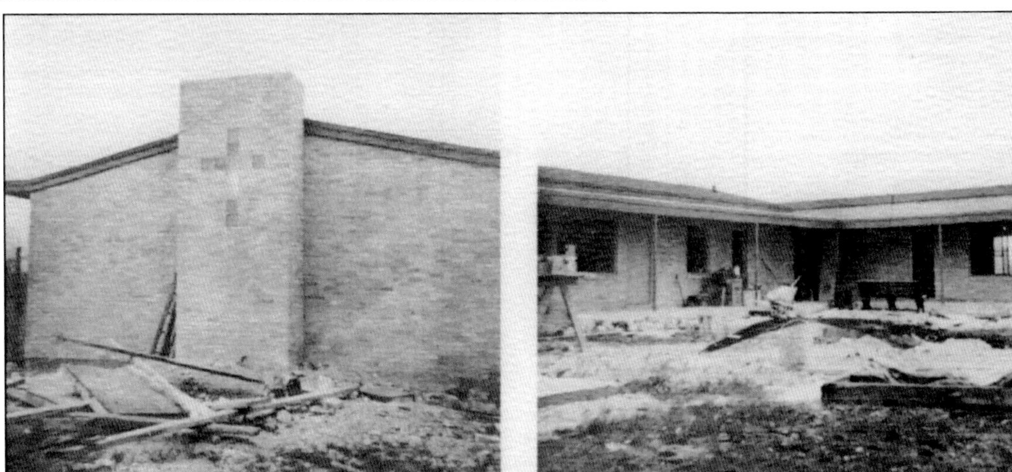

A CHURCH BUILT BY A CONVICT

The old wooden Methodist church was replaced with this brick structure in 1956. The church had materials to build, but no funds to move forward on construction. Russell Brooks, an escaped convict, showed up and offered to brick up the church free of charge. As soon as the last brick was laid at the Sunday school building, Brooks was arrested and taken back to prison. Reverend Turner worked to get Brooks paroled, and Brooks finished the church. (Courtesy Manchaca Methodist Church.)

# *Six*

# Then and Now

As time marches on and the hustle and bustle of modern-day life collides with the past, more and more information is being revealed about the Manchaca area. Research documenting the various old cemeteries in the area tells the stories of the many families who called Manchaca home. Further investigation into old newspapers of the 19th century tells the stories of those founding families. These chronicles reveal a community of neighbors back to the 1840s, experiencing Indian depredations along with the usual, and unusual, relationships and tiffs between families. One such disagreement led a man to shoot two of his neighbors during the 1850s. Many pioneering families still have descendants living on land that has been passed down from generation to generation.

As building increases along the I-35 corridor south of Austin, more areas of historical significance are expected to emerge. For example, the development of Southpark Meadows shopping center revealed a farm and cemetery established in the 1850s. These graves were relocated to enable further development to take place on the land.

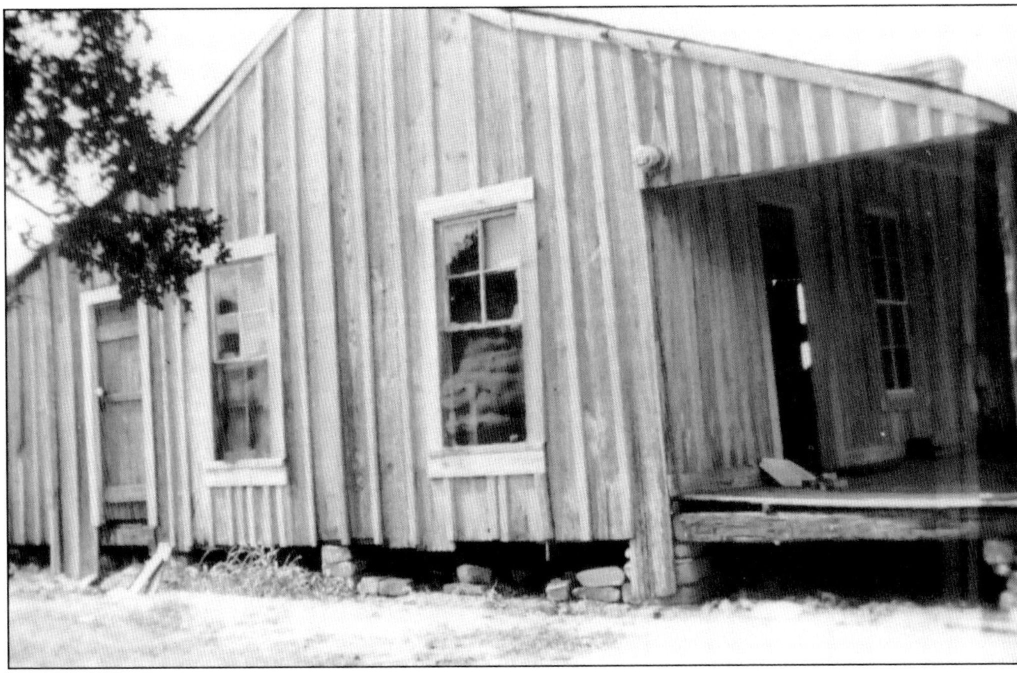

Thomas and Louisa Matthews built this home in 1850 on land that is now part of Southpark Meadows shopping center, just west of I-35. They farmed the land there and raised 10 children. This image was taken around 1950, a few decades after electricity had been added to update the old homestead. The oak trees below were a familiar sight for the family whose home was just west of where PetSmart is today. Youngsters in the family have fond memories of climbing on the tree to the left as it bent down toward the earth to make access easier. (Above, courtesy Virginia Dunahoo; below, courtesy Marilyn McLeod.)

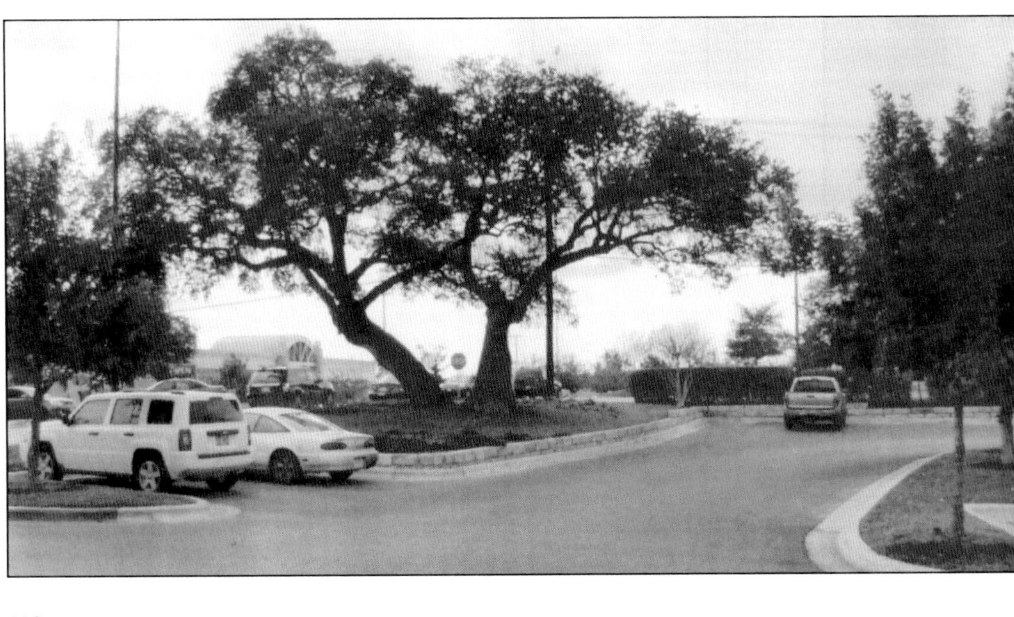

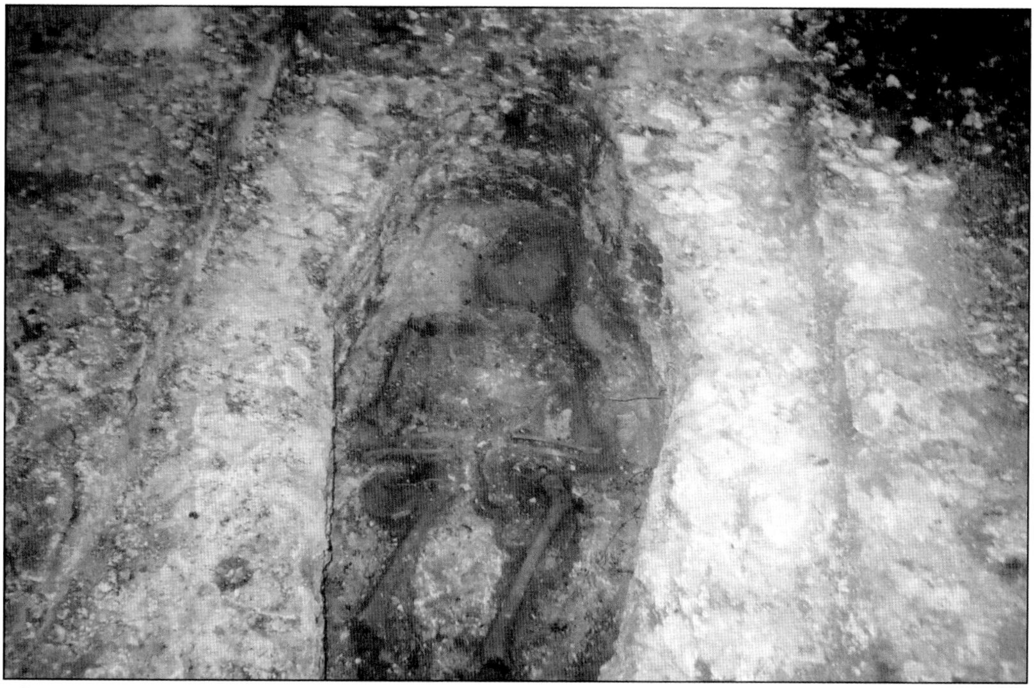

The Matthews family, who settled on land in the 1850s where Southpark Meadows is today, buried three of their family members on that property, a child named Sue Matthews, who died in 1854, Sue's mother, Louisa Matthews, who died in 1864, and Louisa's husband, Thomas Matthews, who died in 1885. Before construction could begin on the planned shopping center, the bodies had to be moved. Archaeologist Kerri Barile took on the job. The best-preserved remains were those of Louisa, which are shown above. All of the bodies faced to the east, due, perhaps, to their strong faith that their savior would return from the east and raise the dead to life. The square nails shown below were found with the bodies; remnants of the coffins they had been laid to rest in. (Above, courtesy Victoria Daywood; below, courtesy Marilyn McLeod.)

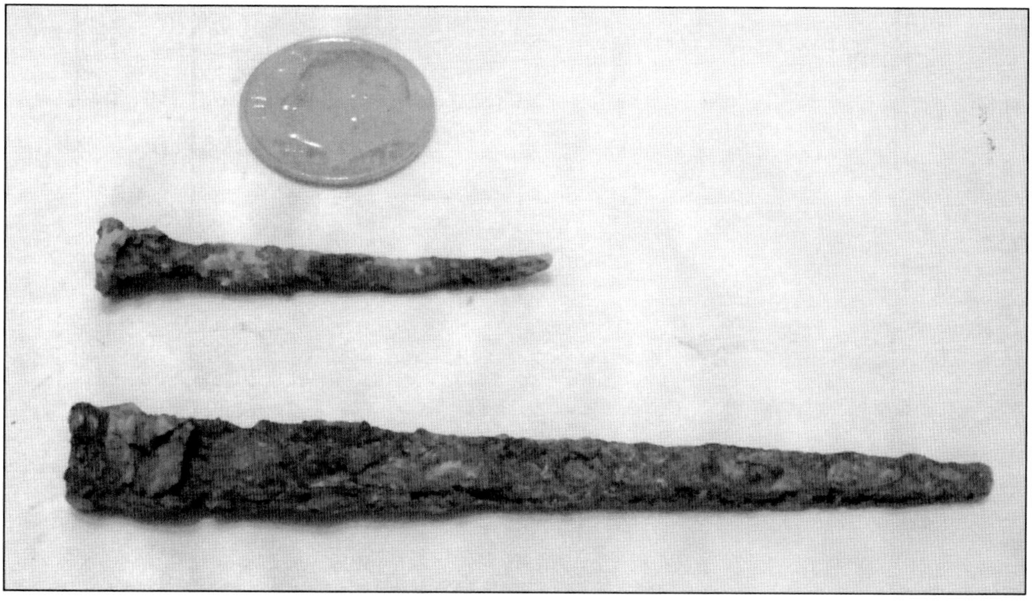

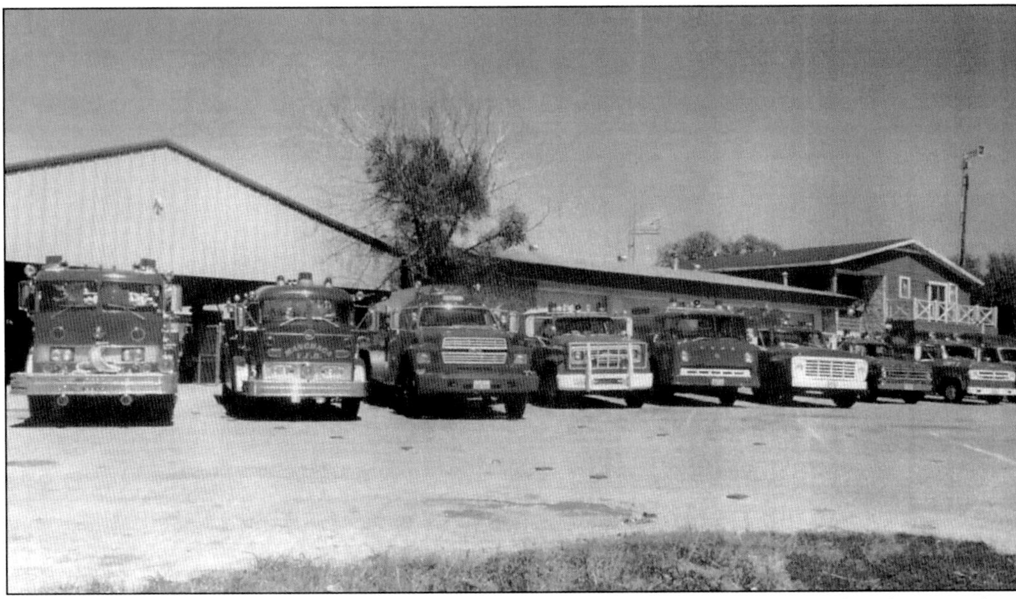

The catfish dinners prepared each Friday and Saturday evening by Clarence Vogel at the Manchaca Fire Hall Kitchen are fond memories for many. Before the Fire Hall was a restaurant, it was home to the Manchaca Volunteer Fire Department, shown above, where Mr. Vogel served as fire chief for a time. That building is a stark contrast to the state of the art facility, shown below. On March 31, 2012, over 1,000 people attended the grand opening of the new Manchaca Volunteer Fire Department Station No. 501, located at 665 W. FM 1626. This facility encompasses approximately 12,000 square feet. The station responded to over 700 calls in 2012. Fire Chief Chris Barron has been instrumental in the planning and implementation of this new facility. Currently, there are "49 volunteers (which include 21 new probationary volunteer firefighters) plus 26 part-time staff." The staff also operates out of another new station, No. 503, located at 12010 Brodie Lane. (Both, courtesy Manchaca Volunteer Fire Department.)

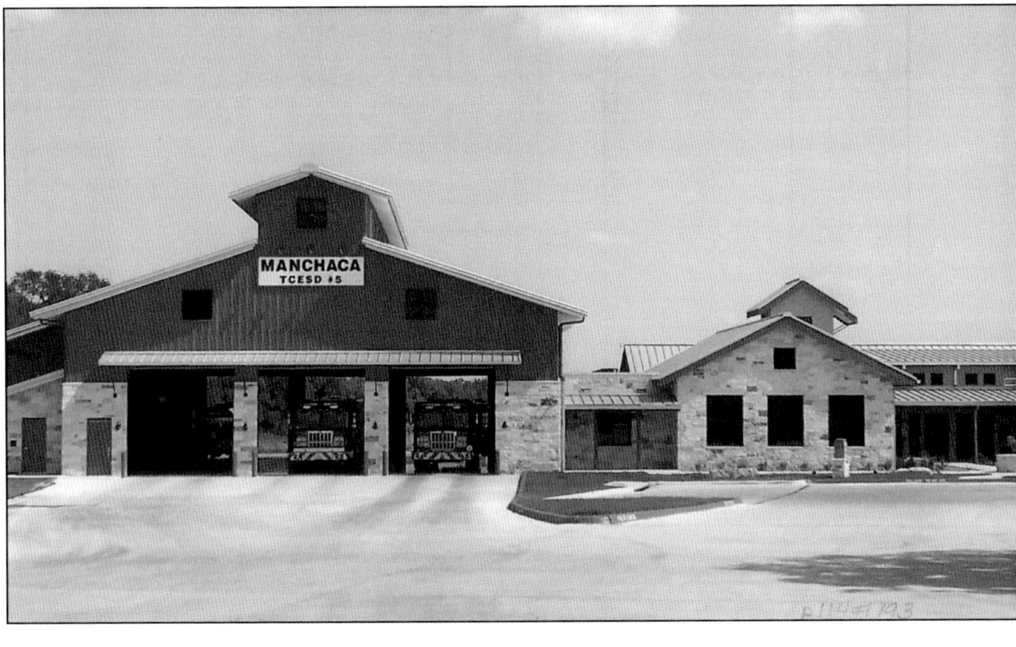

Manchaca constable Tom Dunnahoo is shown at right in 1929, standing along the main road through town, just to the left of where Manchaca Methodist Church was located. That road would later be named FM 1626. The view behind him is to the east, toward the railroad tracks. At that point in time, there were no paved roads in Manchaca, and most of the roads were not formally named. Manchaca resident Barry Trask stood in approximately the same spot along FM 1626 for this 2012 photograph. To the east, behind him on the right-hand side, the sign for the Manchaca Methodist Church is visible. (Above, courtesy Marilyn Dunnahoo McLeod; below, courtesy Ann and Barry Trask.)

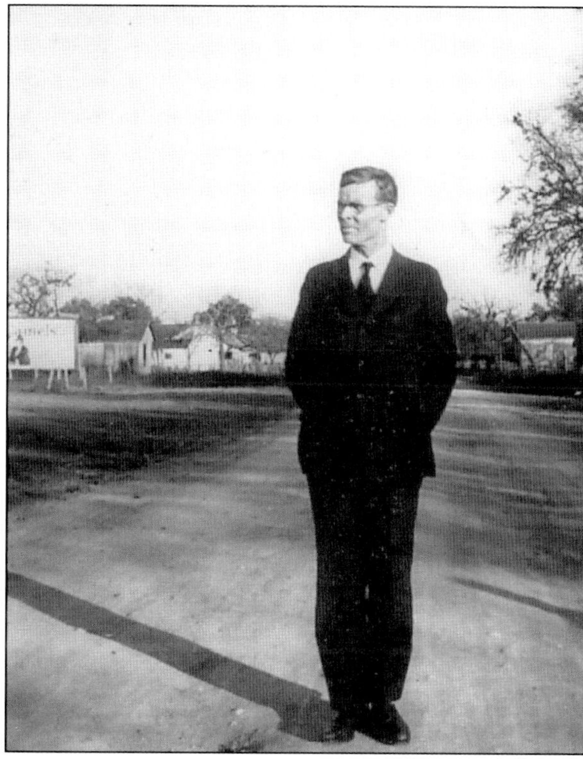

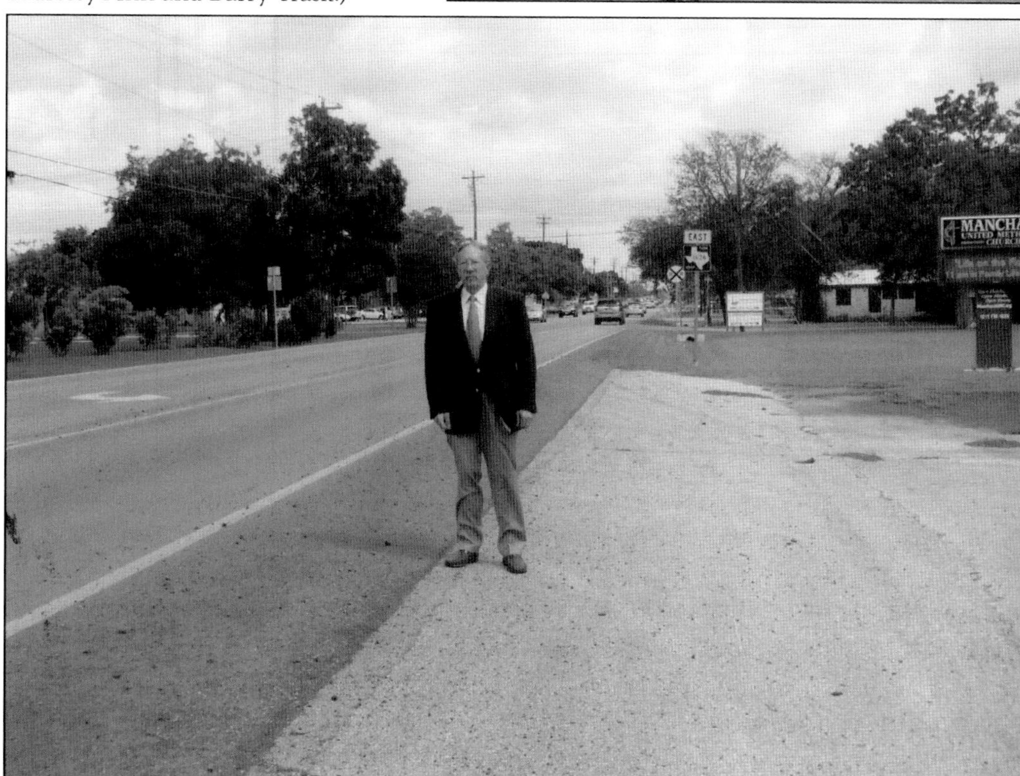

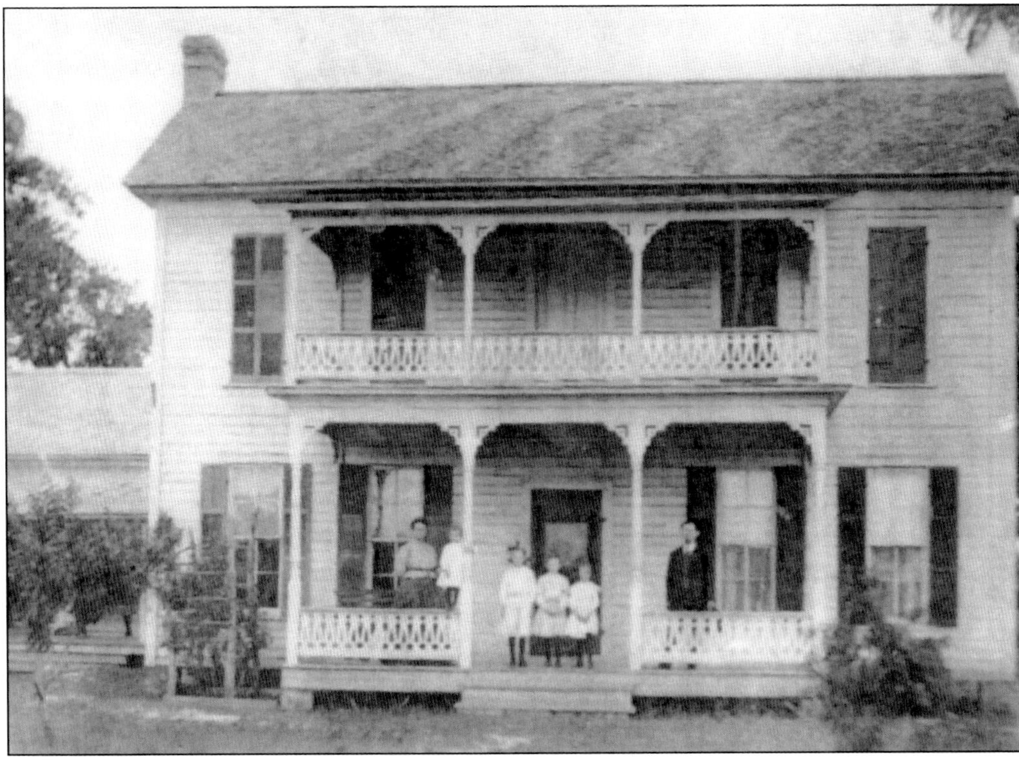

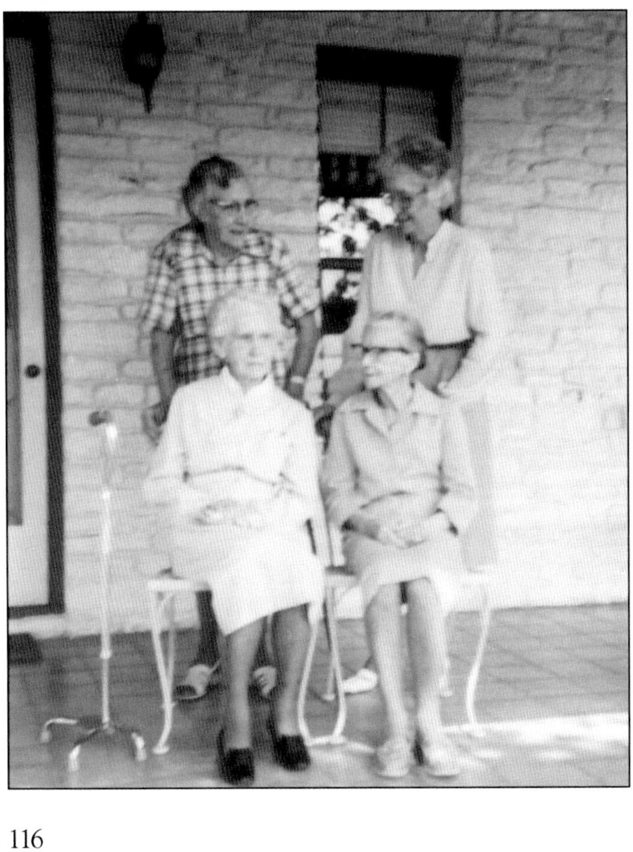

Frank Blackwell was a pharmacist and store owner in downtown Manchaca. In 1896, he built this lovely Victorian home that stood next to the Blackwell Store. Shown on the porch from left to right are Hannah, Blanche, Bruce, Bernice, Beatrice, and Frank. The daughters of Hannah and Frank Blackwell gathered again years later in the photograph at left. They are shown on the porch of Martha and Chester Johnson's home. Martha is the daughter of Bruce Blackwell Johnson. Shown from left to right are (first row) Bernice Green and Bruce Johnson; (second row) Beatrice Toombs and Blanche Howard. (Both, courtesy Joanne Deane.)

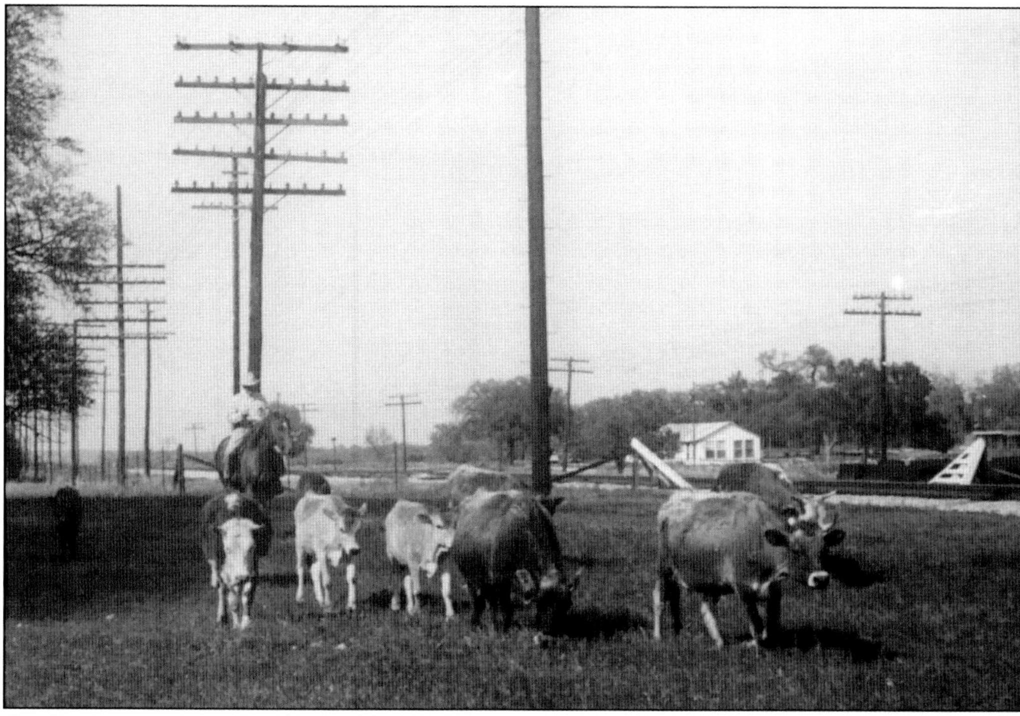

Cattle were a common sight in old Manchaca. The local ranchers used the railroad to get their beeves to market. Here, William Cruze drives part of his herd along the railroad tracks toward their destination. The home of Vera Polk is in the background. Below is that same area as it appears today. According to the February/March 1973 issue of *Frontier Times Magazine,* the train in Manchaca was once the target of infamous train robbers known as the Cornett Whitley Gang. In the fall of 1887, they planned to rob both the northbound and southbound trains when they stopped at the Manchaca station. Thanks to former Texas Ranger Jim Martin and his posse, they were not successful, and one gang member, John Ensall, was captured and put in jail. (Above, courtesy Joanne Deane; below, courtesy Ann and Barry Trask.)

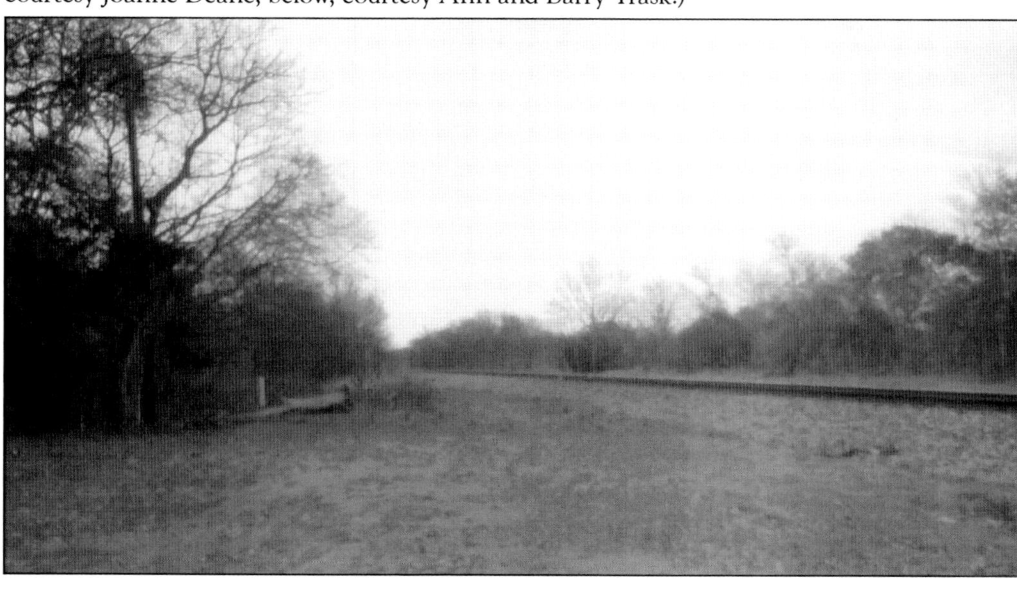

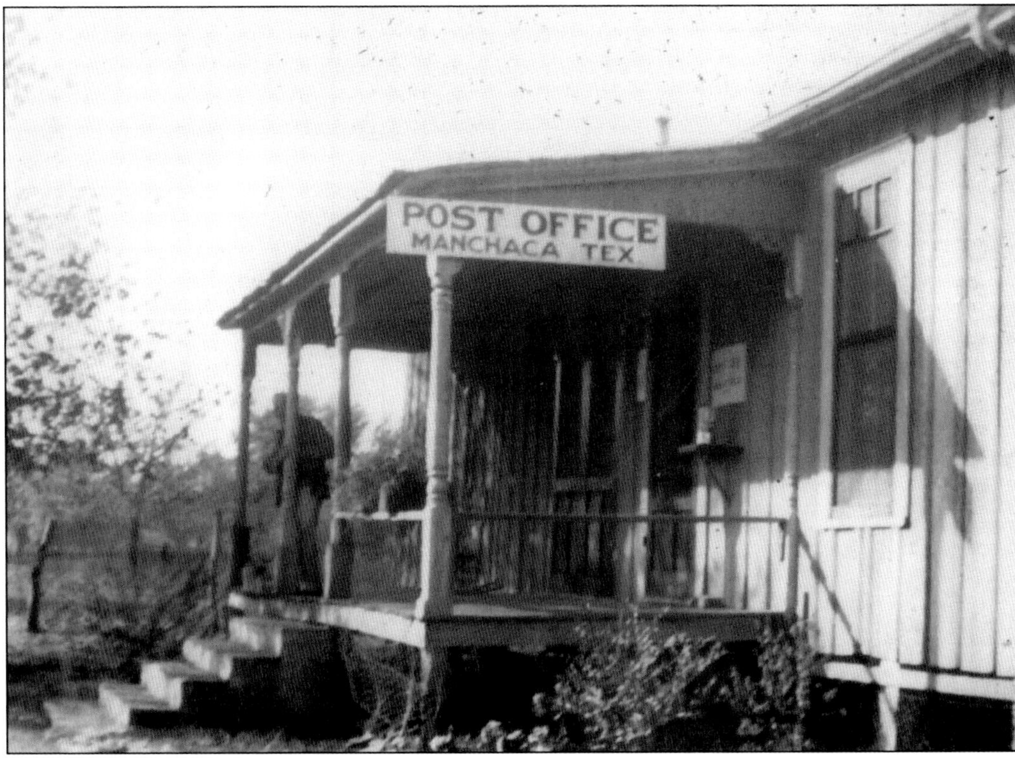


The Manchaca Post Office, shown above, was located on Wirth road in the home of Annie and Festus Biggs. Mrs. Biggs was postmistress of Manchaca from 1937–1968. The post office remained in that location even after Mrs. Biggs retired. A local postal patron can be seen here on the porch. When Annie was appointed postmistress, the facility was a fourth-class station. She encouraged everyone to increase the volume of mail they sent out, and it was soon upgraded. The ground-breaking ceremony for the present post office, shown below, was held in October 1998. It claims 6,000 square feet of space nestled on a two-acre lot located on the north side of FM 1626 and has 900 boxes for its customers. (Above, courtesy Lillie M. Moreland; below, courtesy and Ann and Barry Trask.)

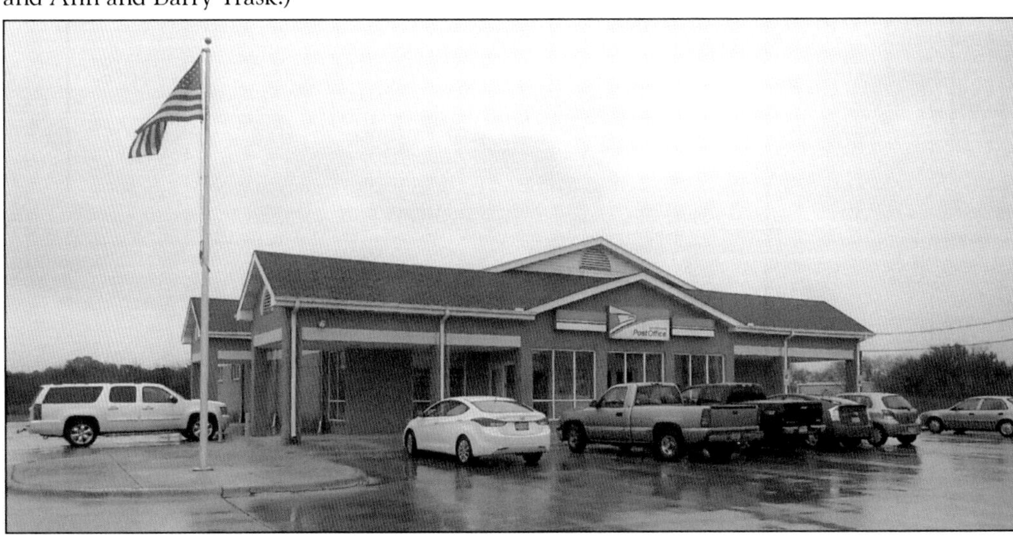

The antique brass mailboxes at right were first located in the Blackwell Store in the early 1900s, and then were transferred to the post office on Wirth Road, located in the Biggs family home. In 1975, when a new post office was built, items from the Wirth Road location were offered for sale. Manchaca resident Liz Higgins purchased the fixtures from the old post office, including the brass mailboxes. Liz had the boxes installed in her home. She wanted MOCHA ultimately to have them for preservation. After Liz passed away, Peggy Pryor purchased her home. Through Mrs. Pryor's generous donation, the mailboxes are now owned by MOCHA. Today's post office, built in 1997, is shown below. It sports a hall of 900 sleek post boxes offered to its patrons. (Both, courtesy Ann and Barry Trask.)

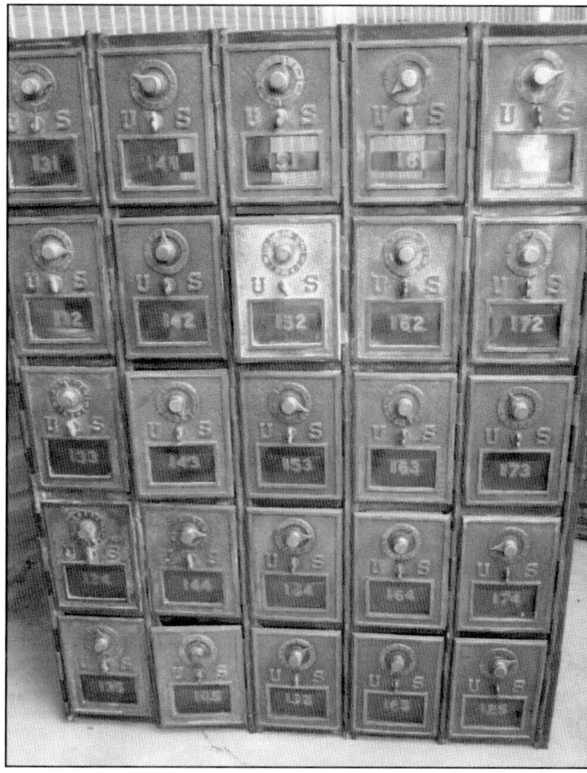

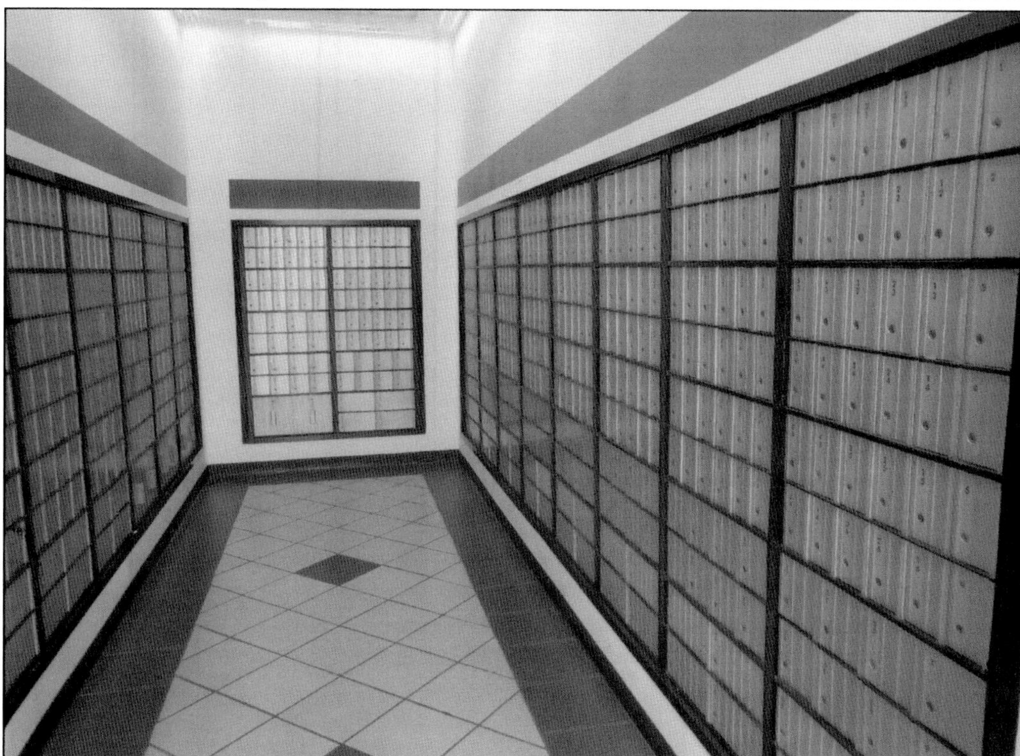

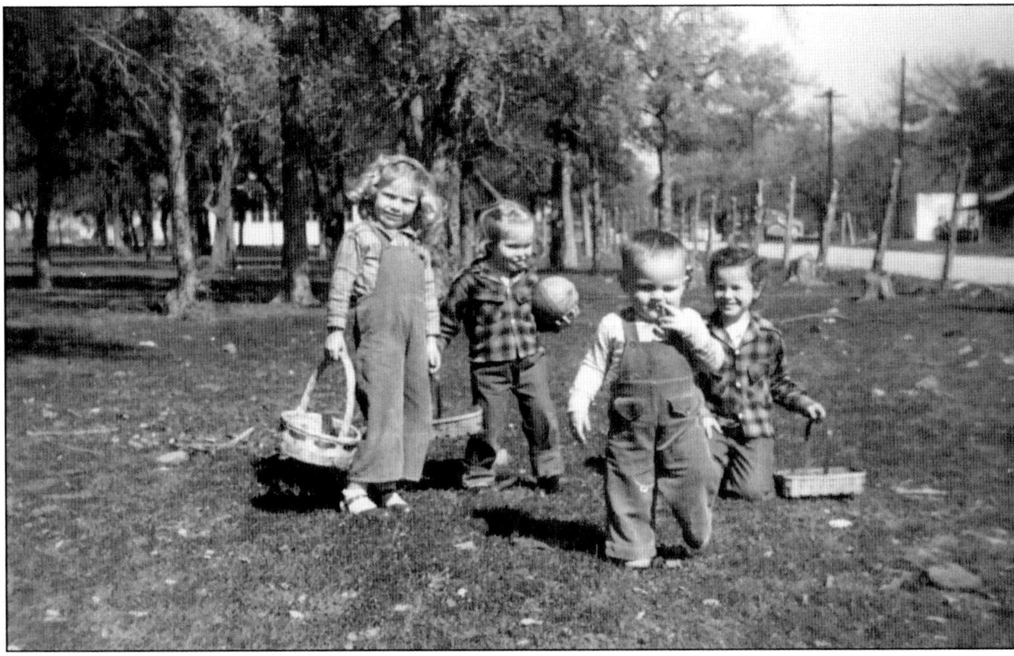

On Easter day in 1948, these children thoroughly enjoyed themselves while having an Easter egg hunt in Dodson Park. Shown from left to right are Diane Cassidy, Sharon Barho, Nealen Moreland, and Patricia Barho. Dodson Park, owned by Mary and Jack Dodson, was available for parties and family functions. Below is that same place today, which is now part of the Manchaca Elementary School grounds. At one point in time, the Dodson family owned the property along the west side of Manchaca Road from what is today Frate Barker Road to FM 1626. (Above, courtesy Joanne Deane; below, courtesy Ann and Barry Trask.)

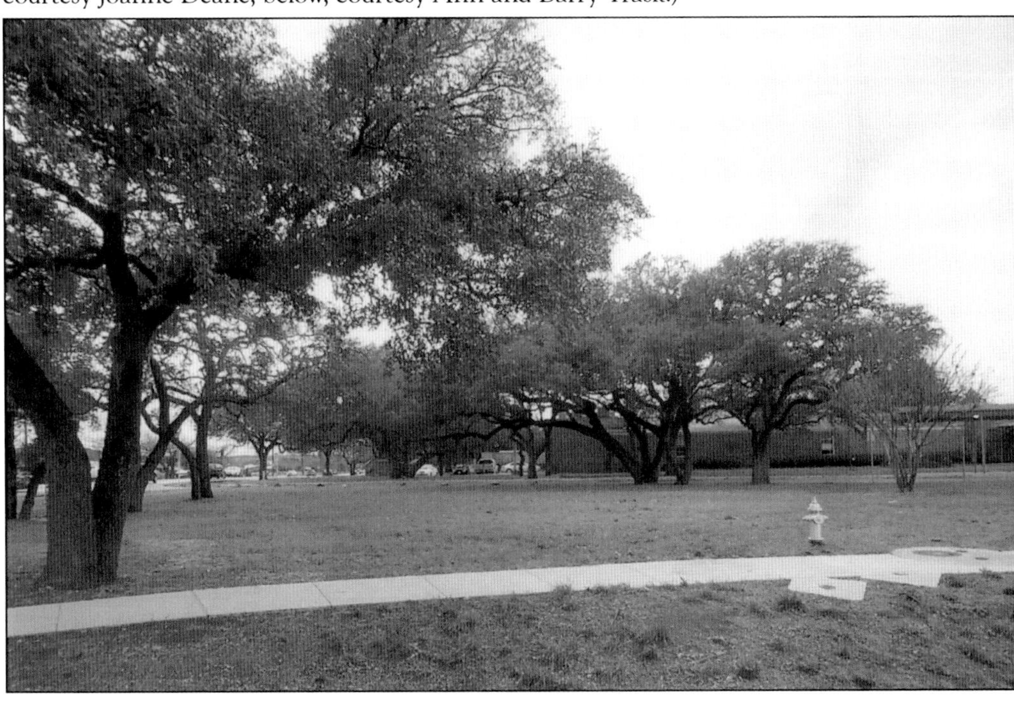

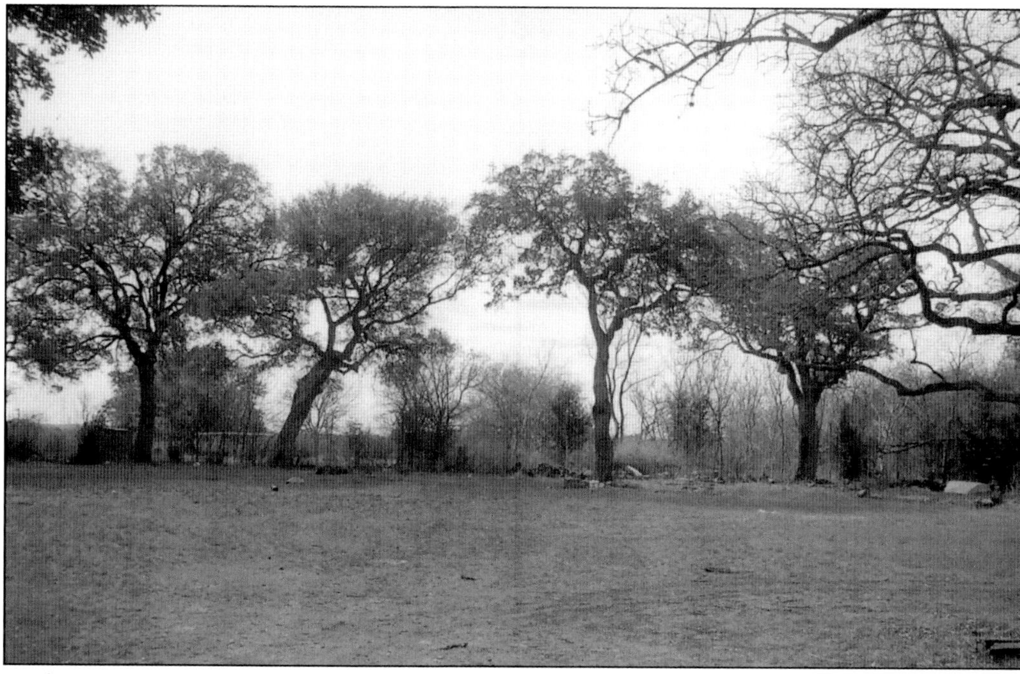

In the early days, Manchaca had three schools: the Mexican American school, the African American school, and the Caucasian school. The image above shows where the African American school used to be located, on a lot that today bears the address of 753 FM 1626. The Mexican American school was situated close to the railroad tracks off of Polk Road. That location is shown below as it appears today. The majestic oaks on those lots are all that remain. They were, no doubt, silent witnesses to the giggles and laughter of children as they joyously played during recess. (Both, courtesy Ann and Barry Trask.)

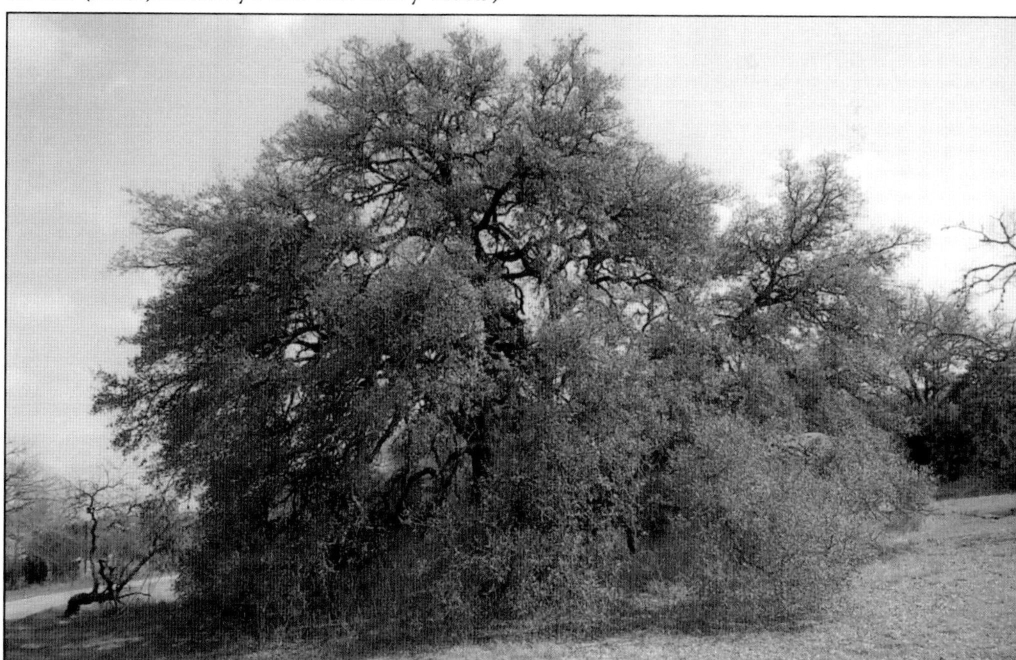

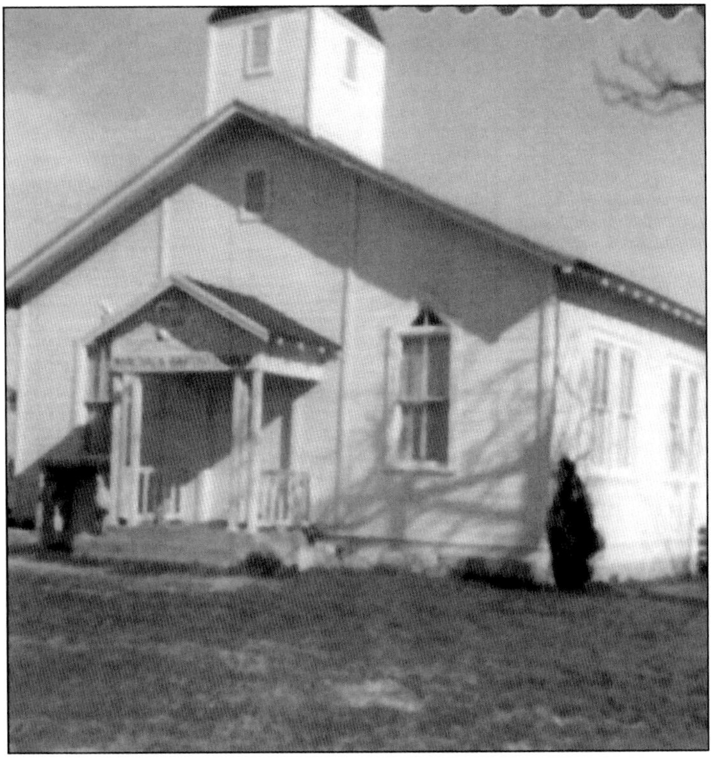

Manchaca Baptist Church has a rich history in the community. The church was organized in 1918 and quickly grew through the years. The old structure, shown at left, was built in 1925 for a cost of $1,800. The beautiful building shown below, located at 1215 FM 1626 in Manchaca, is home to the present congregation. During the process of building this new facility, it caught fire and had to be completely rebuilt. (Left, courtesy Lillie M. Moreland; below, courtesy and Ann and Barry Trask.)

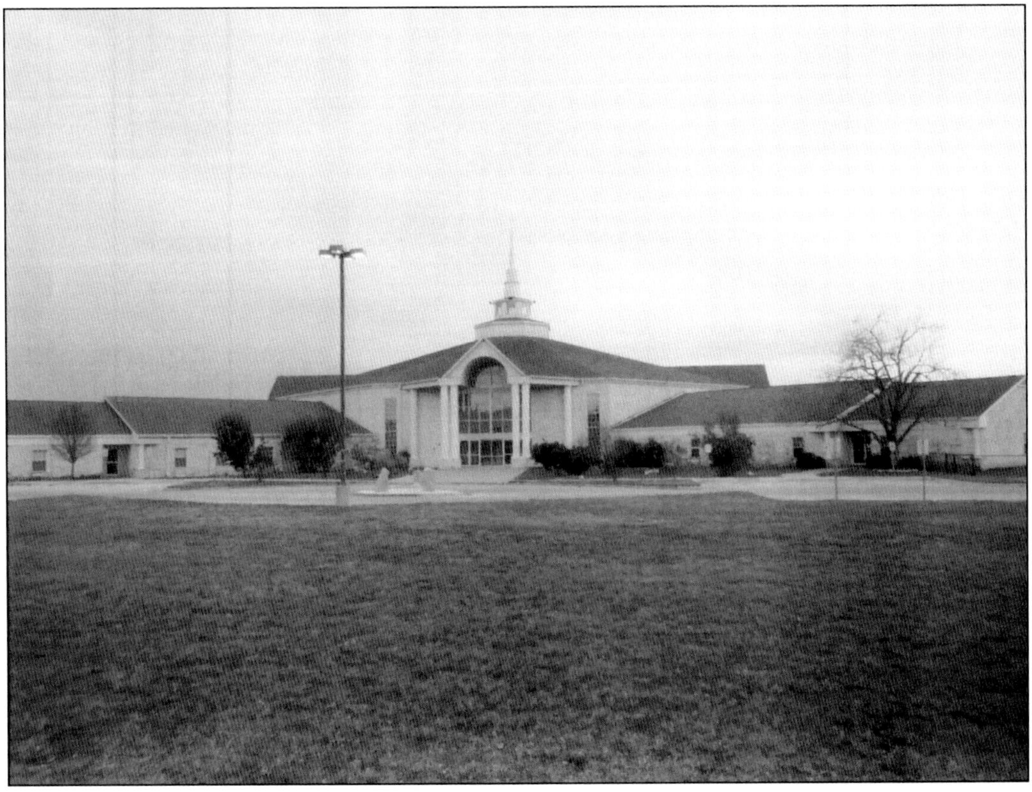

When Pastor Sam Whipple organized Manchaca Methodist Church back in 1874, he had no idea it would grow into the large congregation it is today. The old wooden church stood from 1892 to 1957, when it was torn down to make way for a new brick building. The photograph below is the result of several additions and updates made through the years to accommodate a growing congregation. The church is located at 1011 FM 1626 in Manchaca. (Right, courtesy Lillie M. Moreland; below, courtesy Ann and Barry Trask.)

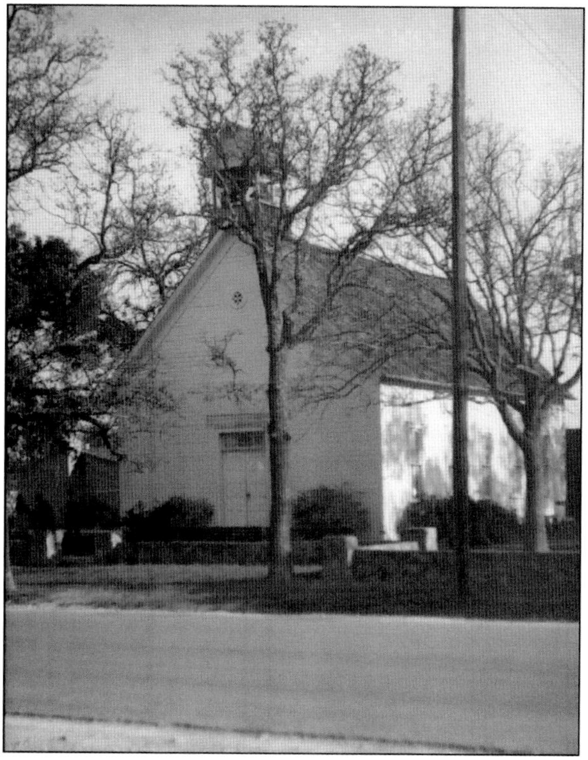

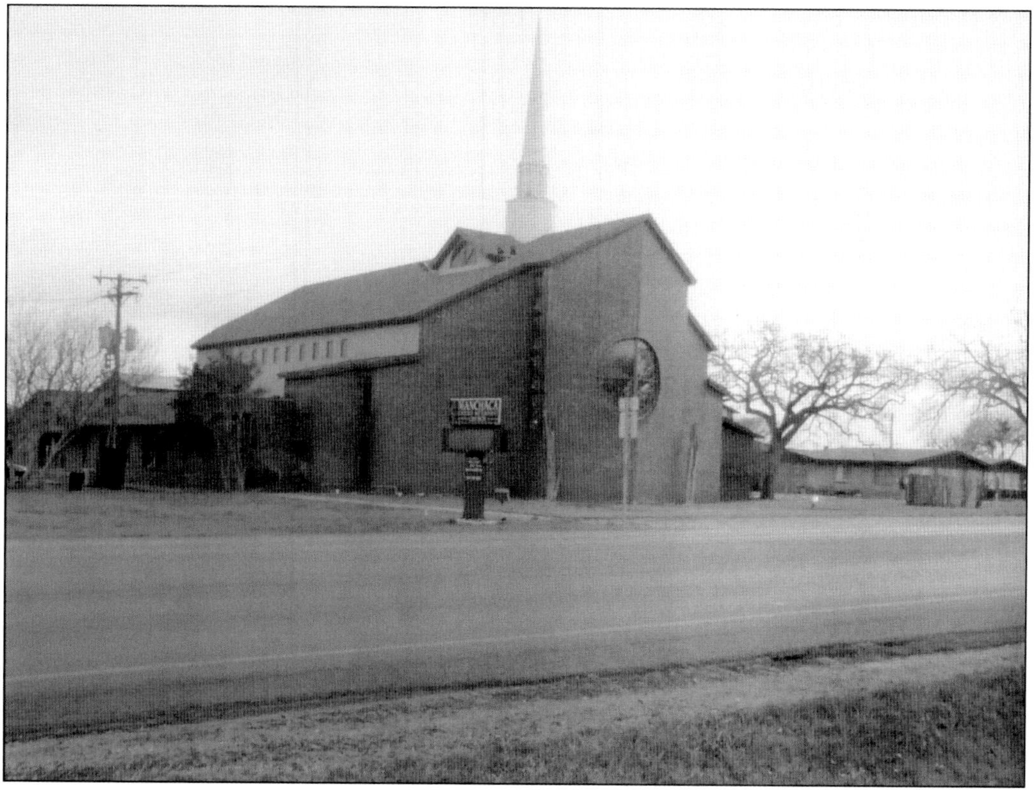

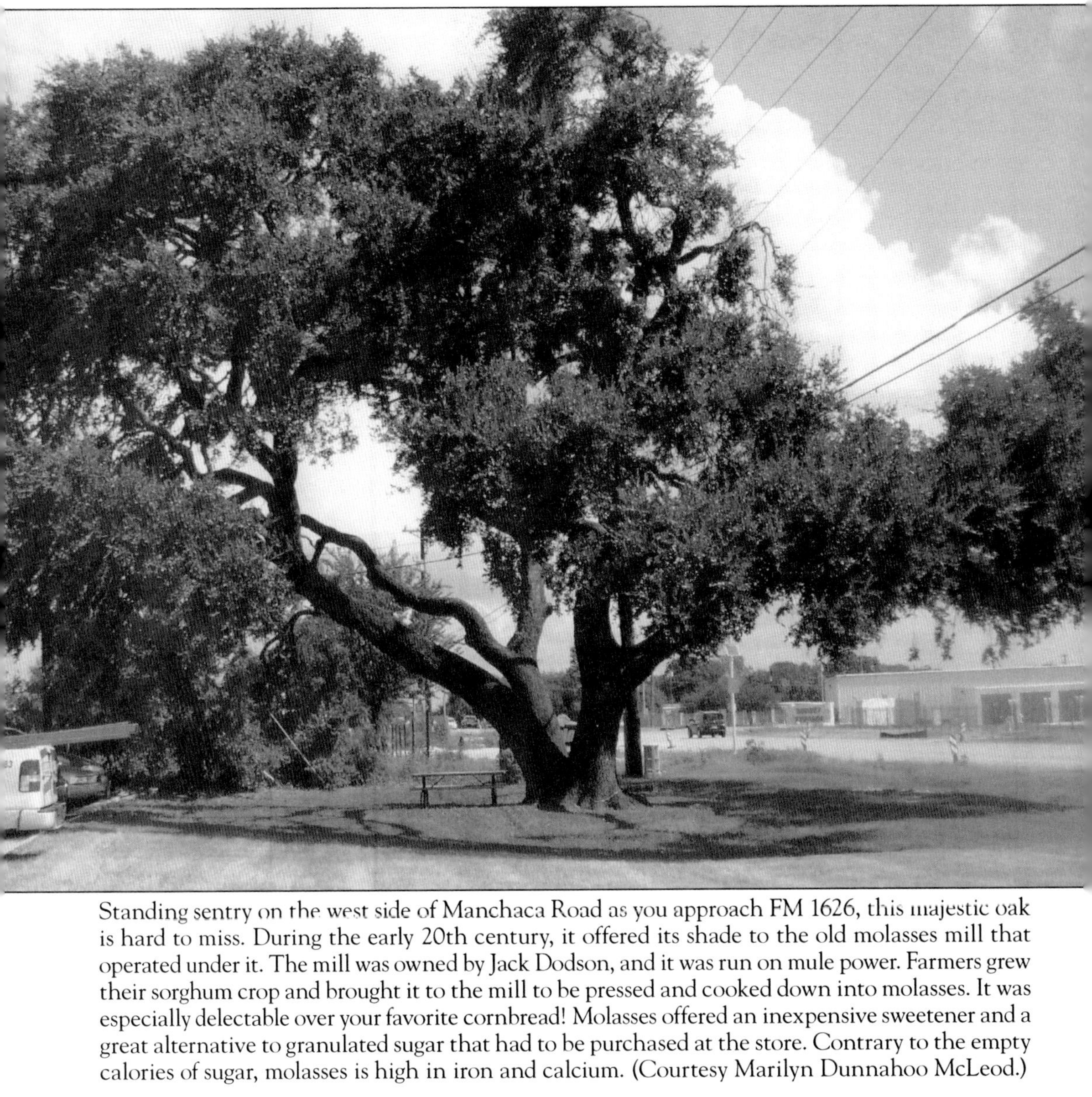

Standing sentry on the west side of Manchaca Road as you approach FM 1626, this majestic oak is hard to miss. During the early 20th century, it offered its shade to the old molasses mill that operated under it. The mill was owned by Jack Dodson, and it was run on mule power. Farmers grew their sorghum crop and brought it to the mill to be pressed and cooked down into molasses. It was especially delectable over your favorite cornbread! Molasses offered an inexpensive sweetener and a great alternative to granulated sugar that had to be purchased at the store. Contrary to the empty calories of sugar, molasses is high in iron and calcium. (Courtesy Marilyn Dunnahoo McLeod.)

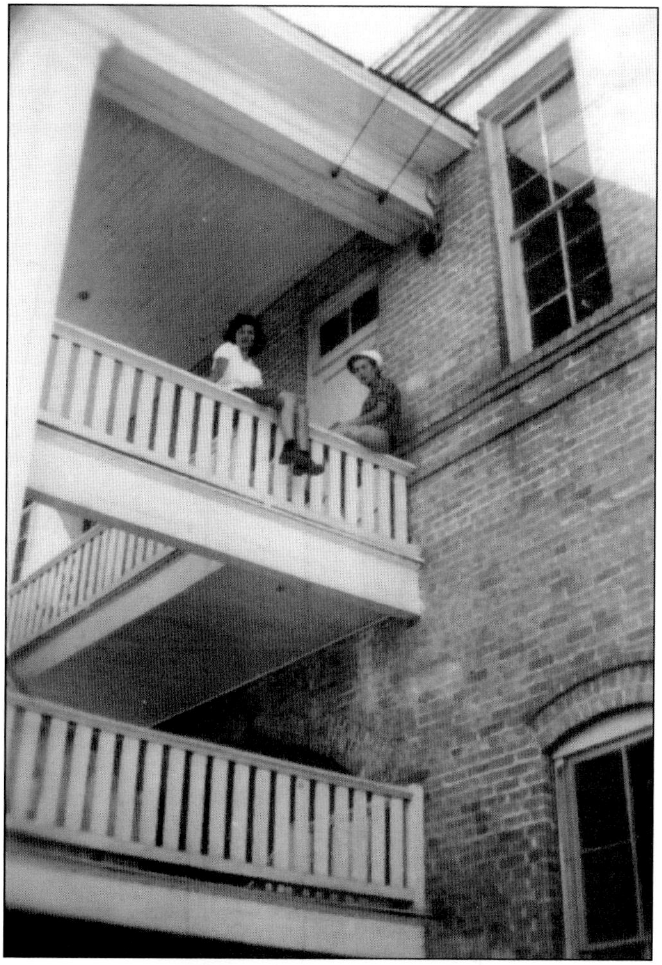

The photograph at right shows the stairway in the old two-story Manchaca School building. There is a stark contrast between that image and the modern elementary school attended by the children of Manchaca today, shown below. (Right photograph, courtesy Lillie M. Moreland; below photograph, courtesy Ann and Barry Trask.)

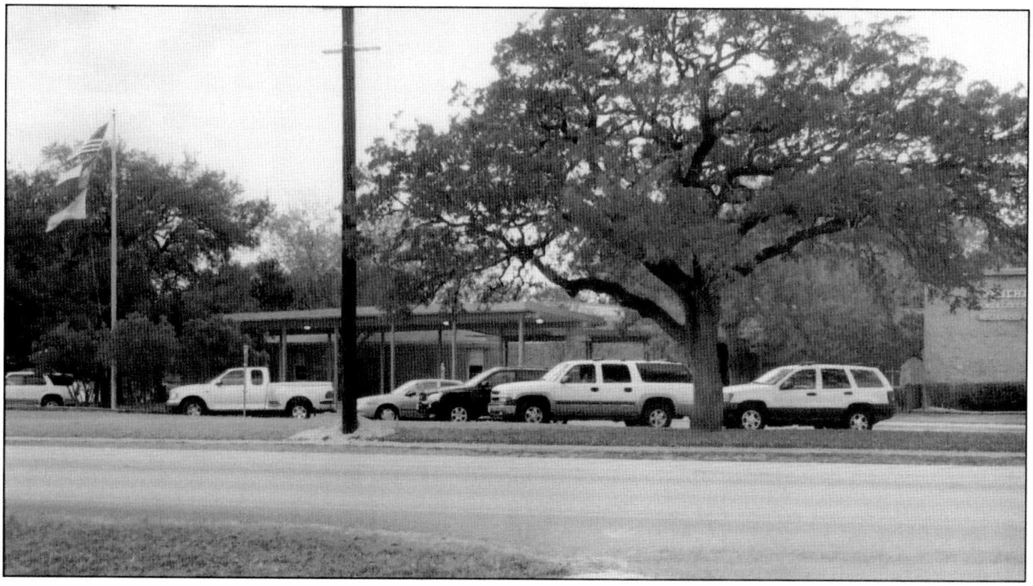

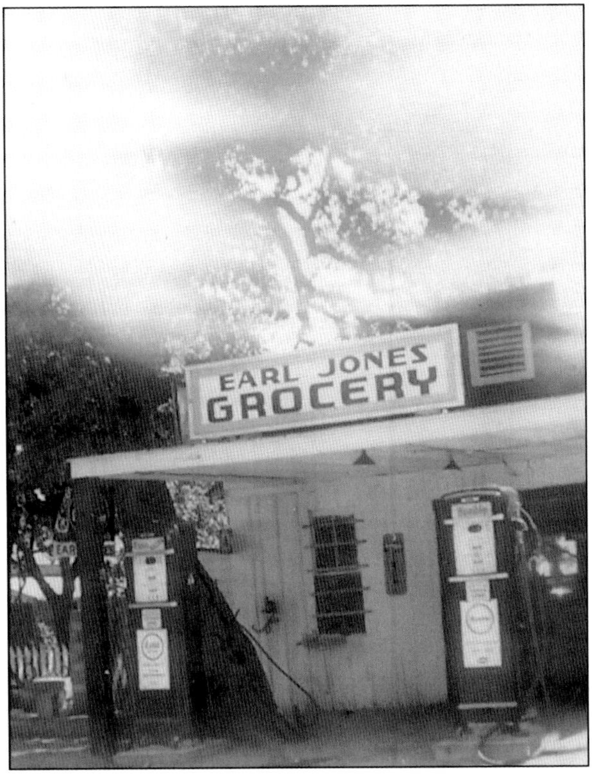


If you were driving through Manchaca in the 1930s, you may have stopped at the Earl Jones Store, shown in the photograph at left. The little grocery offered gasoline at the pumps, plus an array of food. The building below serves the community today as the local Motor Vehicle Inspection Station in Manchaca and is located at 817 West FM 1626. (Left, courtesy Linda Bell; below, courtesy Ann and Barry Trask.)

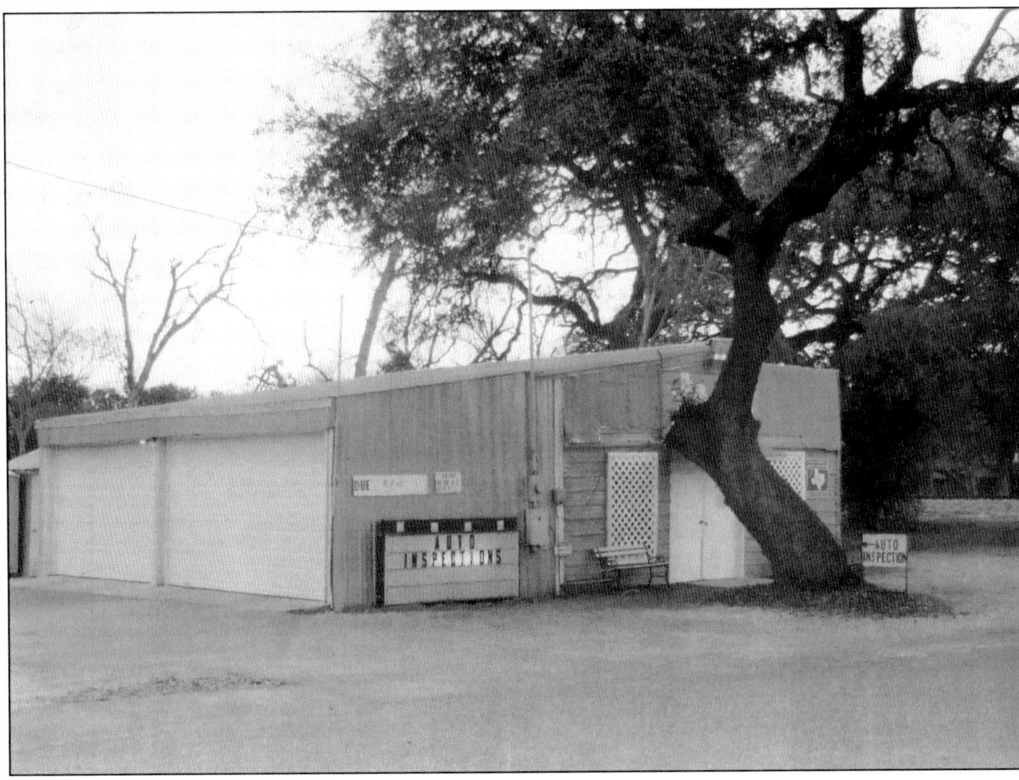

# Bibliography


Coalson, George O. "Menchaca, Jose Antonio [1800–1879]." *Handbook of Texas Online* (www.tshaonline.org/handbook/online/articles/fme12), accessed February 19, 2013. Published by the Texas State Historical Association.

Dodson, Mary. "Slave Narratives" (freepages.genealogy.rootsweb.ancestry.com/~ewyatt/_borders/Texas%20Slave%20Narratives/Texas%20D/Dodson,%20Mary.html).

Hartley, Mary Mae, *A Hand on Their Shoulder—The Special Love Story at Marbridge Ranch*. Austin, TX: Eakin Press, 1989.

Hastings, Robert W. *The Lakes of Pontchartrain: Their History and Environments*. Jackson, MS: University Press of Mississippi, 2009.

Hogan, Bill and Jane Hogan. *Tales of the Manchaca Hills, An Unvarnished Memoir*. New Orleans, LA: The Hauser Press, 1960.

Garver, Lois. "Milam, Benjamin Rush," *Handbook of Texas Online* (www.tshaonline.org/handbook/online/articles/fmi03), accessed February 19, 2013. Published by the Texas State Historical Association.

Marshall, John, ed. *State Gazette*. (Austin, TX), Vol. 11, No. 43, Ed. 1, Saturday, June 2, 1860, newspaper, June 2, 1860; digital images, (texashistory.unt.edu/ark:/67531/metapth81436/), accessed February 19, 2013. University of North Texas Libraries, The Portal to Texas History, (texashistory.unt.edu); crediting Dolph Briscoe Center for American History, Austin, TX. Found page 2; article on murders of W.H. Jones, Mark DeLoach, and Charles Harvey.

Ragan, Cooper K.. "Irvine, Josephus Somerville." *Handbook of Texas Online* (www.tshaonline.org/handbook/online/articles/fir08), accessed February 19, 2013. Published by the Texas State Historical Association.

Roeder, Fred L.S. "Surveyor of the Public Domain—A Portrait of William Pelham." *The American Surveyor* (www.amerisurv.com/content/view/6050/136/), last modified April 11, 2009.

Siebert, Doris. "History of Manchaca, Texas: 1880–1940." Manchaca, TX: Self-published, 1990.

"Statue Honoring Barbara Jordan Unveiled on the University of Texas at Austin Campus" (www.utexas.edu/news/2009/04/24/barbara_jordan_statue_unveiled/) University of Texas at Austin, last modified April 24, 2009.

"Williamson, Robert McAlpin [Three Legged Willie]." *Handbook of Texas Online* (www.tshaonline.org/handbook/online/articles/fwi42), accessed February 19, 2013. Published by the Texas State Historical Association.

## Discover Thousands of Local History Books Featuring Millions of Vintage Images

Arcadia Publishing, the leading local history publisher in the United States, is committed to making history accessible and meaningful through publishing books that celebrate and preserve the heritage of America's people and places.

Find more books like this at
**www.arcadiapublishing.com**

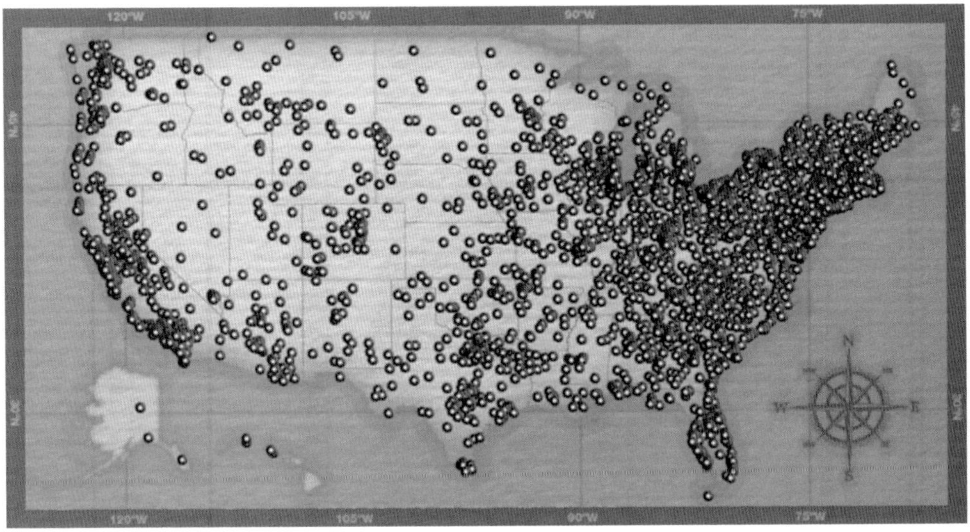


Search for your hometown history, your old stomping grounds, and even your favorite sports team.

Consistent with our mission to preserve history on a local level, this book was printed in South Carolina on American-made paper and manufactured entirely in the United States. Products carrying the accredited Forest Stewardship Council (FSC) label are printed on 100 percent FSC-certified paper.

MADE IN THE USA